The Ethics of Citizenship in the 21st Century

David Thunder
Editor

The Ethics of Citizenship in the 21st Century

Springer

Editor
David Thunder
Institute for Culture and Society
University of Navarra
Pamplona, Navarra, Spain

ISBN 978-3-319-50414-8 ISBN 978-3-319-50415-5 (eBook)
https://doi.org/10.1007/978-3-319-50415-5

Library of Congress Control Number: 2017934072

Printed on acid-free paper

This Springer imprint is published by Springer Nature
The registered company is Springer International Publishing AG
The registered company address is: Gewerbestrasse 11, 6330 Cham, Switzerland

Preface

This collection of essays discusses a range of important challenges confronting the theory and practice of citizenship in a globalized, socially fragmented, and multicultural world. Issues addressed include the ethical and practical value of patriotism in a globalized world, the relation between civic allegiance and religious commitment, the standing of conscience claims in a morally diverse society, and the problem of citizen complicity in political injustice. We analyze the practice of citizenship through the lens of diverse philosophical traditions and perspectives, including Confucianism, Platonism, Thomism, and pragmatism. Although the contributors find their bearings in very different traditions, they nonetheless share the conviction that the crisis of modern citizenship, whatever else it may be, is most certainly a crisis of the ethical values that give shape, form, and meaning to modern social life.

At least since the emergence of the Athenian polis over two millennia ago, citizenship has played a central role in the self-understanding and internal organization of Western societies. Most obviously perhaps, citizenship has served as a marker of "insiders" and "outsiders," that is, those who have the full panoply of political and civil rights, including self-government and (in more recent times) welfare, and those who have a more restricted set of rights. In addition, ideals of citizenship, including virtues of law-abidingness, public service, tolerance, and civic friendship, have traditionally played a significant role in guiding people's behavior and attitudes and in establishing shared parameters of social order.

However, it is no longer obvious how or precisely in what form citizenship can continue to serve these functions: the traditional concept of citizenship as a shared ethnic, religious, and/or cultural identity has limited relevance in a multicultural world, and even the connection between citizenship and national belonging has been put in jeopardy by increasing social mobility and the pervasive influence of a global economy and mass media, whose symbols and values often seem porous to national boundaries. A universal, cosmopolitan conception of citizenship seems scarcely more promising, given the natural human need for rootedness and engagement with an embodied community. Enlightenment ideals of a fully secularized citizenship are acknowledged by the staunchest defenders of Enlightenment rationality, such as Jurgen Habermas, to be unsustainable at this historic juncture, insofar as they presuppose a form of rationality "cleansed" of religious and faith-based assumptions, a proposition many post-Enlightenment philosophers no longer find plausible, and a form of "secularized" public morality purged of all traces of civil religion, another proposition that many sociologists and philosophers would find implausible. Thus, the concept and practice of citizenship, in spite of its continuing relevance as a source of normativity and shared belonging, appear to be suffering a deep crisis.

This volume is conceived fundamentally as a constructive response to this crisis. As such, one of the distinguishing features of the volume is its intensely practical orientation—it is focused on providing the sort of conceptual and normative clarification that can prepare the ground for constructive solutions to our civic crisis. In this respect, though it inevitably involves some intellectual history, sociology, and comparative political theory, it is first and foremost an exercise in *practical philosophy*. Each contributor, after his or her own manner, seeks to penetrate beneath the lived experience of contemporary citizenship, to uncover the ethical principles and values that make it intelligible and sustainable over the long haul. It is this practical orientation that explains the contemporary focus of our investigation.

Second, resisting the habit in contemporary discussions of focusing overwhelmingly on the novel dimensions of citizenship and politics, our investigation does its best to respect the dual character of contemporary problems of citizenship—the fact that they are perennial in certain respects and quite novel in others. In some respects, citizenship must accommodate itself to a fast-changing and increasingly globalized world, and this brings its own peculiar set of problems with it, both problems for the interpretation of citizenship itself, which is a concept "in motion," and problems for the moral loyalties of citizens, who inhabit multiple social groups and may have great difficulty identifying with the official civic identity of the state. In other respects, however, we are no different from our medieval and ancient Greek predecessors: we too have to confront political injustices and decide how to reconcile fidelity to our conscience with responsible participation in a political regime that does not always honor the claims of justice. Whether novel or perennial, the questions raised by citizenship today are worthy of careful and sustained scrutiny, and that is the object of this collection.

Third, while citizenship could be addressed in a more abstract manner, for example, as a way of imagining the commitments of a perfectly reasonable set of agents who need to set the terms of mutual cooperation (this is the approach we find in Rawls's original position and in Habermas's discourse ethics), in this volume, we have generally approached the problem of citizenship as a problem for the practical identity and emotional life of the agent thrust into a social network not of this own choosing, rather than as a problem of choosing an ideal community structure or impartially fixing the content of one's civic duties in a highly idealized context. We are interested in understanding what citizenship means for those who call themselves "citizens" and how the values and commitments woven into this role interact with the agent's neighboring values and commitments. All of our contributors, in one form or another, whether tacitly or expressly, pose the question, "*What is it like to be a citizen* today, and what does this imply for the lives of citizens *as human persons*?"

A fourth distinguishing feature of this volume is that rather than studying modern liberal democratic conceptions of citizenship on their own terms, for example, within the context of modern Western states and their traditional philosophical foundations (which is fairly typical in contemporary discussions), we aim to frame modern citizenship in a broader cultural and philosophical context, whether in terms of the fact of cultural pluralism and social mobility or against the backdrop of ideas and values that either are partially recovered from classical sources (such as the idea of the worthy life) or have been developed in non-Western traditions (such as Islamic ideals of submission to God's sovereignty or Confucian ideas about moral virtue and its social configuration). The point of this dialogic encounter is not to reject one of the interlocutors, but rather to see if a richer and more adequate conception of citizenship can emerge from the encounter. It seems fair to assume that all of our authors have a strong commitment to certain aspects of the Western civic inheritance, ideas such as equality before the law and freedom of conscience and association, and in this sense this volume is indeed in important respects a "product" of Western culture. However, our authors are eager to learn from the dialogic encounter with other ideas and values and would undoubtedly acknowledge that learning does not only flow in one direction!

So much for the distinguishing marks of our approach to the problems of citizenship. Now, to the specific themes we address. The essays selected for this volume address four important problems that affect the meaning and practice of citizenship in contemporary societies: (i) first, the nature and purpose of the activity of theorizing citizenship and specifically its relation to contemporary *practices* of citizenship; (ii) second, the types of emotional and moral attachment that constitute and define the civic bond, in particular in the context of modern mass societies; (iii) third, the potential tensions between the demands of civic life and the demands of the individual *conscience*; and (iv) fourth, the challenge of forging a civic ethos capable of embracing a religiously, morally, and culturally diverse citizenry.

The first two contributions address some meta-theoretical questions concerning the general content, motivation, and limitations of an ethical study of citizenship. In the introductory essay, "What Is the Use of an Ethical Theory of Citizenship?," David Thunder frames the general activity of theorizing citizenship against the fact that we humans are reflexive beings: beings who interrogate the meaning of our own activities and lives. As such, inquiry into the ethical value of citizenship is proper to the sorts of beings we are and meets a deep need to render our commitments and actions both intelligible and justifiable to ourselves and others. This need is of course deeply engrained into our psyches, as Frankl's *Man's Search for Meaning* demonstrates. However, it is more than just a psychological drive: it is a philosophical impulse to know the truth and live our lives in accordance with it. A theory of citizenship that acknowledges this philosophical impulse, illuminates the basic questions behind it, and uncovers even in a preliminary way the values and purposes served by civic identity and engagement can act as a stimulus to further reflection and serve to give some basic orientation to moral conduct. On the other hand, Thunder is at pains to point out that an ethical theory of citizenship cannot bypass the need for practical wisdom nor dispense with the task of moral formation. It can only illuminate and inspire people who have participated in, or learnt vicariously from, communities in which norms of civility and *convivencia* ("living together") are taught through example and patient instruction.

In "Varieties of Citizenship and the Moral Foundations of Politics," Bill English argues that a focus on questions of citizenship is likely to impoverish our political understanding unless we recognize the plural character of citizenship and the ways in which citizenship claims are intricately related to ethical allegiances. Attending to the varieties of citizenship, however, is difficult given the primacy of the modern state as a political unit. We can, in fact, be citizens of multiple polities and communities, depending on the kinds of allegiance each requires, and understanding this truth is crucial if debates about citizenship are to illuminate political discourse, rather than simply recapitulate existing political differences in less precise terms. By examining the kinds of state functions that are bound up with citizenship debates, we can better grasp the larger scope of this concept and its implications. What these debates show—whether they concern economic distribution, cultural identity, or cosmopolitan travel—is that the bounds of citizenship are inherently moral and that citizenship is a marker of community, which, as Augustine points out, is constituted by common objects of love. Rightly understood, questions of citizenship concern the bounds of communities and the moral obligations and opportunities that accompany them.

The next two contributions fall under the general theme of "Citizenship and Attachment." In each case, the special attachments of citizenship are discussed, and an effort is made to connect them coherently to more universalistic impulses such as the pursuit of truth and justice. In "Civic Motivation and Globalization: What Is It Like to Be a Good Citizen Today?," Simon Keller proposes a pluralistic model of civic loyalty which he claims does greater justice to the complexity of our emotional lives than standard accounts, which tend to link civic identity and loyalty quite strongly with national identity and belonging. He points out that the flourishing of states is often linked to the forging of national identities: "creating Italians" or "inventing Australians," for example. Under the associated model of patriotic citizenship, it is hoped that citizens will give a primary and far-reaching loyalty to the state and hence find motivation to act well as citizens. In the twenty-first century, states continue to be legally and morally significant entities, and there is good reason to want people to have particularized commitments to their own states. Yet, as states lose their connections with identifiable ethnic histories, as people receive more of their news and entertainment from international sources, and as the major problems we face are increasingly transnational in nature, the conditions that maintain allegiance to the state as a primary form of identity are ever further undermined. Patriotic citizenship, furthermore, has always brought with it ethical and epistemic dangers, which are arguably exacerbated by recent global changes.

What could take the place of the familiar model of patriotic citizenship? We should start, Keller suggests, by understanding the complexity of our emotional lives as citizens. A loyalty can be derivative yet very strong, and there are significant forms of emotional commitment apart from loyalty to one's state or nation. Keller sketches a broad picture of the good citizen on which she is not patriotic and does not identify primarily with her country, but on which she nevertheless holds a strong commitment to her country, grounded in an accurate understanding of her place in her local community and the wider world. This model of citizenship, he suggests, is both recognizable and widely achievable.

Emma Cohen de Lara, in "The Affective Dimension of Citizenship: A Platonic Account," offers a complementary exploration of patriotism in light of Plato's *Laws*, which, like Keller's discussion, is especially attentive to the affective bonds through which civic allegiance is realized. Contemporary literature on citizenship, Cohen de Lara observes, tends to define citizenship as rights-based, that is, as political membership by means of which one is entitled to certain civic, social, and political rights. But this approach does not do full justice to the *affective* dimension of citizenship, or citizenship defined as the emotional experience of a collective bond. In this essay, Cohen de Lara conceptualizes the affective dimension of citizenship by reappropriating insights from Plato's dialogue *Laws*.

Cohen de Lara shows how Plato, in the *Laws*, develops an interesting psychology of the citizen. Being a member of a political community, for Plato, means that one has internalized the laws of the political community, both on a cognitive and affective level. This process of internalization occurs through participation in public festivals where the laws of the polity are set to music and recited. The rhythmic bodily agreement that is part of the choral performances creates the affective bonds between the citizens. Moreover, the affective bonds between the citizens are directed toward a common object of affection, namely, the laws of the polity. These laws, furthermore, have so-called preambles that explain the reasoning behind the law. Hence, both on an emotional and a rational level, the citizens are, as it were, molded together. Cohen de Lara recognizes some of the limitations of Plato's theory when it comes to the modern, liberal democratic polity. Still, she argues that Plato helps us to conceptualize the affective dimension of citizenship that we can observe today in one's own subrational affection for one's country and fellow citizens but also, in a negative sense, in the tensions that develop between long-term citizens and newcomers. The affective dimension of citizenship is part of the empirical reality which we inhabit. Plato's insights help us recognize, articulate, interpret, and possibly change these emotions.

The third theme to be considered in this work is "Citizenship and Conscience," that is, the place of conscientious judgment and action in the political arena. In "Conscientious Citizenship: Arendt and Aquinas on Conscience and Politics," Angela Miceli argues that a Thomistic approach to conscience and its public standing can help us give the claims of conscience some normative grip in the political arena, the sort of grip they would lack if understood in purely subjective terms. She begins by observing the need, acknowledged by many political thinkers, for a space in the public sphere for moral reflection and conscientious objection, in order to resist pressures to conform to unjust political and legal norms. Hannah Arendt points to Socrates as the paradigmatic citizen—a citizen who, in her view, is responsible solely to himself and to his own internal dialogue. Miceli argues that Arendt's account of Socratic conscience fails in two important respects: first, Socratic conscience is limited to the individual and has little or no political influence, nor can convictions of conscience be shared among citizens. Second, such an account of conscience does not solve Arendt's own dilemma on the failure of conscience; that is to say, she cannot explain why Eichmann's collaboration with the extermination of the Jews was *wrong* and reprehensible.

Miceli offers a different account of conscientious citizenship by examining the theory of conscience offered by Thomas Aquinas, a theory that holds much in common with Arendt's. Since the two thinkers are not considered to hold much in common, she first demonstrates the similarities between their respective theories of conscience. Then, she argues that Aquinas offers a solution to the two problems identified in Arendt's theory. Specifically, she argues that by focusing on a *relational* aspect of conscience, citizens can share convictions of conscience with political potency. For Arendt, this is an impossibility since she believes that conscience is too personal to give rise to political action. Further, by distinguishing between true and false conscience and by offering a set of criteria with which to judge true and false convictions of conscience, Aquinas offers an answer to the problem of the failure of conscience, i.e., to the typological possibility of Eichmann.

Like Miceli, David Thunder, in his essay, "An Ethical Defense of Citizenship," is concerned with the ways in which political participation inevitably draws citizens, for better or for worse, into morally significant actions and relationships. The starting point for Thunder's argument is the observation that in many parts of the Western world, we have reached a low point in public confidence in the moral value and relevance of citizenship, in the integrity of our political institutions, and in the nobility of public office. Consequently, if we are to secure the political field for those among us virtuous enough to serve the common good, we need to restore public confidence in the ethical value of citizenship and public service. One small step in this direction would be to allay understandable moral qualms about the practice of citizenship. And that is precisely what Thunder aims to do here. He hopes that by defeating or at least weakening some serious ethical objections against citizenship, he can at least help pave the way for the larger task of developing an ethical ideal of citizenship that can inspire citizens to put their talents at the service of the common good. The three objections he addresses are rooted in (i) the alleged complicity of ordinary citizens in a range of collective and institutional evils, (ii) the alleged necessity of ruthless utilitarian reasoning in political life, and (iii) the alleged incompatibility of modern citizenship with the Christian way of life. Each of the three objections, according to Thunder, can be answered or at least significantly deflated.

The final theme to be explored is "The Ethics of Citizenship in a Multi-cultural Society." The first two essays in this section consider the virtues and character traits citizens require in order to engage constructively in a political space marked by moral and cultural heterogeneity, while the third essay explores the possibility of articulating civic norms sufficiently capacious to accommodate Islamic religious beliefs without endangering the core values of a liberal society. In "Virtue Politics: Developing Confucian Citizenship and Confucian Citizens," David Elstein considers the resources available within Confucian thought for developing an ideal of civic virtue suitable for the conditions of a modern constitutional democracy and argues that Confucian thought could support a thin theory of civic virtue capable of appealing to diverse religious and philosophical schools of thought. Although consensus about moral virtues is a serious hurdle in pluralistic societies, Elstein argues for a thin conception of Confucian moral virtues which would have a better chance of securing wide agreement. Elstein also makes the case that this line of thought can reconcile more successfully the cosmopolitan aspect of Confucian philosophy with loyalty to a particular moral and political community. The result is a theory of citizenship grounded in classical Confucian thought, but that takes democracy as a necessary condition for the full realization of Confucian virtues. Insofar as a plausible case can be made for the generality of these virtues, Confucian citizenship can make a case that there are common goods and common standards of behavior all people can share.

Paolo Monti is interested in the practice of citizenship in the context of a specific form of moral disagreement, namely, disagreement that involves religious differences. In "From Social Practices to Reflective Agency: A Postsecular Ethics of Citizenship," Monti argues that instead of thinking of the ethics of citizenship as a static set of secular norms, we ought to think of the norms of citizenship as the outcome of a dynamic interaction between coequal citizens, each of whose perspectives and values are informed and transformed by the interaction. No single person or group—whether secular or religious—controls the meaning of citizenship, and consequently, the notion of a dichotomous choice between a purely secular and purely theological ideal of citizenship does not make sense. In this sense, Monti advocates an ethic of citizenship that transcends the traditional secular-religious divide.

Monti's account of citizenship is grounded in the analysis of our condition as "co-practitioners" in civil society. As active members of society—workers, activists, consumers, players, etc.—we constantly participate in a number of social practices, and these practices come with sets of embedded beliefs, rules, habits, and values. Within this framework, Monti suggests that a reflective consideration of the web of practical cooperative relationships that ordinarily characterize our agency as actors of civil society may adequately ground a normative ethics of citizenship. Every citizen is in fact dependent on social cooperation and is in some way responsible for it, yet nobody enjoys a complete monopoly of its constitutive cognitive and motivational resources. This reflective awareness affects the self-understanding of both religious and secular citizens and calls for an epistemic and practical disposition to cooperatively rearrange and reformulate one's own arguments and actions in the light of the structural co-implication of one's own belief with the beliefs of others within the same public spaces. On this approach, the notion of citizenship is also multilayered as is our belonging and participation in civil society, at a local, national, and global level, not necessarily bound to membership in a single political entity.

The third essay in the section on citizenship in a multicultural world is entitled "Liberal Citizenship and the Search for an Overlapping Consensus: The Case of Muslim Minorities." This essay, by Andrew March, tackles a question of increasing relevance across the world, not least in Europe, where the Muslim population is projected to grow significantly over the next few decades and global Jihadist ideologies have sought legitimation in the religion of Islam, namely, the possibility of reconciling Islam with the basic commitments of citizenship in a constitutional democracy. This question is crucial, and its resolution will be decisive, for better or for worse, for the political role of Islam in both established and nascent constitutional democracies. March is not interested directly in what policies a liberal state should have toward Islam nor in what practices on the part of citizens are compatible with justice and equality, but rather in what *views* held by citizens—in this particular case, Muslim citizens—are reasonable responses to the liberal terms of social cooperation. His aim is to investigate under what conditions Islam could provide its adherents with authentically moral (rather than merely instrumental or pragmatic) reasons for signing onto the terms of social cooperation in a liberal society, and what sorts of concessions a liberal society could reasonably make to Muslim minorities with a view to winning their loyalty, without endangering the core values of a free society.

Interestingly, all three approaches to the ethics of citizenship in a multicultural society are united in (i) their implicit acceptance of the permanence of deep disagreement as a constitutive feature of modern polities; (ii) their rejection of the notion that civic morality can or ought to be neutral among competing conceptions of the good; (iii) their belief that civic morality is inevitably shaped in its content, if not exclusively, certainly in part, by the moral demands of cooperating with people with significantly different points of view; (iv) their evident concern with the reconciliation of morally substantive commitments and loyalties with the moral and practical exigencies of living in a culturally and morally heterogeneous society; and (v) their refusal to treat the norms and virtues of citizenship as entirely sui generis or independent from the norms and virtues of a good human life.

Although this collection does not pretend to offer a systematic treatment of the ethics of citizenship, it does offer some careful and original discussions of specific questions raised by civic life in the twenty-first century, in particular questions that implicate our sense of purpose, meaning, and identity as human beings inserted, for better or for worse, into the warp and woof of social life. Another distinguishing feature of this collection is that rather than working exclusively within the context of liberal theory or state-based institutions, we aim to situate contemporary challenges of civic life in a broader cultural, philosophical, and historical context, bringing "Western" ideals of citizenship into dialogue with Confucian, Islamic, and classical concepts and confronting our inherited statist paradigms of citizenship with the facts of globalization and social mobility. Attending to this broader context can potentially free our minds from lazy assumptions and blind spots that may creep into our understanding of citizenship and enrich our philosophical imagination as we attempt to adapt the theory and practice of citizenship to a fragmented, culturally diverse, and globalized world.

Pamplona, Navarra, Spain David Thunder

Contents

Part I
Theorizing the Practice of Citizenship

What Is the Use of an Ethical Theory of Citizenship?

David Thunder

Developing a coherent normative account of citizenship is a risky endeavour. The natural impulse of the political theorist is to discover order in disorder, unity in disunity, intelligibility in apparent confusion. And we theorists would like to think that we have something useful to say to those who practice citizenship yet do not engage in much systematic reflection about it. These aspirations, noble and worthy as they surely are, carry with them the risk of imposing order where there is none, stipulating a fake unity to cover up disunity, rendering intelligible what is mysterious and resistant to analysis, and adopting a patronizing and superior stance toward those who "do" citizenship rather than theorizing it, categorizing and sorting their "doings" before taking the trouble to find out what these doings *mean* to the doers. In stepping back from the practice of citizenship, and attempting to separate out the "noise" from the substance, we risk trapping the practice in a sterile theoretical framework, or seeing in the practice what we *want* to see, rather than sincerely reflecting on the values that are embodied in it.

Notwithstanding these risks, theorizing citizenship at its best is nothing but an extension and clarification of the ordinary act of self-interpretation that is incumbent upon all of us, regardless of our profession or degree of intellectual prowess. As such, while we should theorize citizenship with our eyes wide open to the risks such a venture entails, philosophical reflection upon citizenship and its demands is a noble and worthwhile endeavour, and should not be cast aside lightly. The risks of oversimplification, prideful and patronising attitudes, ideological imposition, and the exaggerated sense of self-importance, can be substantially offset if those who

---

The original version of this chapter was revised: This chapter was previously published as non-open access. It has now been changed to open access under a CC BY 4.0 license. The correction to this chapter is available at https://doi.org/10.1007/978-3-319-50415-5_10

D. Thunder (✉)
Institute for Culture and Society, University of Navarra, Pamplona, Navarra, Spain
e-mail: dthunder@unav.es

D. Thunder (ed.), *The Ethics of Citizenship in the 21st Century*,
https://doi.org/10.1007/978-3-319-50415-5_1

theorize the practice of citizenship approach political and social phenomena wanting to learn and be enlightened, not just wanting to reform, enlighten, or render intelligible. We must temper our philosophical ambition with a generous dose of humility and intellectual flexibility.

Above all, we must clarify for ourselves what we can reasonably hope to achieve by our theoretical reflections, as well as acknowledging to others and to ourselves certain limitations inherent in the philosophical enterprise. In this paper, my goal is not to develop a specific account of citizenship, but to offer some reflections on the nature of that enterprise. In this sense, this paper could be considered an exercise in "meta-theory" – theory about theory. There are two basic questions I wish to address, in the hopes of providing some reasonable parameters for the enterprise of studying and theorizing citizenship: First, broadly speaking, what is the positive contribution such an enterprise might make to our lives as human beings? Second, where are the outer limits of the transformative power of a theory of citizenship?

Q. 1 What Might a Theory of Citizenship Usefully Contribute to Our Lives as Human Beings?

As moral and political theorists, it is worth stepping back from time to time from our craft, to ask, *what exactly are we doing, and why?* If we aspire to do more than "paint a pretty picture" of the good citizen, to be dusted off and admired from afar, if we pretend to have something to say of interest to practitioners—as I believe most of us do—then what exactly is it that we hope to *contribute* through our theorizing? What end or ends do we hope to advance when we develop normative accounts of citizenship? Developing an account of the good citizen, however tentative or partial, is a human activity, and human beings do not willingly undertake projects for no reason at all. Of all of the possible reasons that might motivate such an enterprise, is there any that can adequately illuminate the relationship between *theories* of citizenship and the *practice* of citizenship on the ground, in a way that explains how theorizing has some interesting bearing on practice, even if the relationship is complex and problematic? Are there reasons underlying the theoretical enterprise that can make a bridge between the theoretical and practical enterprises without simplistically assuming that theory either simply mirrors practice or stands entirely aloof from it?

Although one could attempt to make some modest generalizations about the practice of citizenship, recording people's attitudes toward some more or less conventional notion of citizenship, this is certainly not what we are doing when we develop a normative account of citizenship. A normative account of citizenship aims to illuminate the possible value of the activities and relationships associated with citizenship, from the perspective of a person who strives to live a worthy and worthwhile life.[1] Now, if the value of citizenship was a given, as obvious as the value of

[1] The perspective of the villain is useful insofar as it helps to bring into relief that of the responsible, honourable citizen. The perspective of the person who seeks to live a worthy life is described in greater detail in Thunder 2014, chap. 2, "The Concept of Ethical Integrity."

water for a tree, or the value of milk for an infant, then elaborate discussions and debates about the ethics of citizenship would not make much sense. But as it happens, citizenship is a human role which is susceptible to diverse interpretations and enactments and subject to disagreement among reasonable and responsible persons. And we human beings are reflective and reflexive by nature. We do not simply actualize our potentialities, but we pose ourselves questions like "Who am I?," "What is my potential?," "What do my relationships mean for me?" and "What ought I do?" Citizenship, insofar as it gives expression to the meaning of our relationships and duties, our standing in the public square, and the meaning of our lives as persons, is necessarily an interpretive and self-interpretive category.

If we add to this the fact that there is something important at stake in how we live our lives—that we may do so with more or less justice, generosity, magnanimity, kindness, and so forth—then the activity of interpreting our role as citizens is not merely of theoretical interest, analagous to the interpretation of a mathematical theorem, but of intensely *practical* interest. After all, how we interpret our citizenship and its demands will shape the type of person we become, for better or for worse. This is true not only of the professional political philosopher, but of any man or woman on the street. Nobody, save infants and those deprived of cognitive functions, escapes the fate of being a self-interpreting being, and nobody escapes the fate of personal responsibility for their self-interpretations and corresponding actions.

If this is so, then we all have an interest, in Harry Frankfurt's words, in "getting it right," (Frankfurt 2006) both in regard to our overall way of life, and in regard to our relationship with the communities of which we form a part. We *all* have an interest in sifting through candidate answers to the question, "how should I live?" and selecting one that is acceptable, all things considered. Reflexivity and reflectiveness are thus imperatives of the human condition, once we accept that each of us bears personal responsibility for his or her own choices, and once we accept that those choices are not simply predetermined by circumstances independent of the agent.

Obviously, many people do not take seriously the demand to take themselves seriously, to ponder the meaning of their lives, to act with a sense of responsibility. Instead, they may settle for easy and unreflective answers about the meaning of their lives. Nonetheless, this does not make it any less true that our language, institutions, and habits presuppose, for the most part, that we are indeed answerable for our own choices and actions, and that a person who deserves the respect and admiration of others is a person who *takes himself seriously*, and takes care to "get it right" when it comes to understanding who he is, how he relates to others, and how he should act on a day-to-day basis.

If we accept that this interpretive imperative is a valid feature of human life and is binding upon all—even upon those who wilfully ignore it—then the activities of the ethicist begin to look a lot less divorced from the activities of ordinary people than they might at first appear. Theorizing about the value of citizenship and its place in a worthy life begins to look more like an extension of the self-interpretive activities of ordinary persons than the specialized craft of a professional guild. The theorist, after all, is not only a theorist, but a participant in political and social life, and thus he has a practical interest in clarifying the meaning of his relation with the political community. And the citizen, for his part, may not be a professional theorist, yet he too is a participant in political and social order, and has an obvious practical interest in grasping its meaning and its demands upon him. In short, the task of interpreting the meaning and implications of our participation in social and political life is incumbent, to a greater or lesser degree, upon all of us, professional ethicist and ordinary citizen alike. Notwithstanding the fact that ethical reflection in academia has a more systematic and comprehensive quality than ethical reflection in the media and in the streets, ethical theories of citizenship are fundamentally extensions of ordinary reflection of the sort that all reflective citizens are capable and well-advised to engage in.[2] As such, political theory can both learn from the reflections of ordinary citizens (there is no necessary correlation between systematicity or logical rigour and good sense!) and serve to clarify, enrich, critique, and make explicit the reflections of ordinary citizens.

Thus far, I have tried to show that the construction of ethical accounts of citizenship is not the strange and idiosyncratic enterprise that it might initially appear to be—that it is fundamentally an extension of the interpretive and self-interpretive enterprise that is incumbent upon all citizens. But to many, it may still appear too "other-worldly," insofar as it attempts to render civic practices answerable to demanding moral norms. Someone might object, for example, that ethical theories of citizenship, precisely insofar as they paint citizenship at its best, irresponsibly disregard the *actual* circumstances conditioning the practice of citizenship in the real world—in particular, the human tendencies toward self-aggrandizement, war, violence, deception, and corruption.

The charge that theories of citizenship are irrelevant in practice is bolstered by a certain view of moral philosophy that sees adaptation of moral principles to the empirical conditions of human life as a sort of adulteration of morality, a "second-class" morality that is not worthy of the name.[3] John Rawls's theory of justice, insofar as it derives the basic principles of justice from a highly idealized "original position" of mutually disinterested bargainers, may be accused of having limited relevance to the actual circumstances of *real* citizens, who find themselves thrust into unjust societies and structures, with limited economic and political power to defend their interests. Something similar might be said of other social contract theories, insofar as they rest on the conceit of an original agreement or act of consent among equals on the terms of social cooperation, something that neither was nor ever could be achieved in real human communities, which rely on tradition, inherited structures, seniority, and the authority of some members over others, even in the most democratically structured societies.[4]

---

[2]This argument parallels, and is undoubtedly influenced by, MacIntyre's reflections on "plain persons" and moral philosophy (MacIntyre 1992).

[3]Certain comments by Immanuel Kant, in particular about the independence of moralty from the empirical data, might lead one to take this view, although to what extent this is a faithful reading of Kant is quite another question.

[4]I do not mean to entirely dismiss the utility of political theories that rest on thought experiments or philosophical conceits. There is, after all, a respected tradition of utopian and distopian literature. Abstracting away from real political and social conditions can sometimes serve to shed valuable light on the real conditions of social life. For example, utopian and distopian accounts of

In light of the excessively abstract and unreal quality of highly idealized approaches to political theory such as those I have just mentioned, skepticism about the practical relevance of ethical theories of citizenship is quite understandable. However, there are ways to approach the question of citizenship that do not fall into the trap of abstracting away from the difficult and messy conditions of real societies. There are ways of theorizing citizenship that are neither flat-footed, uncritical descriptions of the social landscape (an enterprise whose possibility is at any rate highly debateable[5]), nor elaborate structures of principles that conveniently disregard salient empirical conditions of political life. We can approach citizenship with a blend of realism and hope, striving to understand the practice at its best, without turning a blind eye to the difficulties of implementation in an imperfect world partly dominated by evil and unjust persons and organizations. I would characterise such an approach as broadly Aristotelian in spirit, not in the sense of embracing all the nuances of an Aristotelian picture of social order, but in the sense of sharing Aristotle's passion for discovering not only what is pleasing to behold from a distance, but what real societies and human beings are capable of achieving, consistent with the constraints of human nature and the lessons of history.[6]

This approach accepts that systematic inquiry about political and social order is not merely oriented toward theoretical knowledge, but toward the improvement of self and society. To study citizenship may bring the satisfaction of a more refined understanding of oneself and one's community—a benefit not to be underestimated—but it is also, of its very nature, a critical study of our commitments and priorities as human beings. After all, to exercise one's citizenship is to attempt to bring oneself into a "right relation" with the surrounding community. As such, the study of citizenship cannot be indifferent to the quality of our lives as human beings. To use Christine Korsgaard's language, a theory of citizenship is a clarification of our "practical identity," "a description [of yourself] under which you value yourself, a description under which you find your life to be worth living and your actions to be worth undertaking" (Korsgaard 1996, 101).

We are led to inquire into the meaning and values implicit in the practice of citizenship not for its own sake, but because as human beings, we can neither live virtuously nor make sense of our lives outside of the structure of a human community and outside the structure of a system of law and order. The commitment to personal growth and virtue naturally leads us to inquire into the conditions under which personal and social development is *possible*. This is what leads us to the study of political community, and concomitantly, to the study of citizenship. The preconditions

social order may serve to render certain values or disvalues more salient in our imagination. Nonetheless, building utopias and thought experiments is a risky endeavour, and is no substitute for the task of thinking through the conditions facing agents in real societies.

[5]Cf Finnis 1998, 40–42 for a succinct refutation of the viability of "value-free" social science.

[6]Aristotle's discussion of oligarchic and democratic regimes is a good example of this grounding of theory in history and praxis. Aristotle does not simply stipulate the proper mix of oligarchic and democratic principles. Rather, he begins by adjudicating historically familiar debates among oligarchs and democrats. See Aristotle's *Politics*, bk. 3, esp. 1280a6-1284b34; and bk. 6, esp. 1318a10–1318b5 (Aristotle 1984).

for personal and social development naturally include culture—here understood broadly in terms of moral dispositions, habits of mind, and ethical ideals—and institutions, or rule-governed practices. The ethics of citizenship connects relatively seamlessly with the cultural question, but not all accounts of citizenship are adequately attentive to the institutional context of citizenship. Any attempt to discuss the ethics of citizenship while ignoring or by-passing the institutional question would be a piece of other-worldly speculation or an exercise in utopian thinking.

One of the closing passages of Aristotle's *Nicomachean Ethics* is instructive in this regard. It points out that "discourses" alone will not suffice to persuade people to act justly and virtuously—a point that marks the transition to politics, which complements philosophy and high culture with law and punishment. A normative theory of citizenship must attend not only to the moral values and virtues of community life such as justice and cooperation among equals, but the institutional conditions under which these values can in fact stand some chance of being *realized* and respected by the community at large.

> Now if what has to do with happiness as well as with the virtues, and also with friendship and pleasure, has been sufficiently discussed in outline, ought one to assume that our chosen task has its end? Or, as has been said, is the end in matters of action not contemplating and knowing each of them but rather doing them? Then it is not sufficient to know about virtue, but one must try to have it and use it, unless there is some other way that we become good...if discourses by themselves were sufficient for making people decent, then justly "they would take many large fees," as Theognis says, and one would need to provide them, but as things are, discourses appear to have the power to encourage and stimulate open-natured young people, and would make a well-born character that loves what is truly beautiful be inspired with virtue, but they are unable to encourage most people toward what is beautiful and good. (*Nicomachean Ethics*, bk. X, 1179b1–10 (Aristotle 2009))

An Aristotelian respect for the basic constraints of human nature, for those aspects of our existence that are integral to a meaningful and worthwhile life and those tendencies that are part and parcel of our mortal condition, does not entail that theories of citizenship and political order must blindly ape the patterns of human behaviour or indulge man's most depraved instincts. Nor does it mean that theories of citizenship must put political expediency and survival above all other human goods. A normative account of citizenship, at its best, calls forth our better selves, reminding us of the goodness we are capable of, in spite of the temptation to capitulate to selfishness, and in spite of our participation in institutions and social structures that may penalize us for putting our lives at the service of the community. A normative account of citizenship, while it refuses to close its eyes to existing social, cultural, and institutional constraints, tries to imagine a form of civic life that is humanly dignifying and tries to devise strategies for making society and culture more hospitable to that dignifying vision. In this sense, a normative account of citizenship is constructive and future-oriented, not merely critical of the status quo.

Q. 2 Where Are the Outer Limits of the Transformational Power of a Theory of Citizenship?

So far, I have suggested that the enterprise of developing a normative account of citizenship, far from being a pure exercise in utopian thinking, is at its best an engagement with the facts on the ground, an attempt to develop an interpretation of the practice of citizenship that respects its operating conditions but also calls forth the agent's higher self. It is now time to consider the other side of the coin, namely the limits inherent in theory as an instrument of moral, political, and social transformation. We political philosophers are quite susceptible to the temptation of exaggerating our own role in political life, or overestimating the transformative power of our intellectual craft. We may even be tempted, from time to time, to imagine ourselves in the role of a philosopher-king, contemplating the revolution our own ideas could effect in the political landscape and the public mindset—if only people would pay more attention to them!

This temptation rests on at least two errors: (i) first, the error of exaggerating the power of theory to soundly motivate action and direct practice; and (ii) second, the error of thinking that the values defended by the theorist can be implemented through an act of power emanating from one center, say a powerful agent with the "right ideas." By considering each of these errors separately, we can get a clearer picture of some of the limitations of political theory as an instrument of social change.

Political theory can undoubtedly *clarify* motivation and *illuminate* the values at stake in the practice of citizenship. However, we human beings are on the one hand largely (though not entirely) creatures of habit, highly influenced by our early education and socialization as children and adolescents, and on the other hand capable of directing our lives according to our own preferences and desires, for better or for worse. The force of habit and personal commitment (for better or for worse) is typically just as powerful as the ideas we are exposed to as adults. For this reason, theory, while it can clarify and to some extent channel existing motives, cannot usually defeat opposing motives or make up for missing motives. For example, if a person has become desensitized to beauty and goodness, or hardened to the suffering of others, reading about values or aesthetics is unlikely to suddenly open his eyes to beauty and goodness. Such a person needs a conversion of the heart and mind, and this is occasioned either by a personal crisis or a dramatic and moving encounter with beauty or goodness, frequently revealed in another person or in an unmerited insight apparently granted from on high.

Similarly, the vantage-point of the political theorist, however informed by practice and conversation and reading, is nonetheless the vantage-point of a single person, and insofar as it aims to embrace a wide array of phenomena under a single coherent idea or theory, necessarily stands at a certain distance from the vantage-point of the political actor who must make decisions that are highly conditioned by his own unique role in the political system, and of course by cultural and institutional constraints as they operate upon *him*. The strength of political theory is that it can provide an account of citizenship and political action that is valid for a large number of political actors. But for this very reason, it must leave generous leeway for the practical wisdom of citizens, who are not constructing general accounts of citizenship, but deciding how to act *here and now*, with all of their personal baggage involved, including their capacities, talents, sense of calling, institutional roles, political power, and social networks. Though a theory of citizenship may illuminate and clarify what is at stake in the decisions of the citizen, it must ultimately leave a good deal up to the informed deliberation and decision of the citizen, and it must restrain its inclination to usurp or suppress the pivotal role of practical wisdom in political life.

Besides overestimating the power of theory to guide and motivate practice, another way we might overestimate the transformative power of theory is to think that the step from theory to practice is as simple as putting sound ideas in the mind of a great and wise statesman, so that they might be implemented by him—albeit mediated through his practical wisdom—"top down," like a small piece of yeast that penetrates and transforms the whole dough mix. Unfortunately (or perhaps fortunately!), moral and civic ideals can rarely be properly established in a large, dispersed population through the strategic actions of a few powerful individuals. I do not deny that there may be exceptional moments of crisis in which the heroic or exemplary action of a great statesman can have a powerful transformative impact on public mores and behaviour.[7] However, in the ordinary course of events, transformations in public mores and behaviour cannot be effected rapidly and effectively by a few powerful actors except by means that are irreconcilable with the value of personal freedom, such as fear-mongering and ideological (i.e. irrational, epistemically suspect, manipulative) propaganda.

Moral and political transformation in a free society is achieved through persuasion, education, and example. It aims to engage not only the passions, but the *reason* of the citizen. The citizen must—proportionate to his age and reasoning abilities—become actively and rationally complicit in his own transformation, otherwise that transformation is build on the external manipulation of his passions, rather than on genuine rational reflection, and is liable to be reversed when the passions find another object that is more satisfying or pleasurable.[8] But speaking to the reason of citizens is an extended and gradual endeavour, which normally requires the free cooperation of educators, parents, and communities. It is one thing to shift people's

[7] Martin Luther King, Mahatma Ghandi, and Abraham Lincoln come to mind as possible examples. Let the reader think of his or her own favorite exemplary and transformative public figures.

[8] My rejection of predominantly passion-driven forms of influence is perfectly compatible with the legitimate and crucial role of the emotions in rational discourse and persuasion. There is a world of difference between the emotional manipulation associated with ideological discourse, which has no serious interest in the pursuit of truth, and rational discourse that appeals to or induces emotional dispositions, whether compassion, fear, affection, or courage, without abandoning the pursuit of truth.

incentives by denying them information or feeding them a "party line," quite another to win them over to a better way of life, responding to their questions and objections along the way.

A state-imposed programme of civic ethics, even if it happens to be based on a more or less sound theory of citizenship, is unlikely to make for better citizens, unless it does the hard work of winning over communities and educators, adapting its curriculum to local conditions, and balancing instruction with inspiring real-life role models that citizens can learn from. In short, civic ideals, however coherent and well-grounded, only become securely embedded in the mind and heart of a population when they are *freely* embraced on the ground, supported by the presence of exemplary citizens in local communities, and transmitted from generation to generation through educational institutions that are not simply dictated by government policy, but embraced, adapted, and owned by teachers, parents, and (proportionate to their maturity and stage of development) students.

A tremendous amount of cooperation would be required to successfully and respectfully instill sound civic ideals in a large population, and that cooperation would, of course, be contingent upon the free choices of countless citizens, not just on the opportunities and obligations created by public policies. For these reasons, any political theorist with the ambition of influencing civic culture or transforming society with his or her ideas had better keep in mind that quick-fix, top-down solutions usually rely on manipulative and tyrannical tactics, and that the true friend of freedom will restrain his transformative zeal and patiently advance his ideas through a delicate balance of legislation, rational persuasion and cooperation.

* * *

To reiterate, the purpose of this essay has not been to develop a substantive normative account of citizenship, but to provide a broad framework for thinking through the practical contribution and relevance of a normative theory of citizenship. I have sought to clarify what a theory of citizenship might hope to achieve beyond the intrinsic satisfaction of seeing things more clearly (theoria), and what sorts of limitations confront the theorist's ambitions when we give due weight to the values of rationality and personal freedom. I have suggested that a theory of citizenship is fundamentally a continuation of the task of self-interpretation that is incumbent upon all citizens, and that this task must avoid slipping into utopianism by keeping in mind the basic limitations of human nature. In addition, I have argued that the transformative impact of theory is necessarily limited by the fact that the epistemic vantage-point of the theorist is importantly different from that of many practitioners, as well as by the fact that social transformation is contingent on the free cooperation of many different persons, something that no single person, government, or institution can hope to guarantee. To the extent that these clarifications are found acceptable, they should serve as useful guideposts for the theoretical enterprise, and as sobering reminders of the dangers of philosophical hubris.

References

Aristotle. (1984). Edited by Jonathan Barnes. *The complete works of Aristotle*, Vol. 2. Princeton: Princeton University Press.

Aristotle. (2009). *The Nicomachean ethics*. Trans. D. Ross. Oxford/New York: Oxford University Press.

Finnis, J. (1998). *Aquinas: Moral, political, and legal theory*, Founders of Modern Political and Social Thought. Oxford: Oxford University Press.

Frankfurt, H. (2006). *Taking ourselves seriously and getting it right*. Stanford: Stanford University Press.

Korsgaard, C. M. (1996). *The sources of normativity*. Cambridge/New York: Cambridge University Press.

MacIntyre, A. (1992). Plain persons and moral philosophy: Rules, virtues, and goods. *American Catholic Philosophical Quarterly, 66*, 3–19.

Thunder, D. (2014). *Citizenship and the pursuit of the worthy life*. New York: Cambridge University Press.

Varieties of Citizenship and the Moral Foundations of Politics

William English

I want to begin with the controversial suggestion that debates about citizenship tend to confuse more than they illuminate political discourse. Citizenship is a source of confusion because it has two different sorts of meaning: it has a specific technical meaning in the context of modern states, while it also has a deeper moral meaning as a fundamental political concept. In so far as the moral dimensions of citizenship do not align with the juridical and administrative questions faced by states – and they often do not – we can end up talking about two different things when we debate citizenship, resulting in unnecessary confusion.

The main aim of this essay is to clarify these two senses of citizenship. Rather than forcing us to choose between them, this clarification will show that both serve useful purposes. However, their contrast opens up deeper questions about the ethical foundations of communities and the extent to which these can or should map on to the geographical and juridical boundaries of states.

At their deepest level, debates about citizenship are debates about the fundamental moral commitments that define communities and the proper institutional expression of these commitments. That is to say that debates about citizenship are a way of recapitulating a range of basic political debates. In some instances, the community in question will be coincident with the population encompassed by a state, in which case the two sense of citizenship can happily coincide.

However, we can coherently talk about citizenship in political communities that are not states; and our discussions of state based citizenship can lose sight of the moral dimensions of citizenship, focusing instead on more narrowly juridical questions related to administrative functions and capacities. Not only is it helpful, for the sake of clarity, to differentiate between these different meanings of citizenship. Reflecting on the distinctive concerns surrounding citizenship offers insightful lessons for political theory concerning the principle of subsidiarity, the scope of state

W. English (✉)
McDonough School of Business, Georgetown University, Washington, DC, USA
e-mail: william.english@georgetown.edu

D. Thunder (ed.), *The Ethics of Citizenship in the 21st Century*,
DOI 10.1007/978-3-319-50415-5_2

power, and the tensions between universality and particularity. As debates about citizenship become increasingly heated in both Europe and America, I believe it is valuable to delineate the different meanings of citizenship and call attention to their inherently moral dimensions.

Indeed, my argument sheds light on political phenomena that have recently caught ruling elites by surprise concerning the popular backlash against refugees in Europe and immigration in the United States. Many in the political class have approached these issues through the lens of conventional state-based policy analysis, examining the economic and bureaucratic burdens of accepting new populations, and concluded that this is at least benign if not constructive. However, significant proportions of current citizens have perceived the influx of "foreigners" as an attack on their identity and way of life, to a degree that has provoked moral outrage and political mobilization. Both sides have a point. On the whole, as policy analysts have noted, immigrants make significant contributions to the economy and do not burden state functions (public goods, welfare, law enforcement) more than existing citizens. However, as critics have lamented, immigrants can have different mannerisms and values that transform certain social practices on a local level and may even challenge existing political coalitions over time. The grand question for our current political moment is how to reconcile what I will describe as the juridical and moral dimensions of citizenship reflected in these different perspectives.

Consider three sorts of questions that are routinely asked in public debates about citizenship:

1. Who should be considered a citizen of a particular state and what rights and duties should attach to that designation?
2. Is citizenship an outdated concept, one that should be abandoned in favor of more cosmopolitan accounts of political identity, human rights, and more fluid state borders?
3. Can a thick and compelling notion of citizenship serve as a basis for reinvigorating the political, cultural, ethical life of modern societies?

These are good and seemingly coherent questions, but they invoke both juridical and ethical conceptions of citizenship that must be disentangled for us to adequately address them.

The juridical conception of citizenship is the most common and straightforward. On this account, citizenship concerns who has access to the rights, benefits, and duties provided by the sovereign political authority of a state. The sovereignty of a state consists precisely in its power to create and enforce law, as well as to administer state functions such as the collection of taxes, the distribution of benefits, and the enforcement of justice. For a variety of historical and practical reasons, geographically defined states are the locus of political sovereignty in the modern world. The development of international institutions like the United Nations and International Criminal Court, as well as cooperative political, economic, and military bodies such as the European Union and NATO, complicates state based sovereignty but has not fundamentally replaced it- at least not yet.

Citizens of modern states hotly debate what rights, benefits, and duties citizenship should entail. For example, should all citizens be required to do military service? To what degree should rich citizens be taxed to support poor citizens? And should some crimes disqualify citizens from exercising certain political rights, like the right to vote? Since modern democratic states are constituted by citizens, most contemporary political debates are in some sense debates that concern citizenship.

Also, hotly debated is the question of who can become a citizen and under what circumstances. In many developed countries, the number of people who would like to immigrate and become citizens far outnumbers the number permitted to do so. One obvious reason for restricting immigration is that the resources of any country are scarce and can be strained by the immigration of poorer populations if they draw more from social welfare programs than they contribute in terms of economic growth.

A number of states have responded to this concern, in part, by allowing rich individuals to simply buy citizenship. For example, one can become a citizen of Malta for a mere 650,000 euros. In exchange for citizenship, one receives a number of valuable benefits, such as an EU passport and visa free travel to the US as well as a modestly low tax rate.

If citizenship is simply a bundle of rights, duties, and benefits, it's not clear that there is anything wrong with commodifying it and selling it to the highest bidders. Indeed it is worth noting that the juridical character of state based citizenship lends itself to such transactions. The point of citizenship is it that it renders rights and duties legible, makes distinctions between who is in and out, and clarifies organizing principles of a polity and who can participate in government. There is no ambiguity about the legal dimensions of citizenship, making citizenship easy to evaluate, price, and sell. So long as the terms of sale benefit the state and the individual in question, this sort of transaction appears a win-win for all involved.

Such a perspective conceives of the state as administrative body whose *raison d'être* is to coordinate a stable and productive society. This trades on what the political theorist, Joan Lockwood O'Donovan describes as a "Functional" account of the state. The state enables some group of people to live together in a sustainable manner with "effective government, military capacity, constitutional order, unifying cultural traditions, social stability, and economic development (2004a, 281)." In so far as the concerns of modern states are primarily economic, then citizenship ought to be open to anyone who can make a net economic contribution to a state without compromising its principles of social order.

This perspective is repugnant, however, to those who view citizenship in more than economic terms. Citizenship, it is argued, is a matter of political identity, and identity cannot simply be bought and sold. But what is the basis of this identity? There is a long tradition of thought that conceives of a "people" or nation that exists as an organic unity prior to the state, which a state then gives juridical form to. It is for this reason that we commonly talk of a "nation state" rather than simply a state.

Joan Lockwood O'Donovan identifies this vision with the "romantic nationalism" of the nineteenth century. Romantic nationalism conceives "the nation as a unique communal totality, at once natural and historical, [that] gives rise to and morally justifies the sovereign state. Constitutive of this prior totality, on the romantic view, are such features as a common language and ethnic inheritance – shared sentiments, mores, spiritual capacities, and historical memories – and a continuous relationship to a particular soil (2004a, 287)." The immediate political implication of this view was summed up by the nineteenth century Italian nationalist Giuseppe Mazzini: "Every nation a state…only one state for the entire nation." Note that the question of citizenship does not arise in the same way for romantic nationalism for it is already settled. Citizens are simply members of the nation, and nationality is a matter of ethno, geographical, cultural inheritance. One can't buy citizenship, it is only acquired through birth and communal formation.

There are elements of romantic nationalism that appear as a valid corrective to the thin view of citizenship associated with the functional state. The grain of truth contained in romantic nationalism is that there are social realities that are distinct from the state, which the state properly expresses and serves. Moreover, political identity generally involves much more than a mutual interest in social stability and economic prosperity; and the moral convictions that are bound up with a people's political identity play an essential role in making a state successful. This is simply to recognize a sociological fact that Charles Taylor among others has drawn attention to, namely, that a society "cannot hold together simply by the satisfaction of its members' needs and interests. It also requires a common, or at least widespread set of beliefs which link its structures and practices with what its members see as ultimately significant (459)."

Where romantic nationalism errs is in the attempt to reify such beliefs, structures, and practices into a monolithic identity, often with an ethno-racial foundation. In the first place, this tends to rule out the very idea of immigration, for citizenship must be a matter of birth and not choice. Moreover, the idealization of the nation is liable to impose more conformity than naturally exists and draw stricter boundaries between insiders and outsiders, suppressing pluralistic debate. Finally, the identification of state and nation tends to spiritualize the state, and fuel totalitarian movements.

The identification of state and nation creates additional problems when multiple ethnic populations are contained within a single state, or when such populations cross state borders. The recent crisis between Ukraine and Russia, which resulted in Russia's annexation of Crimea, has not only highlighted the challenges of governing a country with latent ethnic divisions torn between European and Russian identities. It has also made clear that Russia still harbors some aspiration to protect and perhaps repatriate ethnic Russians in other states. Similarly, the ongoing Syrian refugee crisis, which raises the question of whether European states should accept large numbers of non-European refugees, has called attention to the challenge of integrating populations with different religious, cultural, and ethnic backgrounds.

If we reject romantic nationalism, is there still a way to address the sociological truth that a flourishing state requires the allegiance and contributions of its citizens beyond calculations of strict self-interest and the minimal requirements of law? I think the most attractive formulation of an alternative response is characterized by what Joan Lockwood O'Donovan describes as "civic nationalism," according to which the nation is:

> "regarded not as a prior cause of the state but as coterminous with it and, to some extend, the work of it. The civic nation comprises the ongoing moral political reality of the 'popular will' as a vital community of faith, sentiment, and devotion. A rational communion, the civic nation is formed over time through the operation of political and legal institutions according to the principles of universal justice. But it is also a deliberate project of public education and mobilization: of educating citizens in the principles of liberal-democratic political culture and mobilizing them for political action (2004a, 279)."

We can recognize in this vision elements of both classical republicanism and modern communitarianism, buttressed by the institutional forms of liberal democracy. Crucially, the civic nation is based on reasoned principles, not blood, and thus it is possible for citizenship to be open to anyone who shares those principles, consistent with other pragmatic constraints.

However, also critical to this vision, is an understanding that adherence to principles of justice is cemented through shared sentiments, educational formation, and a broader political culture. Thus it is possible to talk, as Samuel Huntington did in the case of America, of both creed and culture being essential to a civic nation.

The United States is often said to be the first country founded on the basis of an idea, and indeed its founding documents are the source of a powerful creed. However, its culture has proved a powerful independent force, one that has been able to assimilate a remarkable range of immigrants. American citizens may celebrate their ethnic ancestry, be it Irish, Italian, Chinese, Persian, or Moroccan, but within a generation immigrants tend to thoroughly identify as American citizens as their children happily adopt American culture. Also, it is worth nothing that there are a variety of paths to citizenship in the US, but one way citizenship can be earned is through military service, one of the most powerfully acculturating experiences in the modern world.

The idea of the civic nation stands between the high idealism of romantic nationalism and the minimally demanding functional state, but it still begs the question as to how the moral commitments that define citizenship are to be developed and what can be expected of them in the context of larger debates concerning legitimate state power.

The philosopher Hegel famously developed the concept of "*Sittlichkeit*" to describe the ethical feelings and judgments that become a second nature to people who inhabit common practices and institutions (see his *System der Sittlichkeit* [*System of Ethical Life*] p.146 and *Hegel* by Taylor p. 376). At an abstract level, it is not hard to identify the origins of these feelings and judgments. Religion, schools, culture, art, literature, family, friends, clubs, sports, and common enemies all contribute to the development of *Sittlichkeit*. These all play crucial habituating and communicative functions that can engender deep-seated normative commitments. The question, though, is to what degree they can be deliberately shaped as part of state-led agenda aimed at developing certain sorts of citizens and common moral purposes.

Consider, on this point, a claim made by the Italian fascist leader Benito Mussolini, in an essay entitled "The Doctrine of Fascism" (published in 1935): "the nation is created by the State, which gives to the people, conscious of its own moral unity, a will and therefore an effective existence." In distinction to romantic nationalism, on this view the nation does not precede the state. Rather the state creates a nation, providing its citizens with a sense of meaning and purpose that can inspire their allegiance and aid, beyond what is required by mere economic self-interest.

Mussolini continues:

> Fascism sees in the world not only those superficial, material aspects in which man appears as an individual, standing by himself, self-centered, subject to natural law, which instinctively urges him toward a life of selfish momentary pleasure; it sees not only the individual but the nation and the country; individuals and generations bound together by a moral law, with common traditions and a mission which suppressing the instinct for life closed in a brief circle of pleasure, builds up a higher life, founded on duty, a life free from the limitations of time and space, in which the individual, by self-sacrifice, the renunciation of self-interest, by death itself, can achieve that purely spiritual existence in which his value as a man consists.

I quote Mussolini at length to illustrate both attractive elements in his attempt to articulate a thick moral concept of citizenship, as well as the dangers that such a project could involve.

Modern liberals rightly reject the radical subordination of the individual to the state. "All men are created equal… and endowed…with certain unalienable rights," reads America's Declaration of Independence, and liberal democracy claims not only to enable government "of the people, by the people, [and] for the people" but also to establish political institutions that promote justice. Mussolini's Fascism is easy to dismiss based on its manifest injustice, which involved the repression of minority languages and cultures, the annexation of foreign lands with ethnic Italian populations, and the totalitarian subordination of individual interests to state interests.

However, the aspirations of "civic nationalism" survive in contemporary political discourse and can be understood as staking out a position in a larger debate about the nature and promise of liberal democracy. Specifically, this debate concerns what moral convictions citizens must share in order for a polity to flourish and where these convictions come from. It's useful to step back and take a broader historical view to understand the development and importance of this debate.

Modern European states owe their emergence to the wars of religion, which destroyed two older principles of transnational political order, namely the Holy Roman Empire and the Catholic Church. The solution to the tremendous bloodshed of that time, fueled by rival religious convictions and politically ambitious princes, was articulated in the Treaty of Westphalia. The treaty involved political separation and containment, seeking to minimize latent conflict by dividing peoples according to their dominant conceptions of the good, in this case, religion. The Westphalian system by no means ended conflicts, but it reconfigured the political geography to separate peoples with deep rival ethical convictions that led to conflict. It is not surprising then, that modern political theory has often been suspicious of deep ethical convictions, seeing them less as a source of social virtues and more as threats to peace.

The concept of toleration, which has become so central to modern liberal theory, represents a sustained attempt to work out both what kind of ethical difference is acceptable in liberal societies and what sort of ethical commitments are legitimate for modern states to require. For example, for John Locke, toleration meant relaxing the demand of religious uniformity in England, a policy for which he provided both theological and practical arguments (see his *Letter Concerning Toleration*). Chief amongst the latter was the claim that enforcing religious conformity was itself a cause of civil unrest. The state does not have the right to ask of its citizens that they all profess a certain religion, and when it does it puts those who hold other religious convictions in unnecessary enmity towards the state (Locke 99).

Crucial to Locke's argument was the claim that many of the demands of religious uniformity in fact bore no relationship to being a good citizen. Protestants of various stripes could be good citizens, and tolerating them would diffuse social conflict. Catholics and atheists were another matter, since their respective allegiance to a foreign power and inability to take oaths were subversive of the political order.

Toleration thus conceived was not an open door to all manners of difference, but a calculation about what sort of ethical convictions were essential to a political order and about which convictions, although perhaps contentious and misguided from various perspectives, could nonetheless be tolerated, however reluctantly. Moreover, many religious faiths came to see tolerance as theologically important, since faith that was coerced might not be genuine. Toleration was also a way of exploring the limits of the state's competence to pronounce on matters of fundamental controversy such as religion.

Debates about the relationship between church and state persist today with great passion, but the terms of these debate have changed dramatically from Locke's time, to which very few would like to return. However, analogous questions surfaced in the context of campaigns of ideological indoctrination in the twentieth century, which saw Fascist Italy, the Leninist Soviet Union, and Maoist China pioneer official state philosophies and re-education programs while persecuting dissenters. It is not difficult to understand the perceived utility of ideological conformity from the perspective of a totalitarian leader. Indeed, there is a latent temptation in all politics for those in charge of social order to want either to control the dominant ethical convictions or suppress their ungoverned sources in civil society.

Western liberal democracies have defined themselves in opposition to the totalitarianisms of the twentieth century, and this has entailed a commitment to toleration conceived both as a limitation on government as well as an openness to ethical pluralism. Democratic institutions have been understood as a way to give expression to diverse ethical commitments in the political arena in the process of arriving at determinate political judgments. At the same time, overarching liberal frameworks supposedly provide non-negotiable ethical foundations for the political order, under the guise of human rights and other basic freedoms. Perhaps the most central dialectic in contemporary political theory concerns whether liberalism or democracy should have priority, and what exactly liberal justice requires. The guiding idea has been that there are certain requirements of justice that are universal, and thus citizens of any state can reasonably be asked to endorse and follow them. Then, there are a host of more particular allegiances and disagreements that can be expressed and adjudicated based on democratic representation.

The social unrest unleashed by the recent democratic revolutions of the Arab Spring has rekindled these old debates about the ethical foundations of successful democracies. Put simply, must citizens share some common ethical convictions in order to sustain peace and prosperity? Partisans in this debate often, and unfortunately, tend towards extremes: either conservative moralizing or technocratic optimism. On top of this, many contemporary liberals are reluctant to affirm the importance of a common ethical framework beyond basic human rights and democratic procedures, for one of the hallmarks of classical liberalism was supposedly the toleration of diverse conceptions of the good. As Will Kymlicka notes, "A distinctive feature of contemporary liberal theory is its emphasis on 'neutrality' -the view that the state should not reward or penalize particular conceptions of the good life but, rather, should provide a neutral framework within which different and potentially conflicting conceptions of the good can be pursued (Kymlicka 883)." As conservative scholars such as Mary Ann Glendon (2008) and Richard John Neuhaus (1986) have argued, liberal neutrality, if actually practiced, robs the public discourse of significant moral resources. Others, like Robert George, have suggested that neutrality more often operates as rhetoric, masking ideological agendas that are themselves particular concepts of good (see George 2014). Ultimately, however, liberals are mistaken to deny an underlying ethical core to liberalism; conservatives have underappreciated how substantial and good this core is; and technocrats have grossly underestimated the degree to which our social institutions depend on behavior motivated by ethical convictions.

Recognizing the importance of ethical convictions has, however, raised two related concerns. First, some question whether it is proper for the state to support, directly or indirectly, the development of thicker ethical attachments amongst its citizens.[1] This question is often animated by an aspiration in liberal theory that would have the state be formally neutral towards thick conceptions of the good. Second, there is a concern with the fundamental indeterminacy of such support. Granting greater autonomy or resources may empower institutions in civil society that produce "social capital" but cannot hope to direct the development of their ethical concepts. Thus, subsidies to educational institutions may support both the Montessori school and the Madrasah; use of public facilities by private associations could benefit both the NAACP and the Ku Klux Klan. There is a fear that subsidiary institutions may develop allegiances that are in conflict with broader principles of good citizenship.

[1] For a useful overview of this question see Macedo 2009 and Garsten 2009.

However, as many political theorists as diverse a Michael Sandel (1998), Seyla Benhabib (2002), Robert George (1993) and Alasdair MacIntyre (1984, 1988) have argued, it is impossible for the state not to endorse and promote some ethical conceptions over others. Moreover, successful liberal democracies depend on citizens who are motivated to make constructive contributions to the social order beyond the requirements of strict self-interest and liberal justice.

Here, I can finally focus the larger argument of this chapter. Regarding the modern state, we can affirm that it has a legitimate interest in demanding certain ethical convictions of its citizens. In the first place, as the locus of military and police authority, the state has to determine what sorts of actions are intolerable. That is, the state has to identify who society's enemies are and protect against them. Second, beyond these minimal requirements of justice and social order, there are reasons for a state to care about fostering more extensive, positive ethical commitments amongst its citizens, for these commitments help both societies and individuals flourish. But how thick should these convictions be, and what are their authentic sources? This is where the second, older conception of citizenship provides invaluable insights.

As I have already suggested we generally discuss questions of citizenship today with the assumption that citizenship corresponds to membership in a state. There is a good reason for this, in so far as states are the juridical bodies with the power and responsibility to ensure basic political, economic, and social order. However, there is an older, classical conception of citizenship that simply refers to membership in a community. This is the sense in which Paul of the New Testament writes in Ephesians 2:19 "you are no more strangers and sojourners, but you are fellow-citizens with the saints, and of the household of God." Or again in Philippians 3:20 "… our citizenship is in heaven."

The Greek term "politeuma" that Paul used, derives its meaning from the Greek *polis*. The early Christian community was understood in explicitly political terms, and the concept of the "City of God" was developed extensively amongst Patristic thinkers, most notably Augustine (in *The City of God, vol.1 p.1*). One implication of the ancient use of this concept was that Christians and others could have multiple citizenships, and the question obviously arose as to how allegiances to different communities could be compatible or conflicting.

Augustine's more interesting claim for our purposes was that, as a matter of social ontology, communities are constituted by common objects of love. This is an insight that the English theologian Oliver O'Donovan has explored in recent writings (in particular O'Donovan 2004b) in order to highlight the particular rather than universal nature of so many of our deep-seated ethical commitments. According to O'Donovan's reading of Augustine, we develop moral commitments through our membership in communities that share common objects of love. This has significant implications for how we understand the promise and perils of liberal democracy.

Membership in a state certainly involves membership in a community that shares certain values and loves, but in most modern nation-states what is shared is likely to be fairly minimal and thin. The deepest springs of meaning and attachment will flow from what Edmund Burke described as the "little platoons" of society. As Burke wrote: "To be attached to the subdivision, to love the little platoon we belong to in society, is the first principle (the germ as it were) of public affections. It is the first link in the series by which we proceed towards a love to our country, and to mankind (Burke 75)." It is from these subsidiary communities that the thicker conceptions of citizenship develop. In some cases these attachments will benefit only the subsidiary communities from which they flow and these attachments may even exist in tension with demands that the state makes. However, it is also possible for these attachments to spill over into the service and love of the larger society.

The liberal state needs to recognize the limits of its own moral authority and create space for subsidiary institutions to be a locus for more extensive ethical formation. Citizenship in these subsidiary communities is the organic source of much of the social capital on which the larger state depends. The older conception of citizenship is useful because it calls attention to the multiple communities and multiple citizenships that exist within the state but are not coincident with it. By their very nature, subsidiary citizenships have a moral character. Much of the hope placed in constructive work that thicker notions of citizenship might do in modern societies is misplaced if it focuses on citizens of a state as a whole. Rather, it is from more local, particular, and voluntary communities that we are likely to see thick conceptions of citizenship develop that might in turn contribute to society at large.

Students of Catholic social thought will recognize that this diagnosis shares a close affinity with the idea of subsidiarity – that is, the idea that social concerns should be handled by the least centralized, smallest, and most direct unit that can competently address a matter.[2] Subsidiary social institutions are effective in part because they generate knowledge, interest, and care around common interests of concern in ways that centralized state institutions can't.

The existence of multiple, overlapping citizenships, corresponding to multiple, overlapping communities defined by common objects of love can, however, pose a political problem. Might their multiplicity create a crisis of sovereignty? It need not, so long as their claims on people don't conflict or, if they do conflict, have a clear method of adjudication. Indeed, we are very familiar with political arrangements that involve overlapping jurisdictions and allegiances. Federalism has long been a crucial principle of government in the United States. I can, for example, be a citizen of Boston, a citizen of Massachusetts, and a citizen of the United States. One question that currently confronts the European Union is how traditional state-based citizenship relates to the EU project. What is the foundation of European Citizenship and what rights, benefits, and responsibilities should be accorded European citizens as European citizens? Conversely, what rights and responsibilities should remain within the purview of member states?

I suspect that skepticism towards the European project reflects in part an ambiguity about what it means to be a European citizen, which is to say an ambiguity about the common objects of love that define the European community above and beyond allegiance to member nation states. It is not clear whether there is a real and

[2] For an introduction to this concept see Hittinger 2002.

distinctive community – a real and distinctive people – that deserves to be called European at large. As Oliver O'Donovan suggests, "When the Italian who moves next door is not a foreigner, but merely from out of town; when it requires no comment or explanation that the chief of police for Northern Ireland is hired from Denmark, or a Spaniard heads an elementary school for the children of Prague, and everyone automatically speaks English, then a European people is at hand (2004b, 153)." Of course, if it is not at hand yet, then the aspirations for European political unity should be correspondingly minimal. There may be broad agreement regarding matters of human rights that can form the basis of a common juridical framework, and even broad overlapping economic interests that justify a common currency. However, the lack of a meaningful sense of community is likely to prove a problem when it comes to deciding, for example, what rich European citizens owe to poor European citizens, or why refugees should be accepted by some countries and not others.

We're now at a point where the two threads of this chapter can be woven back together. The modern state performs an invaluable role in providing a juridical framework backed by force that can ensure social order and perform practically necessary administrative tasks. The question of citizenship is, in the first place, a crucial determination for the state to make for the purpose of coordination and administration. We need to know who is in and who is out, and the conditions under which outsiders can become insiders. There is also a sense in which the state encompasses a community united by common objects of love, although these may be rather minimal. In playing this role, the modern state is but one exemplar of the larger classical concept of citizenship.

The classical concept alerts us to the moral dimensions of any human community, and to the ethical allegiances that inspire individuals to contribute to a community's common good. It is our familiarity with this classical concept that is liable to make us hope that thicker notions of citizenship might contribute to the flourishing of an entire state. While there is something to this hope, we need to ask whether a state can authentically draw on and cultivate common convictions, without this turning into an illiberal or totalitarian imposition.

Even if one finds that citizens of some state do not share deep common purposes, with the implication that their identity as citizens must be correspondingly thin, one may still find within the state, subsidiary communities that have thicker notions of citizenship. If these are compatible with principles of social order for the society as a whole, then it would be wise for the state to allow and encourage these subsidiarity communities to flourish on their own terms. Ultimately, although citizenship debates have a valuable roll to play in practical questions of state administration and political disagreements, these debates also call attention to the moral foundations of communities beyond the state.

I can summarize the implications of these two concepts of citizenship in response to the questions I posed at the outset.

1. Who should be considered a citizen of a particular state and what rights and duties should attach to that designation?

This requires an utterly particular answer that will involve a pragmatic calculation regarding what is functionally possible, as well as an assessment of the moral bonds that currently define the people in question. If one is committed to liberal democracy, then at a bare minimum citizenship should involve an allegiance to, and the protection of, basic human rights and liberties. In some cases, states can ask much more of citizens, in some cases not. Moreover, the question of extending citizenship will be inexorably particular to a country's material capacities and the moral allegiances that currently define it.

Ultimately, the cosmopolitan hope of a borderless world, in which the citizenship of any country is open to all who desire it (or, in which all become universal citizens) is at least premature if not simply unworkable. Successful states currently do not have the economic resources and administrative capacity to open up citizenship to all who want it. At the same time, there is a legitimate concern to admit new citizens at levels that will aid their assimilation into the best features of a country's political culture and common convictions. There may, however, be political arrangements short of citizenship that can aid those who desire to emigrate from an unfavorable political regime, promoting their material well-being and inculcating liberal-democratic values even if not providing full political participation in or full geographical access to a host state.

2. Is citizenship an outdated concept, one that should be abandoned in favor of more cosmopolitan accounts of political identity and authority, and more fluid state borders?

It is certainly possible for liberal, cosmopolitan states to flourish, such as Hong Kong did under British rule. There are also reasons to support recently proposed "Charter Cities" – cities developed on land ceded by third world countries, populated through open immigration and ruled according to a liberal charter. However, a conspicuous feature of these proposals is their anti-democratic character. The rights of immigrants are strongly protected, but these new "citizens" do not have the political authority to change the terms of the charter or to engage in many forms of democratic change. So, a certain sort of cosmopolitanism may only be viable if democratic agency is constrained.

Moreover, although cosmopolitan liberalism may be a sufficient juridical framework for certain countries, and even made more feasible through the emergence of a "global culture," there will be a continued need for the administrative apparatus of the state, politics will always remain local, and particular moral communities and allegiances will continue to create determinate forms of subsidiary citizenship. It is also possible that communities will exist that inculcate fundamentally illiberal values, such that their adherents are unable to abide by the requirements of basic human rights and liberal justice. It seems entirely legitimate to exclude such people from citizenship in liberal, cosmopolitan states if they are indeed unwilling to comply with minimal requirements of justice. Put another way, even if cosmopolitanism is conceived as global citizenship, there is still moral content to that citizenship which can serve as a basis for exclusion.

3. Can a thick and compelling notion of citizenship serve as a basis for reinvigorating the political, cultural, ethical life of modern societies?

Perhaps. But thick notions of citizenship have to be a genuine outgrowth of authentic communities, otherwise thick accounts are likely simply to manifest partisan political divisions and be tools of power. The totalitarian lessons of the twentieth century should serve as a warning as we try to balance ethical formation and tolerable pluralism in public institutions. Questions of citizenship concern the bounds of various communities and the moral obligations/opportunities that come with them. Although the obligations of liberal states will always be comparatively minimal, the possibilities for thicker notions of citizenship in subsidiary institutions of civil society are much more extensive.

In conclusion, the fundamental challenge of citizenship today concerns how to reconcile state-based citizenship and the practical necessities of functional government with the reality that many moral allegiances that are crucial for a functional polity derive from communities and institutions that the liberal state does not, and ought not, control, beyond the impartial requirements of the general legal order. With regard to immigration, a state may legitimately deny citizenship to those who do not accept basic tenets of justice and thus threaten the social order, and a state may also deny citizenship to otherwise innocuous populations whose mere presence threatens to overwhelm and undermine the material capacities of good government. The more vexing *domestic* question, however, concerns how a liberal state can encourage and harness virtuous ethical convictions formed in particular communities within civil society and also discourage and expose illiberal convictions – all the while avoiding the dangers of totalitarianism. In short, how can varieties of citizenship be sustainably harmonized? Unfortunately, there is no simple formula to solve this problem because the answer will depend on particular moral judgments that reflect the convictions of existing communities. Ultimately, a deeper consideration of citizenship draws attention to the moral dimensions of politics and suggests that citizenship debates cannot be divorced from the most fundamental problems of political theory.

References

Augustine, S. (1871). *The city of God* (D. Marcus, Trans.). Edinburgh: T. & T. Clark.

Benhabib, S. (2002). *The claims of culture: Equality and diversity in the global era*. Princeton: Princeton University Press.

Burke, Edmund. (2016). *Select works of Edmund Burke*. A New Imprint of the Payne Edition. Foreword and Biographical Note by Francis Canavan (Indianapolis: Liberty Fund, 1999). Vol. 2. 3/15/2016 (*Reflections on the Revolution in France*). http://oll.libertyfund.org/titles/656

Garsten, B. (2009). *Saving persuasion: A defense of rhetoric and judgment*. Cambridge, MA/London: Harvard University Press.

George, R. P. (1993). *Making men moral: Civil liberties and public morality*. Oxford: Clarendon Press.

George, R. P. (2014). *The clash of orthodoxies: Law, religion, and morality in crisis* . Wilmington. Open Road Media

Glendon, M. A. (2008). *Rights talk: The impoverishment of political discourse*. New York: Simon and Schuster.

Hegel, G. W. F. (1979). *Hegel's system of ethical life and first philosophy of spirit*. Albany: SuNY Press.

Hittinger, R. (2002). Social pluralism and subsidiarity in Catholic social doctrine. *Annales theologici, 16*, 385–408.

Kymlicka, W. (1989). Liberal Individualism and Liberal Neutrality. *Ethics, 99*(4), 883–905. Retrieved from http://www.jstor.org.ezp-prod1.hul.harvard.edu/stable/2381238

Locke, J. (2010). *A Letter concerning toleration and other writings, edited and with an Introduction by Mark Goldie*. Indianapolis: Liberty Fund.

Macedo, S. (2009). *Diversity and distrust: Civic education in a multicultural democracy*. Cambridge, MA: Harvard University Press.

MacIntyre, A. (1984). *After virtue: A study in moral theory*. Notre Dame: University of Notre Dame Press.

MacIntyre, A. (1988). *Whose justice? Which rationality ?* London: Duckworth.

Mussolini, Benito. (1935). *The doctrine of fascism*. Firenze: Vallecchi Editore.

Neuhaus, R. J. (1986). *The naked public square: Religion and democracy in America*. Grand Rapids: Wm. B. Eerdmans Publishing.

O'Donovan, J. L. (2004a). "Nation, state, and civil society in the western biblical tradition," in *Bonds of imperfection: Christian politics, past and present*. Cambridge: Eerdmans Publishing.

O'Donovan, O. (2004b). *Common objects of love: Moral reflection and the shaping of community*. Cambridge: Eerdmans Publishing.

Sandel, M. J. (1998). *Liberalism and the limits of justice*. Cambridge /New York: Cambridge University Press.

Taylor, C. (1977). *Hegel*. Cambridge /New York: Cambridge University Press.

Part II
Citizenship and Attachment

Civic Motivation and Globalization: What Is It Like to Be a Good Citizen Today?

Simon Keller

A Troubled Virtue

Good citizenship is an important virtue, from two points of view. It is essential to the health of the state; a flourishing state requires good citizens. It is also a central personal virtue; it is difficult to imagine someone who is a good person but a bad citizen. Good citizenship is also a fairly transparent virtue, in one respect. It is not difficult to say in broad terms what it means to be a good citizen. A good citizen cares about others, follows the law, contributes to community life, and upholds the values of a just state.

Yet, good citizenship is, in other respects, a puzzling virtue. It is a virtue that essentially involves partiality. As a good friend is partial to her own friends and a good parent is partial to her own children, a good citizen is partial to her own state. Virtues of partiality can be puzzling because it looks as though to have such virtues is to treat certain others differently in response to morally arbitrary characteristics. My children are not more valuable than other children, just because they are my children, but, to the extent to which I am a good parent, their being my children leads me to give them better treatment. Virtue, sometimes, involves partiality – but does it not then also involve a kind of blindness to the rights and interests of others? In the case of the good citizen: if I have a special commitment to the flourishing of my own state and its citizens, do I then turn away from the rights and interests of other states, and of other people, just because they happen not to be "mine?"

There are extra reasons to be troubled by the partiality involved in good citizenship, as compared to the partiality involved in good friendship, good parenting, and so on. For one thing, to be a good citizen is to give a special priority to people with whom you are not acquainted. When you are partial to your child, at least you know your child and are intimately aware of his value and his needs. As a citizen, you

---

S. Keller (✉)
Victoria University of Wellington, Wellington, New Zealand
e-mail: Simon.Keller@vuw.ac.nz

D. Thunder (ed.), *The Ethics of Citizenship in the 21st Century*,
DOI 10.1007/978-3-319-50415-5_3

commit yourself to a polity almost all of whose members you will never meet. You can respond directly to your child or friend in a way in which you cannot respond directly to (most of) your fellow citizens. For another thing, good citizenship involves a direct concern with justice, arguably to a greater extent than do other kinds of partiality. A good friend or parent might be moved mostly by a concern to treat her friend or child well, not because she thinks her friend or child morally deserves it, necessarily, but just because she cares about her friend's or child's interests. The good citizen, though, acts out of a sense of duty to her state and her fellow citizens, and has a concern with justice within her state and with giving each of her fellow citizens their moral due. It is puzzling, again, to say how a virtuous person could have a concern that is explicitly about justice, but is also restricted to one state over others and to one group of people over others.

If there is a real puzzle here, then two familiar ethical treatments of citizenship can be interpreted as attempts to solve it. The first treatment says that in its most mature and ethically defensible form, citizenship is not focused on a particular state but rather on humanity or the world as a whole: we should aspire to be world citizens. That story resolves the puzzle by omitting arbitrary partiality from citizenship, but it betrays its contrivance in its own label. What sense does it really make to speak of being a "world citizen?" To say that you are from the world, or that your political community is the world – that sounds as much like being a citizen of nowhere as being a citizen of everywhere.

The second strategy for resolving the puzzle is to reject the assumption that the real perspective of justice and morality is an impartial perspective. Standards of justice arise from within particular communities, we might say, so there is nothing arbitrary or morally obnoxious about the citizen's paying special attention to the community in which her own sense of justice and her own moral identity are grounded – where that community receives its political expression through a state.[1] There are various stories that can be told in filling out the details of this strategy, one of which I will come to later, but a worry about all those stories is that they look anachronistic in a globalized world. It is difficult to maintain, these days, that the individual's "home" is coextensive with any particular state, and hence difficult to say why we should expect a citizen to see the moral world essentially from the perspective of her own state. It is then difficult to justify her giving special moral

[1] In this paper I will try to avoid controversial commitments over what makes something a country and what makes something a state, but I assume that there are differences between a country, a state, and a government. Putting things roughly, a country is something like Spain or Australia: it is compounded out of a relationship between a given territory, a landscape, a community of humans that exists over time, and a distinctive history. A state is an essentially political administrative structure, usually associated with a country: a state claims authority over a territory, sets and enforces laws, has its own set of rules and decision-making procedures, recognizes certain people as its citizens, and claims to be the political representative of a country and its people. A government is made up of particular people and policies and governs on behalf of, or with the authorization of, a state: a government cannot outlast a state, but a state can and usually does outlast a government. It is possible to love a country without loving the state through which the country is given its political expression, and it is possible to approve of a state without approving of the government that governs on behalf of the state presently.

attention to those who happen to be within her state's borders, just out of a claim about where her sense of justice comes from.

My goal in the present paper is to explain in more theorized terms the puzzle facing the virtues of citizenship and then to outline a more promising strategy for resolving the puzzle. I want to proceed through an examination of the good citizen's states of mind. What does a good citizen care about? What motivates her? What does she believe? To what and to whom is she loyal? With what and with whom does she identify? Our emotional and cognitive lives are complex and there are many different ways in which we could be motivated to perform any given action. Informed by an appreciation of the various psychological profiles that could lead a person to act as a good citizen, I want to suggest, we can construct a model of good citizenship that supports genuine state citizenship but does not look anachronistic or misguided in the modern world.

What beliefs, emotions, and motivations should we hope for in a citizen today? I want to distinguish two approaches to this question: one beginning with the nature of the flourishing state and the other with the nature of the flourishing person.

Serving the State

The first approach asks what citizens can do to help the state flourish. A good citizen, on this way of looking at things, is one who acts in such a way as to make the state better. If we think that a flourishing state is an orderly state, for example, then we will say that a good citizen follows the laws. The good citizen will also perform other acts, such as paying her taxes, supporting important community organizations, looking out for vulnerable fellow citizens, and defending the state when it is under threat. In describing the psychological life of the good citizen, then, we can start by asking which beliefs, emotions, and motives will most reliably lead to the performance of acts that help a state to flourish.

Based on that consideration only, it is a contingent question what psychological life we should hope for in a citizen. In Plato's Republic, Socrates recommends that citizens should be told a "noble lie": they should be led to believe that their fellow citizens are their siblings and their country is their parent.[2] That is a lie, but it is a useful lie, because citizens who believe it are more likely to defend the country and more likely to make sacrifices to contribute to the country's flourishing. Socrates' claim aside, the point is that a citizen who has false beliefs or misguided emotions might thereby be more likely to act in ways that help make the country flourish. It may turn out that the best citizen will falsely believe that her country is the best in the world, will wrongly take her identity to be intimately connected with her country, or will have a wholly arbitrary preference for her fellow citizens over other people: perhaps those are the mental states that best produce acts that contribute to the flourishing of a state.

[2] *Republic* 414b. In Plato, Plato: Complete Works ed. J. M. Cooper (Indianapolis: Hackett, 1997). Translators sometimes call the noble lie the "royal lie" or "magnificent myth."

There is another dimension to the task of serving the flourishing state, however, when the flourishing state is imagined to be democratic. In a democracy, the citizen's actions are not just instrumentally related to the state's flourishing but also help constitute its flourishing. A flourishing state is a legitimate state, and a democracy derives its legitimacy from having its citizens govern themselves. So a citizen who serves her state's flourishing will participate in the state's deliberation and government. To contribute in a constructive manner – to participate in a way that leads to the state's being a just state and making good decisions for good reasons – the citizen will need to have right-minded values, at least to some extent, and will need to engage in informed and judicious decision-making.

A good citizen in a democracy, then, cannot be a robot: it is not enough that the citizen performs the acts that contribute to the state's flourishing. The citizen must be a good believer and deliberator, at least over some domains. Nevertheless, when we characterize the good citizen as one who best serves the flourishing of a state, we take the value of good citizenship and the value of the psychological life behind it to be ultimately instrumental. We start with a picture of the flourishing state, then we slot in citizens who will help the state conform to that picture.

Flourishing as a Citizen

The second approach to the task of describing the psychological life of the good citizen begins with ideas about the flourishing person. When we think about what it means to be a good person, we can ask how a person flourishes within various roles. We can ask what it means to flourish as a lawyer, for example, or as a teacher, athlete, musician, or philosopher, and we can ask what it takes to flourish as a parent or a student or a retiree. Asking what it takes for a person to flourish within a particular role, we need to ask, among other things, how that role can fit into a flourishing human life more broadly. On the question of what makes for a flourishing citizen, we need to ask how it is possible for a person to do well in her role as citizen, where her doing well in that role is an aspect of her flourishing as a human.

One component of human flourishing is having correct beliefs and right-minded values. To the extent to which a person's beliefs are false and her deliberations misguided, she fails to perform well the characteristically human activities of forming beliefs and values and making decisions. Beginning from the question of what it takes for an individual human to flourish in her role as citizen, then, there is an intrinsic reason, not just an instrumental reason, to want her beliefs, values, and motives to be correct, or appropriate, or right-minded. If we conclude that a good citizen must have false beliefs or misguided emotions and motives, then we will have to conclude that good citizenship comes at a sacrifice: a good citizen cannot be a fully flourishing human.

That said, it remains possible that in describing the psychological life of the good citizen, we will choose beliefs, emotions, and motives for their instrumental value, even at the cost of their correctness. Perhaps humans cannot handle the truth.

Perhaps an accurate view of our place in the world would leave us depressed or listless or antisocial. An attempt to describe the psychological life of the good citizen, following this second approach, must balance consideration of the consequences of particular mental states against consideration of their correctness. It is at least conceptually possible that a person will be a better citizen for lacking self-knowledge, say, or for lacking a clear-eyed view of her own country.

We now have two questions to ask. First: what psychological states are most likely to cause a person to perform the acts that most contribute to the flourishing of the state? Second: what is the nature of the mental life of the flourishing person who is (as part of her overall flourishing) a flourishing citizen? One problem for citizenship in a globalized world is that under prevailing accounts of citizenship, our answers to those two questions are likely to come apart.

The Case for Patriotic Citizenship

What Is Patriotism?

If you want to make someone into a good citizen of her state, you might try to make her into a patriot. A patriot loves her country and is loyal to her country, so a patriot can be expected to be motivated to do what is best for her country, and hence to advance the flourishing of her country, in its political manifestation as a state. Patriotism is all around us; it appears to be a natural form of human loyalty, and a relatively easy one to inculcate. The model of the patriotic citizen probably stands as the most common and recognizable model of the mental life of the good citizen: a good citizen, so understood, has many virtues, but insofar as she is a good citizen and not just a good person, perhaps her most important characteristic is her patriotic commitment to her country.

Patriotism involves particular forms of love and loyalty. Not just any kind of loyalty to your country allows you to count as a patriot. There are commonalities between patriotism and other familiar forms of love and loyalty, like love between family members and friends and loyalty between colleagues and teammates. Due to its focus upon the state, however, and its importance for shared political life, patriotism has its own distinctive character. In what follows I try to identify the main motivational and cognitive elements of patriotism, as they bear upon the connection between patriotism and citizenship.[3]

Patriotism, first, involves a kind of identification. If you are a patriot, then you take your connection with your country to say something about who you really are. A patriot of France thinks of herself as, in a deep respect, French. An Australian

[3] In describing the psychology of patriotism here, I lay out some claims that I defend in more detail in chapter 3 of my *The Limits of Loyalty* (Cambridge University Press, 2007); and on pages 51–59 of my 'The Case against Patriotism,' in John Kleinig, Simon Keller, and Igor Primoratz, *The Ethics of Patriotism: A Debate* (Wiley Blackwell, 2015).

patriot takes his being Australian to matter for his own self-understanding. As a result of identifying with a country, a patriot characteristically feels the distinctively patriotic emotion of pride in country. The patriot sees her country's virtues and achievements as reflecting, somehow, on her. She can feel pride in her country's virtues and achievements, almost as though they were her own virtues and achievements. The patriot may also feel shame, even embarrassment and humiliation, in her country's failings. To some extent, at least, the patriot sees a little bit of the country in herself and a little bit of herself in the country. This form of identification with country allows a patriot to feel intimately involved in the fate of her own country, and hence of the state of which she is a citizen, and to share with fellow citizens the common bond of identity that can allow a group of disparate people to form a political community.

The patriot, in addition, is willing to make sacrifices for her country. The patriot's concern for her country's interests may compete with and sometimes outweigh her concerns for her own interests and the interests of others for whom she cares. Patriotism, to put it another way, involves a serious commitment to country. The patriot does not see her relationship with her country simply as useful, or simply as a source of fun. She takes her country's interests to provide her with weighty reasons for action. That is why a patriot can be expected to do what advances the flourishing of her state, even when inconvenient, and even when inconsistent with her immediate interests.

Entangled with the patriot's commitment to country is a view about what her country is. The patriot does not commit herself to her country just because it is her own, but also because she takes it to have features that make it worthy of her allegiance. When a French patriot thinks of France, she thinks of it as a country worth defending. Characteristically, the patriot's commitment to her country takes the form of a commitment to an ongoing national project, which usually incorporates the project of achieving ongoing political independence through the maintenance of a sovereign state. A national project of the relevant kind has its roots in the country's history and sets conditions for the country's flourishing in its own distinctive manner. The French patriot may be committed to the flourishing of France as a secular country, the New Zealand patriot to the flourishing of New Zealand as a bicultural country, and so on. To be a patriot, at least usually, is to have a sense of what is good and distinctive about your own country, and hence of what it would take for your country to succeed on its own terms. This makes sense of the specialness of the patriot's commitment to the flourishing of her state, and the particularized standards that her patriotic commitment to country invokes. An Italian patriot, for example, does not simply have a concern for seeing good things happen to Italy and Italians, more than to Germany and Germans; she has a sense of what it would take for Italy to flourish in its own distinctively Italian manner, and of why its flourishing in that manner is something to be valued.

That said, patriotism does not involve slavish devotion to a national project, or to a state. There is such a thing as patriotic dissent. When a person criticizes her country from the standpoint of a patriot, she criticizes the country for failing to live up to its own values, or for failing to be the best that it – in all its distinctiveness – can be. Also, there is room for political and cultural disagreement among patriots. Patriots may disagree about what is good about their country, about how their national project is best understood, and about what it would take for the country to flourish on its own terms. The political contribution of the patriot may include participation in the conversation about what her country truly is and how it could truly flourish.

The Usefulness of Patriotism

Where a good citizen is construed as a citizen who serves the flourishing of the state, there is then clear reason why we might expect patriotism to contribute to good citizenship. Accordingly, states have often construed the task of creating good citizens, and indeed the task of creating a state, as the task of creating patriots. Through various means, but especially through the education system, the state may try to inculcate patriotic beliefs and feelings. To make a person patriotic, you need to give him a certain understanding of himself; patriotic education involves encouraging people to identify themselves as members of an ongoing community that is represented by the state – to see themselves as Italian, for example. You also need to make him willing to make sacrifices for the state; patriotic education involves establishing service to the state as a virtue – it may glorify those who have made sacrifices for the glory of Italy. And, you need to make him proud of his country, in its guise as a country with its own distinctive virtues; patriotic education involves telling a story about the nature of the country on which the country is special and good – it may tell of the special value of the Italian way of life.

The inculcation of patriotism in the service of good citizenship may be used to confront both localism and globalism. Where people are seen to be committed more to their own regions than to the state, patriotic education may focus on forging a larger national identity. Its main message may be that "we are all Italians," for example: it may tell the individual that his character and future are tied to his country, not his local community. Where the concern is that people are in danger of having no communal identification at all – of understanding themselves simply as individuals or just as inhabitants of an enormous world – patriotic education may seek to build a sense of community and social solidarity. Its main message may be that "we (as opposed to they) are in this together." But the project of nurturing patriotism, in any case, is largely the project of nurturing certain beliefs, emotions, and motivations. That is why patriotic education involves learning about the country and its history, as well as involving songs, ceremonies, and symbols. Patriotic education manufactures opportunities for people to have a particular way of seeing their country and the world, and a particular cluster of feelings.

How Patriotism Can Be Correct

If patriotism can be effective in building citizens who advance the flourishing of the state, can it also build humans who flourish in the role of citizen? What is the connection between patriotic citizenship and human flourishing in general? These are tougher questions.

A cosmopolitan picture, gestured at earlier in this paper, says that patriotism, no matter how useful, is not an element of human flourishing. State boundaries, runs the argument, are morally arbitrary. No one gets to be a better person or to have different rights or to matter more just because she is from one country rather than another. The correct moral identity, on this story, is your identity simply as a human, or as a rational agent. When the patriot ties her moral identity to her country, when she takes a special concern for her own state and fellow citizens over others, and when she sees things from the point of view of her own country, she – on this story – fails morally. Perhaps she helps her state to flourish, but she herself does not see things correctly and thereby fails to flourish as a moral agent.[4]

In opposition to that cosmopolitan picture, however, has been developed a different way of thinking about moral identity and the nature of morality, which is closely associated with the defense of patriotism. In his classic paper "Is Patriotism a Virtue?" Alasdair MacIntrye mounts parallel defenses of patriotism and anti-liberal communitarianism.[5] He says that a person's moral sensibility cannot be separated from the truth about where and from whom he learned his morality, and that the most powerful and attractive form of moral motivation comes from within a community-oriented perspective. While MacIntyre presents his view of moral agency as an attack on liberalism, many liberal philosophers accept his basic insights and seek to incorporate them into a more nuanced liberal perspective, and along the way find liberal justifications for patriotism and other forms of group loyalty.[6]

When it comes to the defense of patriotism, the crucial claim for MacIntyre is that the country can be a moral community, and so the state can embody and speak for a moral community. States, often, are the entities most responsible for our education, moral and otherwise. Whether you are on one or the other side of a state border can make a significant difference to how you are taught. Countries also provide a focus for political and social life; which country you come from determines for whom you can vote, in what form you can participate in politics, and how multiple aspects of your life are formed and administered. A country also connects you with a distinctive political tradition and a distinctive way of life. It can provide you

[4] For versions of this criticism, see Paul Gomberg, 'Patriotism is Like Racism,' *Ethics* 101 (1990): 144–150; Martha Nussbaum, 'Patriotism and Cosmopolitanism,' in Nussbaum and Joshua Cohen, *For Love of Country?* (Boston: Beacon Press, 2002) pp. 3–20; and Peter Singer, *One World* (Newhaven: Yale University Press, 2002) ch. 5.

[5] The 1984 Lindley Lecture, reprinted in Igor Primoratz (ed.) *Patriotism* (Amherst: Humanity Books, 2002) pp. 43–58.

[6] See, for example, Yael Tamir, *Liberal Nationalism* (Princeton University Press, 1995); and Anna Stilz, *Liberal Loyalty* (Princeton University Press, 2011).

with an understanding of what it would mean for you to flourish, within the social context from which you emerge.

If we accept that there is a link between a person's moral education and background and her proper moral perspective and identity, then we can – if we are following MacIntyre's argument – picture the patriot as seeing herself and the world correctly. Instead of saying that the patriot is morally blinded or moved by arbitrary considerations, we can say that the patriot shows self-understanding and has a clear-sighted and robust source of moral motivation. If you are an Australian patriot, for example, then you may be quite correct in identifying yourself primarily as an Australian, in having a special concern for Australia, and in being motivated by thoughts like "this is what an Australian would do." To flourish as a human, surely, is partly to understand who you really are. If the patriot has genuine self-understanding and moral motivation – and if the perspective of impartial morality involves alienation and fails to engage with real human motives – then patriotism may indeed be a requirement for good human flourishing, and not a moral mistake at all.

A consequence is that when we provide people with a patriotic education, we can, in the right circumstances, "make it true" that patriotism, for them, is the correct moral attitude. Patriotic education can create moral identities. If it is successful, then it may be self-legitimating. By making you think of yourself as deeply Italian, I may help make it the case that your identity is deeply Italian. I might make it right and proper for you to see the moral world from an Italian point of view.

Let me note again that the vindication of patriotism just sketched does not need to be tied to a self-consciously anti-liberal perspective like MacIntyre's. One way to see this is to see that the source of morality and moral motivation need not determine morality's content: not completely, anyway. From your essentially embedded perspective – your perspective as an Australian, say – you may find reason to care about the rights of all humans, Australian or not; you may commit yourself to the flourishing of Australia as a liberal democracy; you may think that the distinctively Australian concerns that define your identity are concerns with equality and fairness, as manifested in a distinctively Australian context.[7]

Problems for Patriotism, Problems for Citizenship

The state remains the most significant political institution in the modern world. The human world is divided into states. The individual's political experience and the conditions of her political life are determined largely by her state. States are where people vote and can seek to attain the highest political office. Mostly, the parties to international treaties and agreements, and to international dramas and conflicts, are

[7] These sorts of thoughts inform Igor Primoratz's defense of "ethical patriotism." See chapters 3, 6, and 9 of Kleinig, Keller, and Primoratz, *The Ethics of Patriotism: A Debate*.

states. The most powerful individuals in the political world are the leaders of states. If you want to change something important in the world, you will probably have to do it by trying to change states.

As a result, the health of human life in the present world depends deeply upon the health of states. Human life is better and more just where states are better and more just. Whether individuals are able to be happy, to express themselves, to live comfortably, to self-govern, to exercise religious choice, and so on, depends largely upon the character of the states under which they live. It is common to say that in a globalized world, states are not as important as they used to be. Perhaps that is true, but states are still *very* important, and much more important than any other kind of institution when it comes to the political lives of individuals and of the world as a whole.

Still, there are contemporary phenomena that threaten the state, in some sense at least. People move more easily between states, and many states have large immigrant communities. As a result, states tend to be less ethnically and culturally homogenous than they perhaps once were; it is not so clear that boundaries between states mark boundaries between kinds of people. There exist more transnational institutions, like the European Union, and more free trade agreements and international trade bodies, which accumulate political and financial power that would once have been held by states.

Further, people's attention – so it seems – is less and less constrained to their own countries. We are increasingly aware of ourselves as facing global problems. Problems like climate change involve activities carried out in some countries having their greatest effects on other countries, and require truly international solutions. The sources from which we get our news and entertainment are less and less likely to be shared with our fellow citizens; iconic national newspapers and television stations are disappearing or losing business to more scattered providers, and many of us get most of our news from websites and television stations based overseas. It is easier to follow sports leagues overseas, to watch foreign television, and to form communities that cross state boundaries.

To some extent, surely, all of these phenomena are largely about perception. We have long faced transnational political, environmental, and financial problems. Probably, our countries have never been as homogenous and unified as some people would like to believe. We probably still in fact get a decent proportion of our news and entertainment from within our own countries. But when it comes to questions of identity and loyalty, perception matters.

When people are aware of themselves as sharing experiences and problems with people overseas as much as at home, and when people do not consider their experience of the world to be essentially the experience of a citizen of a particular state, it becomes much harder to make them identify with their countries. To give a stylized example: when a person is preoccupied with the problem of climate change, reads the New York Times online, stays up late to watch English football on the web, spends time exchanging YouTube clips with similarly minded people all over the world, and faces a serious question about whether to seek university education or a job in a different country, it is difficult to make him understand himself as deeply and essentially Australian.

It is no longer so easy to represent states as representatives of moral communities. The country is no longer such a natural source of deep moral identity, or of moral motivation. From an individual's point of view, it is harder for her to think of her country as special and distinctive, or as representing a single particular way of life, or as making her the person she is. From the state's point of view, in the face of the individual's awareness of her country as just one among many, it is harder to "make it true" that she is deeply connected to her own country and hence to a state, as a matter of her very identity. As a result, the model of patriotic citizenship – the most familiar and natural model of good state-centered citizenship – does not appear to capture humans as they are. In today's world, among today's citizens, it is harder to see how patriotic citizenship can underlie a robust and accurate form of identity and self-understanding.

Here, then, is my statement of the puzzle of citizenship in the globalized world. We still have every reason to wish for acts of good citizenship, because states are still so politically important; but it is no longer reasonable to wish for people to display the psychological profiles that (we have always thought) make them likely to perform those acts, because people do not identify so naturally with their countries. States still matter and still require committed citizens, but it no longer makes sense to expect people to identify deeply with their own countries and to be committed state citizens as a matter of that identity. If we are asking what it takes for the state to flourish, then we want citizens who treat their own state as special. But if we are asking what it takes for individuals to flourish, then we do not want citizens whose moral horizons are limited by the boundaries of the country: such citizens, in the twenty-first century, would misunderstand themselves and their moral world.

Forms of Commitment

Under the model of patriotic citizenship, the citizen serves the state out of feelings of loyalty. She takes herself to have a special self-constituting relationship with her country, and she honors that relationship by committing herself to the country's flourishing. Her commitment to her country is entangled with her sense of the country as hers: that, partly, is what makes it a commitment of loyalty.

The patriotic citizen's commitment to country is a primary commitment, not a derived commitment. It is not as though the patriot cares first about something distinct from the country – a value or a project or a region or a person – and then commits herself to the country because (and on condition that) the country contributes to that distinct thing about which she cares. A person might care, for example, about freedom and democracy, and may support her country because (and on condition that) it serves the values of freedom and democracy – but that is not the commitment of a patriot. A patriotic citizen is committed to her country in the first instance or for its own sake, not as a consequence of her commitment to something else.

It makes sense to think that a robust commitment to country, of a kind that can motivate acts of good citizenship, will be a commitment of loyalty to the country for its own sake. But there are commitments of quite different kinds that often, in other contexts, produce acts that contribute in positive ways to the flourishing and success of an institution (or other kind of entity). You can be strongly committed to something, and can act well towards it and contribute to its flourishing and success, without being loyal to it, and without having a primary commitment to it.

Imagine the commitment you might have to a political party. You might be strongly committed to the party. You might be emotionally invested in it and prepared to give up your time and money to help it achieve its goals. Yet, your commitment to the political party may be derived from more fundamental commitments to other things. You might support the party because it sets out to protect the lifestyle or the region you love, or because it does the best job of standing up for the values you care about. If the party were to change, so that it no longer protects your beloved lifestyle or region or the values you care about, then you might be ready to abandon it. If the party were to fall apart, but to be replaced by a different party that did a better job of protecting the things you care about, then that might be a perfectly happy result as far as you are concerned. And, it may be that you are not really *loyal* to the party, exactly: your commitment to it may have nothing to do with any sense that it is *yours*. But your commitment to the party, derived from your deeper commitments to other things, may nonetheless be very strong.

(This is not to say, of course, that nobody is ever committed to a political party as a matter of primary loyalty. There are those who do see their identities as entangled with a particular political party and who are committed to the party in the first instance, not just for what it does or supports. But I am not talking about them.)

Conversely, there are primary commitments of loyalty – analogous to that extent to the patriot's commitment to country – that fail to be strong or reliable. You might have a primary loyalty to the football team of which you are a fan, for example. You may see it as *your* football team and you may care about it for its own sake. But that is not to imply that your concern for it is deep, and it is not to imply that you would make sacrifices out of regard for its interests. You might barely care about the football team, but to the extent to which you do, your caring could be an expression of primary loyalty.

Speaking generally, the structure of a commitment is a different matter from its strength. It is a mistake to think that whether or not a commitment is a commitment of loyalty, and whether it is a primary or a derived commitment, guarantees anything about its intensity or reliability.

Speaking yet more generally, our motivational lives are more complex than it can first seem. You can be committed to something in any number of ways and for any number of reasons. In particular, there is not a direct line, in either direction, between identifying with something and being prepared to contribute in significant ways to its flourishing.

Identity and the State

In a globalized world, it is often – increasingly often – a mistake to regard the country as the basis for the individual's moral identity and motivation. It is unreasonable and misleading to tell the individual that her relationship with her country generates her deep moral identity, or that her moral community is coextensive with her country and politically represented by the state. But it would be equally unreasonable and mistaken to tell the individual that her moral identity is constituted simply by her relationship with humanity, or that her moral community is the world as a whole. The network of communities and the cluster of concerns that we each find as individuals are more scattered than either of those descriptions suggests.

Most of us have places where we feel at home: places of which we have special knowledge and for which we have special concern. You may have a special relationship with your town or city, or with a part of your city, or with a region or national park or landscape. If we are honest, then those places, usually, are not whole countries. If you say that you know and love Switzerland, then the truth is probably that you know and love certain parts or aspects of Switzerland. Also, for many of us, the places we know and love are scattered around the world. If you have lived in various places, in various countries, then you may feel that you have an intimate relationship with each of them. There may be several places around the world in which you feel at home.

Similarly, most of us have particular concerns, and most of us have particular communities of which we are part. You may have family members, friends, and wider groups of people that you know and love. You may have special concerns for particular activities – for playing tennis or drinking good wine – or for particular clubs and other organizations, or for a particular profession. You may care about certain political and social causes, and have commitments to them of sufficient strength that you take those causes personally. Again, among your concerns and communities, some will be relatively local, and some will be more scattered; in some cases, you may well feel a closer bond of community and shared interest with someone who lives on the other side of the world than with someone who lives in your street.

The state, as mentioned, remains the dominant kind of human political institution. The health of many of the things you care about will depend on the character of the state or states in which they are located. If you care about the flourishing of your region or local community, then you have reason to take an interest in your state. Similarly, you should want your state to be just and healthy if you want the activities and organizations you care about to survive and flourish. And if you want to achieve progress in the causes you care about – if you want to contribute to anything on a larger scale that will lead to a better world – then you will need to confront and try to influence states and governments. Given its power and the multiple ways in which it influences our individual and shared lives, the state has significance, of one form or another, for many of the things we care about.

States also have significance for the health and justice of the world, and of humanity. Whether people are able to exercise self-government, whether their basic needs are met, whether their rights are respected – and whether valuable communities and ways of life survive and flourish – all depend upon the character of states. So if you have a general moral sensibility expressed as a concern for the rights and interests of all, then you will have reason to want states to be just. You will have reason, indeed, to want them to be secure and prosperous, insofar as their security and prosperity will redound to the moral benefit of particular individuals and communities. And you will have reason to want states to be moral in another sense: you will have reason to want them to act morally and make good decisions on the world stage. Whether the world is fair and peaceful depends largely on how states decide to act.

Here, then, is a kind of commitment that you may conceivably have to your state. You could care about the flourishing of your state because you take its flourishing to be important not for its own sake, or for the sake of the country that the state represents, but because of its consequences for other things for which you care. You may come to the state, so to speak, through your concerns for various places, people, organizations, and causes that rely upon the state (or other states) for their own flourishing. In your interactions with and concern for the state, you may hope not only to get the things you want for the things you care about, but also to get them on fair terms, through a process that respects the rights of all people within the country. You may care about the flourishing of your state because of the good that will follow for the things for which you have more fundamental concerns: the particular things to which you are attached, and the rights and interests of humans generally.

This mode of concern for the state will look contrived at first. I will say more shortly about its psychological plausibility. But first, let me say something about how it compares with patriotic loyalty to country.

If you care about your state in the way described, then you do not care about your country for its own sake, and you do not need to feel any deep identity with country or pride in country. Any commitment you have to your country, of the kind just described, is not a patriotic commitment. So we have here an alternative to patriotism.

The mode of concern for country just described is not really a form of loyalty. It need not involve your seeing your country as yours, in any significant sense. What matters is not the country's being yours, but its significance for the things that are yours. And it is not a primary form of commitment to country. It is a commitment to country derived from deeper commitments to other things.

Nevertheless, it is a mode of commitment to country that can be displayed by a person who has a strong sense of her own situated identity and a strong sense of place and community. It is not the commitment of a pure cosmopolitan. You may have an unapologetically localized conception of your identity, constructed out of your relationships with particular places, people, groups, activities, organizations, and so on. Those relationships may cross national boundaries. They can nevertheless ground reasons for you to care about your state: to care for the state of which you are a citizen and in whose political life you most directly participate.

A derived commitment can be a very strong commitment, and it is possible – at least – that the commitment to country that I am describing could be profound and thoroughgoing. You may not care about the country for its own sake, but you might nevertheless be prepared to make sacrifices for your state and to play your part in keeping it healthy – to defend the state and to participate in its decision-making – because you take it to have great, even if derived, value.

While your commitment to country may be great, and indeed as great as the commitment of the patriotic citizen, it will be different in structure from the commitment of the patriot, and that will have some consequences for how you think of your country and what you are prepared to do for it. First, in approaching your country, you are less likely to think of it as the one special country that is yours and more likely to recognize it as one country among others; with your scattered pattern of more fundamental concerns, you are more likely to have an awareness of your and your country's place in the world and of your country's strengths and weaknesses relative to others. This, probably, will temper your willingness to serve your country when it is in competition with other countries. Lacking the intense first-level devotion of the patriot, you are less likely to think it a matter of absolute moral urgency that your country succeed when its interests clash with the interests of others.

Second, given the structure of your commitment to your country, your willingness to act for it will be conditional. As you might refuse to help your political party in a campaign for a cause in which you do not believe, you might refuse to serve your state when you judge that its policies do not serve the basic rights and interests of its citizens (or other people), when it abandons the regions or people or other things to which you are committed, or when it embarks upon a war of which you disapprove. (You might, of course, choose to support the state even when its harms the things you care about, on the grounds that keeping the state functioning and unified will be best in the long run, given your deeper concerns. But that, still, is a conditional commitment.)

The form of commitment to country that I am trying to describe here can be called "worldly citizenship."[8] It is "worldly" because it involves understanding your country as one among others. It is not "world citizenship" because the form of identity underlying it is not an identity with humanity or with the world as a whole. It is "citizenship," or so I claim, because it designates a cluster of beliefs, feelings, and motivations that can generate robust concern for a state and can be relied upon to produce acts that contribute to the state's flourishing. In closing the paper, I will say a little about why I think worldly citizenship is attainable and why I think it is desirable.

---

[8] I approach worldly citizenship through a different question in my 'Worldly Citizens: Civic Virtue without Patriotism,' in Gillian Brock (ed.) *Cosmopolitanism versus Noncosmopolitanism* (Oxford University Press, 2013), pp. 239–254.

The Case for World Citizenship

Immigrant Citizens

Consider a person who moves from one country to another and becomes a good citizen of the new country. Such people are common. Suppose that you leave India and move to New Zealand, where you stay, and where you eventually become, formally, a citizen. You may still think of India as home. It may be difficult for you to think of yourself as a New Zealander, really, and still more difficult to think of yourself as a New Zealand patriot: any patriotic feelings you have may be directed squarely at India. But you could be a model citizen of New Zealand, involved in community and political life, respecting the state and its laws, and looking after those around you.

Good immigrant citizens, it seems to me, often exhibit the structure of commitments that characterize worldly citizenship. Upon moving to a new country, you cannot claim to know the country, but you can come to know parts of it and aspects of it. An immigrant to New York may find America a large and foreign place, while yet coming to feel at home in New York; an immigrant to a new country may come to know and love a school or a sports club or a neighborhood or a workplace. As an immigrant, you can also recognize the importance that your new country and its government have for your prospects and for the places and organizations and forms of life within the country for which you care. If you are an immigrant who also has a general concern for other humans, you can also be moved to contribute to good causes in the new country, to get politically involved, and generally to act well towards those you find around you.

The source of such good immigrant citizenship is not detached cosmopolitanism, though it is partly an expression of a general regard for others and a preparedness to act well towards other humans in whatever circumstances are faced. Its source is, partly, a commitment to the things within the new country that the new citizen comes to love – things distinct from the country itself.

The structure of motivation found in immigrant citizens can be replicated in citizens who are not immigrants. You do not need to be an immigrant to a country in order to value the country and make a commitment to the state out of regard for the good it does for the more localized things you care about and for its role in advancing human rights and interests generally. The kind of citizenship that I am trying to describe is not too contrived. It can be found around us, most obviously in good immigrant citizens, but also in others.

Nurturing Worldly Citizenship

There is a long tradition of patriotic education, intended to produce good citizens by inculcating patriotic beliefs, feelings, and motives. If we are to take worldly citizenship as our alternative ideal, then education for citizenship will have different goals.

The first task in educating worldly citizens is to encourage them to recognize and appreciate the different places and other influences that make them who they are. Instead of trying to parlay local attachments into a single attachment to the country, we should embrace local and particular identities, in their various different forms. Children should be taught to identify the things they know best and to understand the influence that those things have upon their identities.

The second task is to inculcate genuinely humanitarian beliefs and sentiments: an understanding of what humans have in common; an understanding that there is a large world full of people living their own lives, similar in some ways but different in others; and concern and respect for the rights and interests of all. This is a foundation for good citizenship that can be transferred between states. Under any circumstances, part of what it means to be a good citizen is just to act well towards the humans you find around you.

The third task of an education for worldly citizenship is to explain how the home country works, emphasizing the importance of the state for the health of local communities and places, and for general human rights and interests. The goal is to create citizens who can see how important the state is, given their deeper identities and concerns, and hence can find motivation to support the state and to try to influence it for the best.

Is it possible for an educational system to perform these three tasks? And if it does, will it tend to produce good citizens as a result? I cannot claim to know, but I do think that there is a coherent and in principle achievable conception of good citizenship around which the three tasks can be organized, and – importantly – that none of the three tasks need involve artificiality or deception or trying to build people in the modern world into something they can never be.

Self-Knowledge, the Value of the State, and What It Is Like to Be a Good Citizen

In a globalized world, we cannot presume that the identities of individuals are constituted by their connections with their countries or that it is possible to form individuals whose identities will be constituted by such connections. But that does not mean, as I have stressed, that we are all just humans now, or that each of us has the world – the undifferentiated world – as her home. Something other than patriotic citizenship and world citizenship is required.

A first advantage of the ideal of worldly citizenship, I think, is that it is compatible with an accurate understanding of self. The worldly citizen is able to see herself, by understanding the scattered networks, communities, and institutions that make her the person she is.

If I am correct, in addition, in saying that it is possible for the worldly citizen to have a robust and reliable motivation to perform acts that contribute to the flourishing of the state, then the ideal of worldly citizenship can bring together the two approaches to the question of good citizenship, in ways appropriate for contemporary conditions.

The worldly citizen can be the kind of citizen wanted by the state, because she can give the state what it needs from its citizens in order to flourish; the worldly citizen can support the state and find motivation to participate in its government. The worldly citizen can also be a person who flourishes in her role as citizen, because she can act well within that role while understanding herself accurately, without embracing a purely manufactured identity, and without having misguided beliefs or misplaced motives.

Another virtue of worldly citizenship is that the worldly citizen's conditional commitment to the state is just the kind of commitment that the state deserves. States are not intrinsically valuable and do not demand sacrifices just for their own sakes. The state's role is to serve the individuals and communities and places within its juridstiction, and to contribute constructively to the world more broadly. A citizen who holds the state to account for its treatment of the things within the state for which she cares, and for its performance in serving the rights and interests of people generally, thereby sees the state as it should be seen. A citizen should not be dedicated to the state no matter what and should not consider it unthinkable that the state should cease to deserve her support or that it should go out of existence. A good citizen does not give her state the benefit of the doubt or hold back on criticizing it. To that extent, a person will be a better citizen if her commitment to her state is derived from her commitment to more fundamental values and principles: ones that really do matter. A citizen who identifies with the country in the first instance will find it harder to see her state and its faults clearly.

The conditions we face in a globalized world pose a challenge to traditional ways of thinking about good citizenship. The model of the good citizen whose identity is deeply entangled with her connection to country, and whose commitment to country is a matter of primary loyalty, is not, I think, sustainable. The world is too interconnected and the forces that form our identities – whether we realize it or not – are too internationalized. But that does not mean that good citizenship is less important, and it need not mean that good citizenship is unattainable. A mature citizen in the globalized world is someone who understands her particular formative relationships, who has a general humanitarian moral sensibility, and who understands and values the state for what it is: not a moral community, not a deep source of moral identity, not an organic or intrinsically valuable institution, but instead a vital instrument through which the things that really matter can be served.

References

Gomberg, P. (1990). Patriotism is like racism. *Ethics, 101*, 144–150.

Keller, S. (2007). *The limits of loyalty*. Cambridge: Cambridge University Press.

Keller, S. (2013). Worldly citizens: Civic virtue without patriotism. In G. Brock (Ed.), *Cosmopolitanism versus noncosmopolitanism* (pp. 239–254). Oxford: Oxford University Press.

Kleinig, J., Keller, S., & Primoratz, I. (2015). *The ethics of patriotism: A debate*. Malden: Wiley Blackwell.

MacIntyre, A. (2002). Is patriotism a virtue? In I. Primoratz (Ed.), *Patriotism* (pp. 43–58). Amherst: Humanity Books.
Nussbaum, M. (2002). Patriotism and cosmopolitanism. In Nussbaum & J. Cohen (Eds.), *For love of country?* (pp. 3–20). Boston: Beacon Press.
Plato. (1997). In J. M. Cooper (Ed.), *Plato: Complete works*. Indianapolis: Hackett.
Singer, P. (2002). *One world*. Newhaven: Yale University Press.
Stilz, A. (2011). *Liberal loyalty*. Princeton: Princeton University Press.
Tamir, Y. (1995). *Liberal nationalism*. Princeton: Princeton University Press.

The Affective Dimension of Citizenship: A Platonic Account

Emma Cohen De Lara

The liberal polity tends to define citizenship as rights-based, that is, as political membership by means of which one is entitled to civic, social, and political rights. Liberal theories of citizenship tend to shy away from analyzing the emotions. By contrast, in this essay I aim to explore the meaning of citizenship placing the focus squarely on the affective dimension of citizenship, or citizenship defined as the emotional experience of a collective bond. By affective is meant the emotional dispositions that people develop on account of interpersonal relationships that are strengthened by shared practices. Taking the affective dimension of citizenship into account can illuminate in a distinctive way the extent to which a substantive conception of citizenship is viable in a world where levels of government are shifting away from the nation-state towards both transnational and local levels.

I propose to re-appropriate insights from Plato's dialogue *The Laws* in order to theorize about the affective dimension of citizenship. Ancient philosophy continues to inspire modern theories of politics and citizenship. Aristotle, in particular, continues to be an important source of inspiration for renewing conceptions of citizenship (Wallach 1992; Boyd 2013) and philosophers such as Hannah Arendt and Benjamin Barber have rooted their theories of citizenship in Aristotle as the original source. The republican notion of citizenship defined as an active participation in the public sphere is derived from Aristotle's definition of what it means to be a citizen. Aristotle corrected the conventional Athenian view that defined the citizen as a person born of Athenian parents, by arguing that a citizen is "defined by nothing else so much as by his participation in judgment and offices" (*Politics* 1275a21–22). A good citizen, according to Aristotle, is someone who participates in the offices of the city and develops the civic virtues on account of this practice.

E. Cohen De Lara (✉)
Amsterdam University College, University of Amsterdam, Amsterdam, The Netherlands
e-mail: e.cohendelara@auc.nl

D. Thunder (ed.), *The Ethics of Citizenship in the 21st Century*,
DOI 10.1007/978-3-319-50415-5_4

Plato provides an alternative account of what it means to be a member of a polity and, even though in theorizing citizenship the turn to Plato instead of Aristotle is unconventional, his insights are no less interesting.[1] In the *Laws*, Plato provides the reader with an elaborate psychology of the members of the polity. This psychology includes the emotional dispositions that are developed in shared group practices. The dialogue proposes that being a member of a political community means that one has internalized the laws of one's political community both on a cognitive and an emotional level.[2] This process of internalization occurs through the participation in public festivals where the laws of the polity are set to music and recited. The process of internalization during public festivals causes the members of the polity to bond with one another on an emotional level. The people's shared feelings towards the laws provide the common ties between the members of the polity.

Plato thus provides an interesting resource because, first of all, a conception of citizenship that is based on the psychology of Plato's *Laws* would reject the idea that citizenship is based on outward characteristics such as rights or entitlements. Rather, Plato's psychology takes into account the citizen as a human being who, by being present in the polity and by sharing in its practices, develops specific emotional attachments. Such shared emotional attachments may help explain, for example, possible tensions in contemporary societies between the members of a polity and immigrants or newcomers. These tensions seem particularly difficult to diagnose and resolve because they result from differences in people's emotional make-up, which is not captured well within contemporary theories of citizenship. Involving the affective dimension in theories of citizenship has long been suspect, in particular because it was associated with a perverted sense of nationalism. Liberal theories of citizenship, such as Habermas' *Verfassungspatriotismus*, shy away from

[1] Important exceptions are Bobonich (2002) and Prauscello (2014). The turn to Plato is less common in part because of author anonymity. Plato wrote dialogues in which he does not partake himself and this raises the question whether or not the main interlocutor in each dialogue can be regarded to represent Plato's own views. Another reason may be that Plato acquired a bad reputation with the appearance of Karl Popper's *Open Society and Its Enemies*, which was originally published in 1945 and which depicted Plato as a totalitarian thinker. The question whether Plato proposes practices that are illiberal and undemocratic is a legitimate one, but the idea that Plato should be ignored because he is a totalitarian thinker is no longer taken seriously. A third reason that Plato is sometimes ignored is that he is considered a utopian thinker, which limits the relevance of his ideas for contemporary social and political practices. The current chapter seeks to show that Plato actually theorized a dimension of citizenship that is still present in practices of citizenship today.

[2] Prauscello's *Performing Citizenship in Plato's* Laws was published when the first draft of the current chapter had already been written. The current chapter takes her important work into account as much as possible. One way in which the current chapter differs from *Performing Citizenship*, besides being a much shorter exercise, is that Prauscello has a strong focus on the *form* in which citizenship is expressed in the *Laws*. Also, she emphasizes the erotic side of citizenship, arguing that Plato develops civic practices in order to awaken and strengthen an eager desire to become a perfect citizen in all inhabitants of the city. My own reading differs to the extent that it focuses on the content of the civic practices which, I argue, consists of the written and unwritten laws and customs of the city that are set to music.

conceptualizing the affective dimension, as we shall see later in this chapter. However, the affective dimension is all around us; it is part of the empirical reality in which we live that people develop emotional dispositions on account of civic ties. Adequate moral and political theorizing benefits from taking the emotions and affective bonds between citizens seriously (Nussbaum 1995, 2001). As I argue in this chapter, Plato's conception of citizenship can contribute to contemporary theorizing of the affective dimension of citizenship. As such, the chapter connects to a growing interest in what is called the social psychology or political sociology of citizenship (Johnson 2010; Neuman et al. 2007; Kymlicka and Norman 1994).

Secondly, Plato's account of citizenship may be particularly interesting to the liberal polity because, even though it is based on the process of internalization - which fits uneasily with the liberal paradigm– the object of the civic attachments are the laws and not, for example, ethnicity, history, or a shared nationhood. Law has the potential to be reasonable, universal and inclusive. I write this with hesitation because the ancient Greeks did not separate law from culture; the Greek word for laws (*nomoi*) extended beyond written laws to include unwritten laws and customs (cf. *Laws* 824c). Still, there is a sense in Plato's *Laws* in which the legislator provides the members of the city with rationalized *nomoi*, meaning *nomoi* that are distanced or dissociated as much as possible from a specific cultural context. And this fits easier into the liberal paradigm, which tends to regard citizens as autonomous individuals who are separated from cultural ties and historical context.

In this way, so I will argue, Plato's theory may still inform modern theories and practices of citizenship. In order to explore Plato's contribution, this chapter, first of all, seeks to analyze what it means to be a member of the *polis* in Plato's *Laws* by focusing on three topics in the *Laws*, namely, the psychology of the citizen based on the puppet image in book two, the discussion of the choir festivals in which all members of the city participate, and the so-called preambles to the laws that are meant to persuade or exhort the citizen to obey the law. Secondly, in light of Plato's psychology of the members of the polity, the chapter explores several of the conceptual problems that the development of the affective dimension of citizenship runs into when different levels of governance are taken into account. The chapter concludes with the suggestion that changes in the substantive conception of citizenship need to take place on a level that facilitates the emotional bonding between its members and makes the physical proximity between people possible.

The Psychology of Plato's *Republic*

At first sight, Plato seems close to Aristotle in the definition of the citizen. According to Plato, a citizen "knows how to rule and be ruled with justice" (*Laws*, 644a), a definition comparable to Aristotle's statement that "the capacity to rule and be ruled is at any rate praised, and being able to do both well is held to be the virtue of a citizen" (*Politics*, 1277a25–26). The two philosophers depart, however, in their conception of what it means – and what qualities are involved – in ruling. For Plato, knowing how to rule and be ruled with justice is a result of an internalization of the laws of the polity. For Aristotle, knowing how to rule and how to obey is the result of participation in the offices of the polity. In short, these are two distinct conceptions of what it means to be a citizen.

In order to understand how, in Plato's *Laws*, the citizen internalizes the laws of the city, we need to look at the psychology of the citizen. Here, it is useful to start with an analysis of the soul in the *Republic*, which Plato builds upon in the *Laws*.[3] In the *Republic*, the main interlocutor Socrates proposes that the soul has a tripartite structure and each of the parts stands in a particular relationship to the others. The first part consists of the rational element. This is the reasoning part and the part that the soul uses for learning. The second part consists of what Socrates calls the spirited part. This part is less familiar to modern ways of thinking. The spirited part is a kind of emotion that one may call justified anger. It is this part of the soul, more than the other two parts, that is focused on action. Children already exhibit this type of sensibility, such as a justified anger at promises broken, candy stolen etc. Plato understands this part of the soul as separate from the emotions and desires because it - the spirited part - can be in conflict with the desires. In a well-functioning soul, spirited anger is an ally of reason in the attempt to control and manage the desires. The third and largest part of the soul consists of the desires for the pleasures of food, drink, sex, etc. Socrates calls this part of the soul one that is devoid of reason (*Rep.* 439d). It is also the part of the soul that easily predominates; human beings experience a wide range of desires and emotions, pleasures and pains. Because of this, the desiring part is the part of the soul that is most obviously present in the everyday decision-making process and is also the part, as we will see, that is of central importance to a man's psychology in the *Laws*.

In the *Republic*, ethical behavior is premised on the harmonious ordering of the soul. This ordering is a natural consequence of the soul's tripartite nature and how exactly these three parts relate is the key to understanding Plato's conception of the ordered soul. That there are three parts, and that the soul is not one uniform entity, is clear. Socrates makes the argument based on the principle of opposites. Nothing, so Socrates explains, "can do two opposite things, or be in two opposite states, in the same part of itself, at the same time, in relation to the same object" (*Rep.* 436b). Take, for example, thirst, which may be defined as the desire to drink. Even though a person may be thirsty, there are situations in which he decides not to drink. In that case there must be, in Socrates' words, "something in their soul telling them to drink, and also something stopping them" (*Rep.* 439c). Even though a person is thirsty, he may refuse to drink when the drink is poisonous. Following the principle of opposites, there would have to be another element in the soul that is not part of the desires but that inhibits action. In this case, it is the rational element that – recognizing that the water is polluted – dominates over desire and decides not to drink. Given that one element cannot be in opposite states with respect to the same object,

---

[3] For the purpose of this chapter, a significant amount of continuity between the moral psychology of Plato's *Republic* and the *Laws* is assumed, cf. Kahn (2004); Prauscello (2014).

i.e. the glass of water, it follows that there are at least two elements involved in the process of decision-making.

As to the ordering of the three different parts, Socrates states that it is appropriate for the rational element to rule, "because it is wise and takes thought for the entire soul" (*Rep.* 441e). The spirited part is meant to be an ally of the rational part. A soul may have good judgment, but one generally needs the energy and the courage to impose wise decisions on the desiring part. The spirited part is meant to assist the reasoning part courageously, meaning that "although surrounded by pleasures and pains", it is able to stand up to the emotions and to "keep intact the instructions given to it by reason about what is to be feared and what is not to be feared" (*Rep.* 442c). The desiring part, in turn, should be moderate and obedient. Lacking reason, it should submit to the rule of the rational part. This is possible only if, through habituation, the desiring part becomes moderate. Genuine moderation is defined as a kind of friendship or harmony between the three parts, suggesting that the desiring part agrees to be ruled by reason with the assistance of the spirited part (*Rep.* 442c–d). When each part performs its proper function – the rational element rules over the soul, the spirited part assists the rational part courageously and the desiring part submits to the control of the rational and spirited parts – then the soul is properly ordered and ethical behavior follows (*Rep.* 441e).

The Psychology and Education of the Citizen in Plato's *Laws*

Note that, following the previous analysis, the development of an ordered soul does not entail a complete suppression or expulsion of the desires. The point is – and this is where we turn to Plato's *Laws* – that human life is happiest when one indulges the desires in a reasonable way. As in the *Republic*, the soul in the *Laws* is presented as having a reasonable part, which should rule, and a desiring part, which should obey reason. The middle or spirited part of the soul does not play a prominent independent role in the *Laws*.[4] Following the static conception in the *Republic* about the order in the soul, the *Laws* provides a more dynamic account of what it means to live an ordered life and an account in which the emotions play an important role. One should experience the right pleasure or pain at the right time, in the right amount, and towards the right object (*Laws*, 636e). Desires in themselves do not cause unhappiness, but excessive desires *do* (such as for a whole bag of licorice), and so do desires at the wrong time (such as an alcoholic drink in the morning) or towards the wrong object (such as someone else's wife). In the *Laws*, being in control of one's desires and emotions manifests itself as a kind of musical harmony between the different parts of the soul. Just as a conductor directs an orchestra in a musical performance by way of allowing different musicians to play at the right moment and by unifying the performers into a harmonious whole, so reason decides – in the performance of life – which emotion to act upon, which to ignore,

[4] For an interesting discussion on this topic, see Sassi (2008).

to what degree, and at what time. In this way, the balanced, virtuous person goes through life with his reason and emotions in tune. Moreover, just as the lack of synchronicity of one section of performers results in dissonance in an orchestra, so do the rebellion of pleasures or pains result in chaos in the soul. In a person with a healthy disposition, such disorder causes someone to experience honorable shame (*aidos*), that is a sense of embarrassment at not being in control of one's self (*Laws*, 647a; 648e ff).

The potential for internal struggle and lack of self-control is more evident in Plato's *Laws* than in Plato's *Republic*, given its emphasis on the role of the emotions and desires.[5] With this awareness comes an emphasis on cultivating moderation, which is the virtue that ensures the harmony between reason and the desiring part of the soul, including practices that promote the habituation of the soul towards moderation. The Greek word for moderation is internal harmony or *sophrosune*. Internal harmony or *sophrosune* goes beyond the moral ideal of being in control by repressing certain emotions – the Greek word for this is *enkrateia*, meaning to have control or power (*kratos*) over oneself. Moderation as *sophrosune* reflects the musical harmony that a conductor brings about in the orchestra; the conductor does not dominate over the musicians but, rather, coordinates the orchestra, allowing the different instruments to be played at the appropriate times, in the right intensity, and for the right length of time.

How, then, does the moral psychology presented in the *Laws* relate to Plato's understanding of the citizen? Here, we turn to yet another image. Instead of an orchestra that produces musical harmony with the help of a conductor, the soul is now represented by an image of a puppet on strings (*Laws* 644c-5c). The strings are made of different materials. Most of the strings are made of iron and are tough. They represent the passions that pull the puppet in all sorts of directions. Among the many hard strings attached to the puppet there is one that is soft and golden and that represents reason. The puppet, of course, is meant to follow the soft, reasonable cord, but it is being tossed about by the stronger cords. Therefore, so the story goes, the golden cord of calculation needs helpers. Its main helper is a socially cultivated feeling of shame. We see here that, in an ingenious way, the puppet image connects the internal functioning of the soul to the social context. A well-functioning soul needs the support of an environment that praises noble action and shames ignoble action. By means of social praise for reasonable action and social blame for unreasonable action, the golden cord in the soul that represents reason, receives support because the cords that represent the desire for praise now pull in the same direction. Social customs have an effect on the tug of strings that acts upon the puppet. In a terse yet graphic way, the puppet on strings illustrates the affective dimension of citizenship. The social practices, which differ from polity to polity, make different kinds of behavior more or less pleasurable to the citizen on account of social approval or disapproval. With repeated strengthening of certain strings

[5] Cf. Gerson (2003) and Dorion (2007). Plato's *Laws* is often considered to offer a description of a second-best city, in which reason is less to be relied upon to provide order, whether in the city or the soul. Cf. Laks (2001).

over other strings, the citizen-as-puppet develops a specific disposition or emotional makeup that is shared with other citizens since all are subjected to the same practices and customs.

The laws of a polity play a role in the development of the emotional disposition of the citizen as well. The story about the puppet on strings operates on the premise that the puppet has a golden cord of reason that needs to be developed. The laws of a polity, which should be reasonable laws, support the golden cord until it becomes mature. The golden cord coming into its own means that the individual matures emotionally and intellectually and gains understanding about the nature of the different passions that pull him in different directions. Law, based on this argument, supports the puppet in developing its ability for moral reasoning, which in turn promotes the internal harmony of the soul. One could argue that the cultivation of moral reasoning belongs primarily to the sphere of the family, but in the *Laws* the focus is on the moral development of the person as a member of the polity. The development of *sophrosune* occurs on account of being a member of the political community who is subject to its laws and a participant in its practices. Membership of a political community has meaning for one's internal disposition.

We are now ready to provide a more elaborate definition of what Plato means by citizenship. Plato's *Laws* defines a citizen as someone who lives in a polity, is an active member of the polity and – as a member of the polity – is subject to its laws. The laws of the polity should reflect right reason.[6] This is a prescriptive, not descriptive argument; the interlocutors assume the existence of right reason and do not take into consideration what happens when the laws do not reflect right reason. The citizen is meant – by means of common practices that will be discussed below – to internalize the law and strengthen his ability to reason correctly about the different desires and emotions that he harbors in his soul. This is the psychological process that underlies Plato's definition of the citizen as someone who "knows how to rule and be ruled with justice" (*Laws*, 643e-4a). In other words, there are psychological prerequisites that qualify one as a citizen. Citizenship is not a right or a legal status. Rather, citizenship for Plato in the *Laws* entails an inner disposition that is shaped by the customs and written laws of the polity.

Public Festivals and Moral Education

The process of internalization of the law occurs through a variety of communal practices. The proposal about these practices is demanding, involving public holidays and religious festivals for every day of the year (*Laws*, 828b). For Plato, the education of the citizen is a full-time affair that lasts a lifetime. The demanding nature of the proposal fits uneasily with life in modern societies. Still, the way in which Plato understands the psychological processes that occur during these common practices are informative. The public festivals work on two levels. Music and

[6] For a novel discussion of this argument, see Irwin (2010).

movement affect the emotional part of the soul, while the lyrics influence the rational part of the soul. The poets are meant to set the actual texts of the laws to music and choral dancing that is harmonious, joyful and playful (*Laws*, 811d).[7] The so-called Guardians of the Laws supervise the poets to make sure that they do not interpret the text of the laws in a way that deviates from convention (*Laws*, 801d). These songs are then performed at the public festivals, repeated daily, in which the citizens themselves participate both by singing and dancing to the songs in unison.

Human beings are considered to have the natural ability to perceive and experience rhythm and harmony (*Laws*, 654a). Furthermore, human beings are considered to find the experience of rhythm and harmony naturally pleasurable. Plato is clearly aware that human beings learn and remember things better when they *enjoy* the pedagogic experience. People, especially the young, are averse to seriousness and this is why the texts of the laws should be mixed with pleasant and playful practices, just as a medicine is best taken with a sugar coating. The songs and dances function as enchantments that, in a musical and playful way, help the performer – who is the citizen and who enacts the text of the law in song and dance – absorb the law on an emotional level (*Laws*, 659d–660a; 665c). These performances habituate the people to experience pleasurable emotions whilst singing the texts of the laws. In this way, so the interlocutor argues, the people learn to love becoming a good citizen who *enjoys* obedience to the law (*Laws*, 634e).

One could remark that the notion of citizens singing songs that have the texts of the laws as the lyrics is quite childish. The interlocutor refers to early childhood education, which is mostly concerned with the habituation of pleasure and feelings of pain (*Laws*, 653a ff.). He proposes that children are especially excitable by music and movement and that childhood education depends on the Muses (*Laws*, 654a). Play is the most common and appropriate practice for producing good character at an early age.[8] Furthermore, the interlocutor provides us with the existential argument that, perhaps, human beings are *meant* to be like children who spend their lives at play: "Every man and woman should spend life in this way, playing the noblest possible games" (*Laws*, 803c; cf. 644d). Wine is promoted to encourage those made solemn with age to return to a state of childhood playfulness (*Laws*, 646a; 671b). Not only does playfulness facilitate moral learning, human beings are meant to be cheerful. In the *Laws*, man can be said to be at his best in songs and dance during the public festivals.

On a rational level, so-called preambles to the laws are meant to persuade the citizen of the purpose of the law (*Laws*, 720e). Plato's argument is that free people internalize the law not by force or indoctrination but by being convinced of the

[7] Throughout the *Laws*, Plato plays with the double meaning in Greek of the word *nomos*, which can be translated both as law and as a song that was sung by a chorus or a soloist and accompanied by a string instrument (see especially 700b; 799e). By doing so, he emphasizes the connection between the laws and the songs that are sung and performed at the public festivals.

[8] Throughout the *Laws*, Plato plays with the words *paideia* (the shaping of character), *paidia* (play) and *pais* (child), which have the same Greek root.

soundness of the arguments put forth (cf. *Laws*, 720d). The preamble expresses not a philosophical argument but, rather, an argument from common sense that is meant to show the law's rationale.[9] For example, the preface to the marriage law argues that men should marry between the age of thirty and thirty-five in order to achieve some trace of immortality by leaving offspring. A bachelor of over thirty-five actually has to pay a fine and this is, so the preamble continues, to discourage the idea that not maintaining a family and living the bachelor's lifestyle is worth it. Even though liberal countries would reject such a law on account of interfering in what we would today consider private choices, there is still a kind of logic here that explains the reasoning behind the law. The main point is that the laws that are sung and performed during the public festivals are not dogmatic rules that work by mere threat of punishment.

In considering public festivals, and the emotional bonds developed at festivals, Plato is theorizing a phenomenon that resonates with the findings of contemporary anthropological research. In *Keeping Together in Time. Dance and Drill in Human History*, William McNeill coins the term "muscular bonding", referring to the "human emotional response to moving rhythmically together in dance and drill." (McNeill 1995, p. vi) Bonding occurs, so McNeill argues, due to the pleasurable experience of dance and drill; it is "natural and automatic" to move to the rhythm of music. McNeill refers to the boundary loss that promotes emotional bonding and the feeling of being one as a result of a common "rhythmic muscular" experience of participating in the musical performance (1995, p. 8). One of the original purposes of dance in small, independent communities is that "dancing became an efficacious way of consolidating distinct subgroups within larger communities." (McNeill 1995, p. 42, 52 ff.) In the experience, differences are transcended and previously marginalized persons or complete outsiders "coalesce into new, more or less coherent groups." (McNeill 1995, p. 52) McNeill also recognizes the political implications of the practice. The social consolidation is achieved by including previous outsiders and, at the same time, enhanced by the exclusion of others.

Now, the story of Plato's *Laws* concerns the design of a law code for a new colony. The establishment of colonies was commonplace in ancient Greece. Colonization occurred on account of overpopulation or civil strife, when part of the population migrated or displaced itself (*Laws*, 708b). The case of the story of the *Laws* concerns a situation where the new inhabitants come from all over Crete (*Laws*, 708a), which indicated that there was a lack of tribal unity amongst them. The challenge exists not so much in having this population accept a new code of law. Since they come from different legal systems, they will not all be attached to the same code and are more likely to be open to collectively accepting a new one. Instead, the challenge is – in the words of the interlocutor – to have them "breathe together and grow to be constantly united – like a team of horses, as they say"

[9] There is a dispute about the character of the preambles as rational or sub-rational, with Stalley (1983) arguing that the preambles stay on the level of moral exhortations, Bobonich (2002) arguing that several preambles actually contain philosophically sophisticated arguments, and Annas (2010) proposing that the preambles have a mixture in them of both rational and non-rational elements.

(*Laws*, 708d). The public festivals, where people join in song and choral dancing developing a common attachment to the laws of the polity, are to provide the transformative experience that Plato is looking for while crafting the citizens of the new political community. The rhythmic bodily agreement that is part of the choral performances creates affective bonds between the citizens. Moreover, the affective bonds between the citizens are directed towards a common object of affection, namely, the laws of the polity. Together, they celebrate the written law. In doing so, the citizens are changed internally and are soldered together.

Limitations and Applications

When thinking about the contribution that Plato's understanding of citizenship in the *Laws* could make to contemporary theories of citizenship in liberal democracies, several objections present themselves. Some of the legal content proposed in the *Laws,* such as the marriage laws that were discussed earlier, are illiberal in the sense that they interfere in the private lives of individuals.[10] Also, Plato presents a static theory of law that seems unrealistic and undemocratic. In Plato's *Laws*, change in the law is possible but only under rare circumstances (*Laws*, 772d), which is an indication that laws are not arrived at by democratic deliberation.[11] In particular, the songs and dances are not subject to change and, indeed, are sanctified in their permanence so that the ethos of the polity is the same for different generations of people (*Laws*, 799a). Overall, Plato's purpose is to provide the system of laws with a sacred status in order to exact reverence to the laws. These are all valid concerns. And, yet, the idea that citizenship implies an emotional bond with one's fellow citizens and an attachment to the laws of the city may still provide a correction to liberal, rights-based theories that, in lacking an affective dimension, can be regarded as too abstract and, therefore, divorced from reality in that they fail to capture what for many people constitutes part of the everyday experience of citizenship.

One observation is that the practice in Plato's *Laws* concerns emotional bonding in small-scale communities. The proposal for the new colony in the *Laws* involves a populace of 5040 families (the number has the most numerous and consecutive divisors, see *Laws*, 738a). This, of course, is a very small community. If we accept that the emotional bonding of members of a polity through shared practices is an inherent part of what being a citizen means, then the local, rather than the national,

---

[10] Indirectly, of course, liberal laws also impact the private lives of individuals. For example, tax laws may favor married couples over people who are single. It is often the case that liberal laws implicitly promote one way of life over the other; law is barely ever completely neutral in this respect.

[11] This is not to say that there are no democratic elements in the city. The *Laws* proposes a regime that even allows women over forty who are past childbearing age to run for most offices (*Laws*, 785d). For many of the public offices, the selection procedure is by lot, which was considered to be democratic *par excellence*. Still, even though the city in *The Laws* has a wide range of offices that are open to all citizens, the citizens do not make or change their own laws.

transnational, or global level would be best suited for the reinforcement of citizenship. Given that human beings are embodied beings and accepting the premise that emotional bonding involves physical proximity, the local level may be the primary level at which citizenship develops its affective dimension.

And, yet, there is a way in which Plato offers an account of citizenship that has the potential to transcend the local. The objective of civic affection is the system of laws and, in modern times, laws tend to be primarily a national or international affair. This raises the question whether national and international law may provide the foundation for citizenship in the Platonic sense. One could imagine, with some effort, the musical recitation and performance of the Bill of Rights, the Universal Declaration of Human Rights, and so forth on a local level, in civic groups that are small enough to facilitate human interaction and bonding.

Still, Plato is an unlikely source of inspiration for the conceptualization of any kind of citizenship that claims to go beyond the national level. According to Plato, not only is the practice of citizenship local and communal, out of necessity the law will always have a particularistic aspect because of being language-specific. This argument is not emphasized in the *Laws*, but the connection between reason and language for which the ancient Greek has one word (*logos*) is evident. Human beings have language because they share in reason and because law embodies sound reason, but being language specific will always have different sounds, articulations and connotations across different languages. Therefore, Plato's conception of citizenship is likely to sit uneasily with, for example, the notion that was articulated by the Stoic Diogenes Laertius who called himself a citizen of the world, providing a foundation for what in modern times is called cosmopolitan citizenship (see, for example, Soysal 1998; Nussbaum 2002).

The contemporary theory that comes closest to the idea of citizenship as having internalized legal norms is the theory of constitutional patriotism. The theory of constitutional patriotism has undergone development but broadly understood, can be understood as defending the notion that the citizen is one who is loyal to the democratic state and to the rule of law. The citizen is meant to have affinity with the principles of the constitution and the constitutional culture of the country. The emphasis on the public performance of laws set to music and choreography is not part of the theory of constitutional patriotism; as a liberal theory it shies away from a notion of citizenship that is transformative on account of the public celebrations whereby citizens develop a common attachment to the laws and to each other, even though the theory does allow for a symbolic content and narratives that evoke particular emotions (Müller 2007, p. 62). This raises the question whether Plato's theory of citizenship can inform the theory of constitutional patriotism. Some have argued that the purely academic *Verfassungspatriotismus* of Jürgen Habermas suffers from "emotional abstinence" (Müller 2007, p. 43). According to Müller, Habermas argues that "citizens attach themselves to the norms and values at the heart of the constitution, that is, the constitutional essentials, and, in particular, the fair and democratic procedures producing legitimate law." (Müller 2007, p. 58) The loyalty requirement of citizens to the constitution should show itself in external behavior, not as part of an inner disposition. One question is *how* newcomers are expected to develop their affinity with the principles of the constitution. Moreover, one could question whether the external allegiance involved is substantive enough to last through major challenges and across generations.

Even though the idea of festivals at the heart of which is the public performance of the written constitution may engender awkwardness in a liberal polity, it may also strengthen both people's knowledge of and, especially, attachment to the constitution. Setting the text of the constitution to music may be just as awkward or even less compared to the attempt in the Netherlands in 2014 to celebrate the bicentennial anniversary of the Dutch constitution in a historicized way with battles of knights, people dressed up in costumes of the time period, and random culinary and musical festivals. One could argue that this was a missed opportunity to educate Dutch citizens about the text of the constitution and help them cherish the document, especially because Dutch citizens have little knowledge of the content of the constitution, which makes it difficult for Dutch citizens to become genuinely attached to the document (cf. Oomen 2009).

Another example of a missed opportunity is the Treaty of Lisbon, signed by the EU member states in 2007, which modified the proposed text for a European constitution. The Treaty of Lisbon suppressed all mention of the symbols of the European Union, such as the flag, and the European Anthem, Beethoven's Ode to Joy. The treaty also eliminated the preamble to the draft European constitution, articulating amongst other things an allegiance to democracy, equality, the rule of law, and a commitment to forge a common destiny. The political will did not exist to create a European Union as a polity, but thinking from the affective dimension of citizenship the changes implied significant obstacles that prevent the development of a European citizenship.

Plato's *Laws* may be, in several ways, less illiberal and undemocratic than expected. The citizen internalizes laws that are not perfectly liberal, but are not irrational or subjective either. The preambles to the laws ensure a reasoning aspect to the law. Plato's theory of citizenship helps us reflect on the affective dimension of citizenship and how this is developed. Plato's insights help us appreciate the idea that citizenship is not (merely) a legal status or a ticket to certain rights and responsibilities but also a way of being that affects our emotional relationship to others; fellow-citizens, strangers, and newcomers. Plato's insights help us recognize, articulate and interpret these emotions and perhaps even engage in the craft of citizenship in a more self-conscious way.

References

Annas, J. (2010). Virtue and law in Plato. In C. Bobonich (Ed.), *Plato's* Laws. *A critical guide*. Cambridge: Cambridge University Press.

Aristotle. (1984). *The Politics*. Trans. C. D. C. Reeve. Indianapolis: Hackett Publishing Company.

Bobonich, C. (2002). *Plato's Utopia Recast. His later ethics and politics*. Oxford: Clarendon Press.

Boyd, R. (2013). Boundaries, birthright, and belonging: Aristotle on the distribution of citizenship. *The Good Society, 22*(2), 215–235.
Dorion, L.-A. (2007). Plato and *enkrateia*. In C. Bobonich & P. Destrée (Eds.), *Akrasia in Greek philosophy from Socrates to Plotinus* (pp. 119–138). Leiden: Brill.
Gerson, L. (2003) 'Akrasia and the divided soul in Plato's *Laws*,' in Scolnicov, S. and Brisson, L. (eds.) *Plato's* Laws*: From theory into practice. Proceedings of the VI symposium Platonicum. Selected papers*. Sankt Augustin: Academia Verlag, 149–154.
Irwin, T. (2010). Morality as law and morality in the *Laws*. In C. Bobonich (Ed.), *Plato's* Laws. A critical guide. Cambridge: Cambridge University Press.
Johnson, C. (2010). The politics of affective citizenship: From Blair to Obama. *Citizenship Studies, 14*(5), 495–509.
Kahn, C. H. (2004). From *Republic* to *Laws*: a discussion of Christopher Bobonich, Plato's Utopia Recast. *Oxford Studies in Ancient Philosophy, 26*, 337–362.
Kymlicka, W., & Norman, W. (1994). Return of the citizen: A survey of recent work on citizenship theory. *Ethics, 104*(2), 352–381.
Laks, A. (2001). In what sense is the city of the *Laws* a second best one? In F. L. Lisi (Ed.), *Plato's* Laws and its historical significance. Selected papers of the 1st international congress on ancient thought, Salamanca 1998 (pp. 107–114). Sankt Augustin: Academia Verlag.
McNeill, William H. (1995) Keeping together in time. Dance and drill in human history. Cambridge, MA: Harvard University Press.
Müller, J. W. (2007). *Constitutional patriotism*. Princeton: Princeton University Press.
Neuman, W. R., Marcus, G. E., Crigler, A. N., & Mackuen, M. (Eds.). (2007). *The affect effect. Dynamics of emotion in political thinking and behavior*. Chicago: University of Chicago Press.
Nussbaum, M. C. (1995). *Poetic justice. The literary imagination and public life*. Boston: Beacon Press Books.
Nussbaum, M. C. (2001). *Upheavals of thought. The intelligence of emotions*. Cambridge: Cambridge University Press.
Nussbaum, M. (2002). Patriotism and cosmopolitanism. In M. Nussbaum (Ed.), *For love of country?* (pp. 1–17). Boston: Beacon Press.
Oomen, B. (2009). Constitutioneel bewustzijn in Nederland: Van burgerzin, burgerschap en de onzichtbare grondwet. *Recht der Werkelijkheid, 2*, 55–79.
Plato. (1980). *The Laws*. Transl. by T. L. Pangle. Chicago: University of Chicago Press.
Plato. (2000). *The Republic*. Transl. by T. Griffith. Cambridge: Cambridge University Press.
Popper, K. (1971). *The open society and its enemies: The spell of Plato*. Princeton: Princeton University Press.
Prauscello, L. (2014). *Performing citizenship in Plato's* Laws. Cambridge: Cambridge University Press.
Sassi, M. M. (2008). The self, the soul, and the individual in the city of the *Laws*. *Oxford Studies in Ancient Philosophy, 35*, 125–148.
Soysal, Y. N. (1998). Toward a postnational model of membership. In G. Shafir (Ed.), *The citizenship debates: A reader* (pp. 189–217). Minneapolis: University of Minnesota Press.
Stalley, R. F. (1983). *An introduction to Plato's* Laws. Oxford: Basil Blackwell Publisher.
Wallach, J. R. (1992). Contemporary Aristotelianism. *Political Theory, 20*(4), 613–641.

Part III
Citizenship and Conscience

Conscientious Citizenship: Arendt and Aquinas on Conscience and Politics

Angela C. Miceli Stout

Participation of citizens in political society is considered an essential aspect of political legitimacy, both promoting the common good and fostering civic virtue. However, some theorists question whether increased participation of citizens is a good (Irvin and Stansbury 2004). As more citizens participate in a regime, there may perhaps be more pressure to conform to its principles, even if those principles are unjust or unduly burden other members of society (Wolin 1960). Of course, this assertion presupposes two things, viz. that we understand what a citizen is and what justice is. This paper will not focus particularly on either of these questions, for it is not about a theory of citizenship or of justice, though both of these problems remain in the background. Rather, I assume some basic ideas about citizenship, namely that citizens in a political society have legal status within that regime that affords them certain rights and obliges them to particular civic, social, moral, and political duties.[1] The question in this paper is about how a citizen or citizens ought to act when confronted with injustice that exists in a particular political regime. How does being a citizen in a particular regime, with the rights and duties that come with citizenship, oblige us to order our lives according to the actions and values of the regime or even of other citizens? In short, I intend to explore the concept of *conscientious citizenship:* What is the role of conscience for a citizen? How ought we to live out our moral convictions as citizens in a political society? Moreover, what should one do when one's moral convictions are threatened by a hostile political regime? What happens if an individual's conscience or indeed the conscience of an entire society, fail to object to injustice?

It was precisely reflection on such questions that so troubled political philosopher Hannah Arendt as she struggled to comprehend the political phenomenon of totalitarianism. How could one possibly remain a good man and be a good citizen in

[1] For a more in-depth consideration of the concept of citizenship, see chapter 3 of Thunder 2014.

A.C. Miceli Stout (✉)
Universidad de Navarra, Instituto de Cultura y Sociedad, Pamplona, Spain
e-mail: angelamiceli@gmail.com

D. Thunder (ed.), *The Ethics of Citizenship in the 21st Century*,
DOI 10.1007/978-3-319-50415-5_5

such a regime? The question was of personal consequence to Arendt, for she, as a German Jew, fled Germany after the rise of the Nazi party in 1933. In Arendt's famous coverage of the trial of Nazi Adolf Eichmann, we can see the starting point of her philosophical reflections on conscience and citizenship. She writes, "as for his conscience, [Eichmann] remembered perfectly well that he would have had a bad conscience only if he had not done what he had been ordered to do—to ship millions of men, women, and children to their death with great zeal and the most meticulous care" (Arendt 1994, 25). Arendt finds this disposition of moral conscience incomprehensible. How was it possible that Eichmann never experienced a crisis of conscience for his complicity and collaboration with the Nazi regime? Where was this interior order—his conscience—in Eichmann that should have prompted him to act differently? How had the Nazi ideology so deformed his moral sensibility that he believed murdering Jews was a morally good and conscientious act?

Arendt's philosophical investigation of politics and conscience throughout her career led her to some paradoxical conclusions. Conscience, according to Arendt, is essentially unpolitical and shows commitment to one's *own personal* spiritual welfare and integrity rather than concern with political activity or political commitments. Thus, for Arendt, to be concerned with conscience is to be drawn away from politics altogether, making a conscientious citizen a virtual impossibility (Arendt 1971, 1972, 1990; Kateb 1983; Canovan 1992; Villa 2001). Conscience is not only unpolitical, but convictions of conscience are unable to apply to anyone other than the individual person holding that conviction: "The counsels of conscience are not only unpolitical; they are always expressed in purely subjective statements" (Arendt 1972, 62). We will consider her view of conscience more deeply in the following section. Suffice it to say here that for Arendt political action and conscience appear to be incompatible. That is to say, to be a citizen, i.e. a participant in political life and in a political regime, draws one away from conscience and conscience causes one to withdraw from politics. Arendt, therefore, seems unable to answer her own inquiry that began with her reflection on totalitarianism and on Eichmann. How can one be a good human being, one who maintains his or her moral integrity, and simultaneously be a good citizen? Citizenship and conscience seem to have no place for each other.

I offer Thomas Aquinas's theory of conscience as one that can address the tensions that we see in Arendt's view. Arendt's philosophy in many ways is diametrically opposed to that of Aquinas. She rejects metaphysics, and Aquinas presupposes it and calls it the highest science.[2] It seems that the only point of comparison between Arendt and Aquinas is that both died untimely deaths before finishing their

[2] On the existence of metaphysics, Arendt gives an account of its being discredited in contemporary philosophy and calls Kant's prediction that philosophy would return to metaphysics as unlikely and undesirable. She writes that it is not the metaphysical questions that are meaningless; rather the way they have been framed and answered that has lost plausibility. Cf. her introduction to *Life of the Mind*, volume 1. Aquinas calls metaphysics the highest science in the *Summa Theologiae*, Prima Pars, Art. 1, Q. 8.

great works (Lebech 2003). Yet, as Mette Lebech points out, both thinkers are committed to the life of the mind, bringing them together in a fascinating dialogue, as their approaches and presuppositions differ. Moreover, both thinkers are committed to the idea that the ability to know right from wrong through living a 'life of the mind' was not a task for philosophers alone, but one that pertains to each and every person.[3] Arendt's last work, *The Life of the Mind*, "runs out where Aquinas starts: with the intersection of thinking and willing in the judgement of existence" (Lebech 2003, 1). Their mutual commitment to the life of the mind and the human capacity to discern good and evil is the starting point of our study. Let us first then consider Arendt's position on conscience and its implications for the life of the citizen.

Arendt: Socratic, Secular Conscience

As stated above, for Arendt, a life lived in accord with the convictions of conscience is unavoidably pitted against a life lived in the midst of politics. To say that one could be a 'conscientious citizen' would be for Arendt untrue. She points to the example of civil disobedients in the United States during the Civil Rights movement and the anti-Vietnam demonstrations. These citizens, according to Arendt, were not acting as conscientious objectors (i.e. acting on account of their convictions of conscience), but rather as a group of citizens who band together to make change in their political society. They take responsibility for their political society together because "they have become convinced either that the normal channels of change no longer function, and grievances will never be heard or acted upon, or that, on the contrary, the government is about to change and has embarked upon and persists in modes of action whose legality and constitutionality are open to grave doubt." (Arendt 1972, 74). This is the key point: civil disobedience is not an act of a group of conscientious citizens for Arendt, but rather citizens who are concerned with the *res publica*. The civil disobedient "acts in the name and for the sake of a group" and not for his own sake or for the sake of individual interest (Arendt 1972, 76).

This example seems an odd one, for Arendt herself acknowledges that although "a particular group of civil disobedients may still claim the initial validation-their consciences-they actually no longer rely on themselves alone" (Arendt 1972, 68). This statement points us toward what conscience means for Arendt. In several places

[3] Arendt states that "every sane person, no matter how erudite or ignorant, intelligent or stupid," is capable of thinking (1978a, 13). Likewise, Leo Strauss in his *Natural Right and History* observes that Aquinas's theorization of conscience as consisting of *synderesis* and *conscientia* make the insights of the natural law accessible to every person; that is to say, the ability to discern real, tangible, and universal criteria for judging right and wrong moral action is available to everyone. This is a point of critique for Strauss, who prefers the exclusive natural right as belonging only to philosophers. To be sure, Arendt herself is no advocate or apologist for the natural law. The point is that both Arendt and Aquinas believe that what was considered to be available to only a select few philosophers is available, and indeed *must be* available to every human being. Their reasons for this may differ greatly, but it is another point of comparison.

in her corpus, Arendt refers to Socrates as the model of conscience. Her model of 'Socratic conscience' is very particular and she describes it as 'secular conscience' (Arendt 1972).[4] It is subjective, self-interested, and radically individual. Her analysis of Socratic conscience is based on her interpretation of the central question in the *Gorgias* wherein Socrates considers whether it is better to do or to endure wrongdoing (Arendt 1971). Socrates's insistence that it is better to endure wrong than to perform it, according to Arendt, stems from his concern for being in harmony with himself. And how did Socrates achieve this being in harmony with himself? For Arendt, it is through the activity of thinking. Let us consider what she understands by the activity of thinking.

Thinking, for Arendt, is precisely that activity that enables the human person to know right from wrong. And it is her inquiry about this ability and particularly the question of Eichmann's inability to think that inspires her philosophical investigation. She explains in the beginning of her *Life of the Mind:*

> The immediate impulse came from my attending the Eichmann trial in Jerusalem. In my report of it, I spoke of 'the banality of evil.'… I was struck by a manifest shallowness in the doer [Eichmann] that made it impossible to trace the uncontestable evil of his deeds to any deeper roots or motives. The deeds were monstrous, but the doer-at least the very effective one now on trial-was quite ordinary, common-place, neither demonic nor monstrous. (Arendt 1978a, 3–4)

Arendt characterizes the phenomenon of Eichmann with an inability to think, thoughtlessness, "Might the problem of good and evil, our faculty for telling right from wrong, be connected with our faculty of thought?" (Arendt 1978a, 5). Socrates is the 'thinker' par excellence, the model of one who understands the necessity for thinking in order to discern right from wrong. The tension, as it were, is that this very act of thinking, the very means by which one can know right from wrong, is one which moves the thinker [e.g. Socrates] away from his duties as citizen. Conscience, according to Arendt, moves one out of community and into dialogue with oneself.

But here we have made an assumption. We have conflated 'thinking' and 'conscience.' In several places in her work, Arendt identifies thinking as the activity of conscience saying "the very word 'con-science,' at any rate, points in this direction insofar as it means 'to know with and by myself,' a kind of knowledge that is actualized in every thinking process" (Arendt 1978a, 5, see also Arendt 1971, 1972, 1990). Arendt also calls conscience the 'by-product' of thinking (Arendt 1972). Although she never offers a systematic account of conscience, she does discuss Socrates's statement that it is better to suffer evil than to perform it as a matter of conscience—but conscience of a particular type. Socratic conscience is a discourse that one has

[4]Arendt makes a distinction between secular conscience and conscience that is based on divine revelation or on a source outside of the individual himself. For Arendt, the convictions of secular (Socratic) conscience spring from the individual's interaction and dialogue with himself. It is thus strictly individual. "Moreover, the conscience of a believer who listens to and obeys the voice of God or the commands of the *lumen naturale* is a far cry from the strictly secular conscience – this knowing, and speaking with, myself" (Arendt 1972, 67).

with oneself, a 'two-in-one' "which Socrates discovered as the essence of thought" (Arendt 1978a, 185).[5] Arendt explains, "The only criterion of Socratic thinking is agreement, to be consistent with oneself, its opposite, to be in contradiction with oneself, actually means becoming one's own adversary" (1978a, 188). This being in dialogue with oneself and not contradicting oneself is what thinking accomplishes. Socrates does not do wrong because to do wrong would put him in contradiction with himself: it would violate his own integrity. On the contrary:

> A person who does not know that silent intercourse (in which we examine what we say and what we do) will never mind contradicting himself, and this means he will never be either able or willing to account for what he says or does; nor will he mind committing any crime, since he can count on its being forgotten the next moment. (Arendt 1978a, 191)

With this description Arendt certainly has in mind Eichmann: one who cannot think and thus has no ability to realize that he has committed a wrong.

Arendt also describes thinking and conscience as not being based on the usual rules or customs of society, but rather on the question of "whether I shall be able to live with myself in peace when the time has come to think about my deeds and words" (Arendt 1978a, 191). But because conscience is so personal, subjective, and focused on the interiority of the individual person, Arendt contends that it has no political role, indeed she calls it 'unpolitical' (Arendt 1972). Its contents cannot be universalized and Arendt calls the content or the rules of conscience negative, meaning that it prescribes what *not* to do, but can never tell a person what he or she *ought* to do. Arendt explains:

> [T]he rules of conscience...are...entirely negative. They do not say what to do; they say what not to do. They do not spell out certain principles for taking action; they lay down boundaries no act should transgress. They say: Don't do wrong for then you will have to live together with a wrongdoer.... The rules of conscience hinge on interest in the self. They say: Beware of doing something that you will not be able to live with. (Arendt 1972, 63–64)

---

[5] While Arendt herself does not give us a systematic account of conscience, she does seem to use it interchangeably with her concept of 'thinking' as the ability to know right from wrong. This 'thinking' is extraordinarily subjective and individual and seems at odds with Arendt's political ideal: in fact she frequently describes thinking as destructive of politics. The tension is that thinking (and thus conscience) is at once essential and at odds with political life. It is a tension with which I believe Arendt herself was not fully satisfied. Mette Lebech points out, rightly I believe, that had Arendt lived to finish the third part of her *Life of the Mind* on judgment, she likely would have addressed conscience more fully, perhaps even more systematically. Cf. Lebech 2003, footnote 36. I believe that Lebech is correct based on Arendt's own words in the closing paragraphs of her essay "Thinking and Moral Considerations" (1971). She writes: "It is the faculty to judge *particulars* without subsuming them under those general rules which can be taught and learned until they grow into habits that can be replaced by other habits and rules. The faculty of judging particulars (as Kant discovered it), the ability to say, 'this is wrong,' 'this is beautiful,' etc., is not the same as the faculty of thinking. Thinking deals with invisibles, with representations of things that are absent; judging always concerns particulars and things close at hand. But the two are interrelated in a way similar to the way consciousness and conscience are interconnected. If thinking, the two-in-one dialogue, actualizes the difference within our identity as given in consciousness and thereby results in conscience as its by-product, then judging, the by-product of the liberating effect of thinking, realizes thinking, makes it manifest in the world of appearances, where I am never alone and always much too busy to be able to think" (446).

Thus, for Arendt, conscience can never be the basis for politics, indeed she calls a politics based on the convictions of conscience a politics of 'impotence' (Winters 1987; Arendt 1978a) not only because it cannot incite political action, but also because it is too radically individual.[6]

Arendt almost seems to ban conscience entirely from politics, viewing it as an enemy to civic virtue and even causing conflict in a political community (Winters 1987). Arendt's doing so points toward a fundamental tension. The convictions of conscience to be sure are individual convictions and therefore Arendt recognizes that conclusions of conscience will certainly differ, "What I cannot live with may not bother another man's conscience. The result is that conscience will stand against conscience" (Arendt 1972, 64).[7] The Arendtian concept of conscience has no ability to draw citizens together, to give them any cause for action, or to enable them to avoid the ideological terror that so troubled Arendt. Thus Arendt's problem remains unresolved. She writes that she wants to avoid the possibility of a politics where Eichmann could be a reality, yet the very solution that she proposes is at once too personal, too self-interested, and too politically impotent to effect any real political impact.

However, in *Life of the Mind*, Arendt does make one exception to her own view. She writes:

> [Thinking] does not create values; it will not find out, once and for all, what 'the good' is; it does not confirm, but, rather, dissolves accepted rules of conduct. And it has no political relevance unless special emergencies arise. That while I am alive I must be able to live with myself is a consideration that does not come up politically except in 'boundary situations' (Arendt 1978a, 192).

These 'boundary situations' arise when something forces a person to take into account both past and future—to transcend their own individual existence to judge the past and to create for the future. This kind of thinking, according to Arendt, occurs in situations of political emergency (Arendt 1978a). This exception is curious. Arendt does not explain why this particular kind of thinking—of moral thinking—would only occur during a political emergency, such as a totalitarian political regime. Nor does she adequately explain how or why a person whose thinking led him solely into conversation with himself would, on account of a political emergency, suddenly become more civic-minded. She only explains that it is the

---

[6]One could object to this statement by arguing that political protest or telling an officer that you cannot comply with an unjust law is itself a political action. But Arendt disagrees. She would call the non-compliance with a law political inaction or a conscientious objector politically inactive. Political action, for Arendt, is specific. It arises "directly out of acting together, the 'sharing of words and deeds.'" (Arendt 1958, 198). Thus, according to her understanding of political action, the actions based on conscience, which are exclusively individual, cannot be considered political. Cf. Arendt 1958. Some, including her own friend Mary McCarthy, were not satisfied by this tension in her thinking. Cf. footnote 8 below.

[7]This insight is particularly poignant today in the American regime with claims of violations of religious freedom and freedom of conscience over many social issues (i.e. gay marriage, free coverage of contraceptives in healthcare insurance plans, etc). On both sides of these disagreements, the conflicting parties claim a conviction of moral conscience, and thus prove Arendt's point.

thinking person, the citizen with a Socratic conscience, whose action of withdrawal in moments of 'boundary situations' *becomes* something political because the practice of thinking enables this person to distance himself or herself from the disaster of a politics dominated by ideological dogma (Arendt 1971 and 1978a; Villa 2001). In short, Arendt's own solution to the problem of Eichmann does not seem to solve her problem, except indirectly and in very rare circumstances. How can political disaster be avoided and fought against by citizens?

Let us turn back, for a moment to Arendt's discussion of civil disobedience. Recall that for Arendt, citizens who engage in civil disobedience are distinct from conscientious citizens. In fact, as we have seen, only on very rare occasions can a conscientious citizen exist—and the act of thinking which makes that citizen political in emergency circumstances makes him impotent and unpolitical in normal circumstances. Arendt wants to argue that a truly *conscientious* objector cares only for his own interests, while the group of civil disobedients cares for the things of the common trust (Arendt 1972). Yet, she cannot account for why the group of civil disobedients *cares* for the *res publica* in the first place. What would cause a group of citizens to be concerned with a political problem such that they would demonstrate against it, even risk the consequences of breaking the law? How would they know that a cause was worth fighting for? How would they know that a law is unjust in the first place? The good citizen, or the group of good citizens, must first be good human beings. This is not properly acknowledged in Arendt's work.[8]

Perhaps Arendt herself was aware of this unresolved tension, for in her essay 'Philosophy and Politics,' she tries to link the two-in-one dialogue of Socratic conscience to other persons. She writes,

> Moreover while I am engaged in the dialogue of solitude [i.e. thinking] in which I am strictly by myself, I am not altogether separated from that plurality which is the world of men and which we call in its most general sense humanity (Arendt 1990, 88).

---

[8] Margaret Canovan (1992) and Francis X. Winters (1987) are very good on this point. Arendt argues that concern for the public things is born of consent, giving citizens of a particular regime (the ideal being a republic for Arendt) only one obligation, viz. "to make and to keep promises" (Arendt 1972, 92). Again, there is no explanation here about why we ought to keep our promises. Moreover, Arendt's own close friend and editor, Mary McCarthy, found Arendt's argument separating conscientious objectors from civil disobedients unconvincing. In a personal letter to Arendt on October 14, 1970, McCarthy wrote; "I am not convinced, finally, by your distinction between conscientious objection and civil disobedience. I understand the distinction but am not persuaded that it is so cut-and-dried as you make it sound. To me, civil disobedience remains a matter of conscience and the inner light, whether it's practiced by one person or a group. What stands out in the draft-resistance or tax refusal (or abolitionist activity) is not the collected but the separate individual souls who are saying no. I think that is clear from the fact that nobody could seriously speak of violations of the Prohibition amendment as being instances of civil disobedience (whether one is thinking of bootleggers or private drinkers and speakeasy customers); the reason is that nobody broke the law as a matter of conscience….I see that the whole question of conscience, when religious sanctions are no longer operative, makes civil disobedience a very difficult nut to crack, i.e. as you say, why should my conscience be respected rather than my neighbor's?" (Brightman 1995, 263). Unfortunately, Arendt did not reply to the critique, or if she did it has not been published. The next letter in the correspondence is a telegram from Arendt to her friend announcing her husband's death.

Because the thinking person is in the habit of dialogue with himself, he is more capable of dialogue with others, so Arendt argues (Arendt 1990; Villa 2001). She tries to account for political friendship by saying that because a person is capable of this two-in-one thinking, he or she expects others to be in the same manner by viewing others "in the image of his own action" (Arendt 1990, 88). But it is a strained and undeveloped argument in the essay, although it demonstrates that Arendt was aware of the limitations of her own view of conscience and citizenship.

This is not to argue that Arendt advocates an unmoral *polis* or an unprincipled citizenry. She believes that as human beings, we exist in the world of plurality—a world with other human beings—and as such, we must be accountable to one another. Margaret Canovan explains:

> What makes her thought specifically political…[is] the possibility of taking political action and, amongst us, building and guarding political structures to house men and to protect them against the wilderness…. Totalitarianism had left human beings without moral certainties, in need of a new foundation for human community. But Arendt's contention…was that although no absolute moral rules exist which could provide such a foundation, and although the most authentic of personal moral experiences [i.e. conscience] cannot supply it, nevertheless a foundation for sound human coexistence can be found in the fundamental human condition of plurality itself, in acceptance of the fact that we share the earth with others who are both alike and unlike myself (Canovan 1992, 190–191).

But this claim itself is a moral one, i.e. the acceptance of the fact that we share the earth with others. I cannot know why I ought to establish and safeguard political institutions with others by the fact of plurality alone, as Arendt would have. To be convincing, this claim itself must appeal to the conscience of the citizen, to his or her moral vision that would motivate action. A person must understand *why plurality* matters and why he or she should respect and defend that plurality in his or her actions and dispositions.

Arendt's reflections on citizenship and conscience begin with her experience of totalitarianism and the realization she had that traditional morality had not prevented it. The person of moral conviction might abstain from taking part, but neither "Socratic conscience" nor "Christian goodness" prevented Nazism, and in many cases, justified it (cf. Canovan 1992). Thus it may seem strange to turn to a Christian whose moral vision and philosophical presuppositions Arendt herself both rejected and respected.[9] Moreover, Thomas Aquinas's concerns were not primarily political like Arendt's. He never wrote a systematic treatise on politics and the only small treatise he wrote on the subject he left unfinished (Aquinas 1949). But, as pointed

[9]Arendt critiques Aquinas in a 1973 speech she gave to the American Society of Christian Ethics. She critiques him precisely on the matter of conscience because he wrote that the blessed in heaven rejoice at the suffering of their fellows who are damned. She points to this as an example of conscience being an anarchic concept, lacking the ability to build and sustain a community. Yet, in her second volume of *The Life of the Mind*, likely written about the same time, she extols his brilliancy: "Every philosophical system aims at offering the restless mind a kind of mental habitat, a secure home, but none has ever succeeded so well, and none, I think, was so free of contradictions. Anyone willing to make the considerable mental effort to enter that home was rewarded by the assurance that in its many mansions he would never find himself perplexed or estranged" (Arendt 1978b, 115).

out above, both Aquinas and Arendt were committed to the belief that the ability to discern right from wrong is within the purview of every human person. They speak to the tensions inherent in each other's thought and make for engaging interlocutors.[10] In what ways, then, does Aquinas offer an alternative vision or a complement to that of Arendt? More specifically, what does Aquinas's view of conscience add to Arendt's? I argue that Aquinas offers a theory of conscience that is both individual and relational, giving citizens who share convictions of conscience political potency. For Arendt, this is an impossibility since she believes that conscience is too personal to give rise to political action. Further, by distinguishing between true and false conscience, Aquinas offers an answer to the problem of the failure of conscience, i.e. to the typological possibility of Eichmann. Let us then turn to a closer consideration of Aquinas's understanding of conscience.

Aquinas: Conscience as Individual and Relational

Aquinas discusses conscience in several places throughout his work, but this paper will focus on three of his treatments in the *Summa Theologiae*, *De Veritate*, and *Commentary on Romans*. Within these three works we can frame a wider vision of the impact of conscience on politics – one that, I believe, can offer some correctives to the tensions presented by Hannah Arendt. Like Arendt, Aquinas recognizes conscience to be both deeply individual *and* connected to thinking, or in the language of Aquinas, to the activity of reason and intellect. For Aquinas, conscience is a function of reason and his theory contributes to the tradition of the *lex-ratio*, viz. the idea that human beings *by their nature*, that is, by their common rational and political nature, share basic knowledge and universal inclinations that guide their moral actions. This is precisely what Arendt wants both to reject and maintain when she tries to ground a political ethic on the 'fact of human plurality.' Arendt writes:

> In so far as morality is more than the sum total of *mores*, of customs and standards of behavior solidified through tradition and valid on the ground of agreements, both of which can change with time, it has, at least politically, no more support itself than the good will to counter the enormous risks of action by readiness to forgive and to be forgiven, to make promises and to keep them. These moral precepts are the only ones that are not applied to action from the outside, from some supposedly higher faculty or from experiences outside one's own reach. They arise, on the contrary, directly out of the will to live together with others in the mode of acting and speaking, and thus they are like control mechanism built into the very faculty to start new and unending processes (Arendt 1958, 245–46).

[10] Mette Lebech writes, "Arendt represents everything Aquinas did not yet take into account, such as women and politics, just as Aquinas represented what Arendt did not want to think about, such as metaphysics and religion" (2003, 1).

Arendt tries to ground a morality, a particular one, viz. one where 'to forgive and to be forgiven, to make promises and to keep them' are the only precepts, in the simple fact of human plurality.[11]

But Aquinas's view of conscience may offer insight on this tension present in Arendt. For Aquinas, human beings are naturally oriented in particular ways based on what he calls the natural inclinations. These inclinations have an order to them that is based upon the nature of the human person, and they are *natural* characteristics of human beings that point to the ends that a person pursues *in accordance with reason*. This point on reason is a critical one, because both Aquinas and Arendt contend that human morality is a function of thinking. In Aquinas's theory, the ends that are pursued are *good*, which "is the first thing that falls under the apprehension of the practical reason, which is directed to action: since every agent acts for an end under the aspect of good" (Aquinas 1948, I-II, Q. 94, art. 2, Corpus). Aquinas thus presupposes that human beings act for a good they perceive via reason—reason's very activity being *thinking*. The natural inclinations are the orientation to pursue good and to avoid evil, the desire for self-preservation, procreation, education, and a desire to know the truth about God and to live in society (Aquinas 1948, I-II, Q. 94, art. 2, Corpus). These inclinations also form the basis of the natural law tradition, a tradition that Aquinas helps to develop, as the natural inclinations are both the precepts of the natural law that all human beings have in common and the content of conscience. For Aquinas, that by which human beings both know and subsequently act upon these inclinations is what we call conscience. Perhaps these natural inclinations, in the language of Aquinas, are what Arendt intuits as human plurality: that we somehow recognize a kinship, a connection with others based on our being oriented in similar respects to similar ends. Another important point we shall examine is that for Aquinas, conscience does not mean the universal knowledge of all objective good and bad, a view which Arendt also finds objectionable (Arendt 1958, 1978a).[12]

Conscience, according to Aquinas, consists of two parts, viz. *synderesis* and *conscientia* (Aquinas 1948, 1953). The Greek term *synderesis* remains untranslated in English and is found primarily in the New Testament writings of St. Paul as

[11] Cf. Margaret Canovan (1992), especially chapter 5. Canovan contends, correctly I believe, that Arendt's commitment to these particular standards of forgiveness and promise-keeping likely derives from Arendt's own conviction of human equality which comes from outside politics and cannot be found in politics itself. For, just as human plurality can cause us to seek to live together peaceably, it can also cause us to see other persons as threats to ourselves, a fact that Arendt herself was well aware of. Thus the fact of human plurality is not a self-evident first principle upon which one can ground moral action.

[12] This is not to say that for Aquinas, the natural inclinations and the natural law are without metaphysical foundations or first principles. Undoubtedly, he believes that there are such foundations. As a Christian, he considers God to be that first principle, for it is God who created the human person with his or her natural inclinations. Arendt would certainly disagree. But for Aquinas, having God as the source of truth for the person does not in any way attenuate his or her moral freedom or the necessity to develop his or her moral knowledge and virtue through action and experience. The inclinations are general precepts-first principles. At some point, both Arendt and Aquinas rely on first principles, although Arendt tries to eliminate them. Yet, as we have seen, for her the fact of human plurality becomes a first principle.

syneidesis, although it also appears in Classical Greek philosophy and in the Greek Patristic Church fathers (Kries 2007). The use of *synderesis* and its grammatical variations by the Classic philosophers refers to an awareness (consciousness) and a sense of remorse or approval for a past action called 'judicial conscience,' that is to say; it is what judges an individual's past actions, but does not necessarily have the connotation of a guide to choosing right action (D'Arcy 1961). Such a view of conscience is quite similar to that which Arendt herself understands when she conceives of a negative conscience, viz. a conscience that cannot prescribe action, but only tells us what we cannot do. It is not until St. Paul uses the Greek term in his writings that it takes on a much more *politically* significant meaning:

> In [in St. Paul's writings], however, we encounter something quite new. In the First Epistle to the Corinthians, the problems of certain individuals' scruples concerning the right course of action leads St. Paul to use the phrase, 'Their conscience is uneasy, doubtful;' the context shows that this defective condition is the product, not only of timidity, but of ignorance too. Being a conscience, it imposes a rule of conduct; yet for all that it may be mistaken. Here then are two new features in the use of the word 'conscience': that of having authority to legislate; and that of being subject to error…St. Paul, then introduces an entirely new phase in the history of the term 'conscience' in moral theory, and two new features characterize his use of it. First, it is to play a *directive* role *before* an action takes place. In the pagan writers conscience did not appear on the scene until *after* the action was performed, and its role was purely *judicial*; but in St. Paul, conscience is credited with a legislative function, and it induces an obligation in the proper sense. Second, conscience is fallible: the directions it issues may be mistaken. (D'Arcy 1961, 9, 11)

Instead of having an exclusively negative function, conscience becomes a guide, a consultant for future action. This transformation of conscience into something that has both a negative function and a legislative or positive one is the tradition that Aquinas inherits and develops (and Arendt partially rejects). Its positive function also gives conscience an important role in the lives of human beings *qua* human beings and *qua* citizens because it *prescribes* actions.

But what about the insight that conscience is fallible and its convictions can err? In part, this fallibility is precisely why Arendt wants to limit the role and scope of conscience and sees it as anarchic and dangerous to politics. On the one hand, she recognizes it as the essential faculty for moral thinking—the kind of thinking that would prevent the existence of an Eichmann. On the other, she views it as so radically individual that the conscience can have no impact on the greater political and civil society, and could *hardly* play a role in the prevention of totalitarian ideology. Aquinas too, recognizes such a problem, and his solution, though not without tensions of its own, merits our consideration.

First, as previously mentioned, conscience contains two parts, *synderesis* and *conscientia*. Aquinas calls *synderesis* the natural habit by which we know the first principles of practical reason (Aquinas 1948, 1953). That Aquinas recognizes this first part of conscience as a habit is a critical point. It is not something exclusively objective, imposed from the outside, or innate knowledge of good and evil. Arendt found such a view of conscience untenable (Arendt 1958, 1971, 1972, 1973).

Rather, the content of *synderesis* is the natural inclinations; it is a natural habit or disposition—raw, undeveloped, and general—and thus in need of education, order, training, and practice. This classification of *synderesis* as a natural habit was, according to Hittinger,

> ...a deft interpretation, allowing Thomas to avoid conflating innate habits with innate knowledge. Like other medieval masters, Thomas knew that, for Aristotle, the intellect does not naturally know anything without experience of extramental reality, beginning in the senses. Seeing that he couldn't front-load knowledge of moral principles ahead of experience, he hit on the solution of positing [*synderesis* as] a habit. (Hittinger 2009)

What is given are the natural inclinations themselves but they are guided by human experience and the activity of reason.

Conscientia, the other part of conscience, is also connected to experience and the activity of reason. *Conscientia* is a judgment and application of conscience to a particular situation (Aquinas 1948, 1953).[13] It is the practice and training of *synderesis*, and Aquinas classifies the *conscientia* as part of the intellect and connected to the function of reason. He understands it to be the consciousness or awareness of an act that was done, but it is also that which judges whether an action is right or wrong and ought to be pursued. When we speak of *conscientia* in this sense, Aquinas states that it functions in two ways. First, it is that by "which we are directed through the habit of scientific knowledge to do or not to do something" (Aquinas 1953, Q. 17, art 1, Corpus).[14] It also functions as a judge of past action, again "with reference to the habit of knowledge" that is supplied by *synderesis*. Aquinas thus acknowledges both the judicial and legislative (or negative and positive) functions of conscience (Aquinas 1953 Q. 17, art 1, Corpus). However, the judgment of *conscientia* can be in error, that is to say, a person can apply the knowledge of *synderesis* in the wrong way (because for Aquinas the content of *synderesis* cannot be wrong as it is made up of natural inclinations shared by all persons). It is not a lack of thinking in the Arendtian sense, but rather a misapplication of our thinking that leads to the wrong judgment of *conscientia*.

The failure of conscience is a failure to judge correctly, causing a person to go astray because of such things as ignorance and attachment to vice. For example, an intemperate desire for food can cause someone to eat more than he should, even if he knows it is bad for his health. Aquinas explains, "Error, however, can occur in this application in two ways; in one, because that which is applied has the error within it, and in the other, because the application is faulty." Aquinas further explains:

---

[13] I am here referring to the passage from Arendt quoted in footnote 5 above. Her relation between thinking and judgment is very similar to Aquinas's relation between *synderesis* and *conscientia*.

[14] By 'scientific knowledge,' Aquinas follows Aristotle in defining 'science' as an intellectual virtue through which the agent grasps knowledge that can be demonstrated by a set of certain premises or first principles. Cf. Aristotle's *Ethics*, Book VI.

> We must remember that in some things conscience can never make a mistake, namely, when the particular act to which conscience is applied has a universal judgment about it in *synderesis*. For, as in speculative matters, error does not occur when we are dealing with particular conclusions which are derived directly from the universal principles and expressed in the same terms—as for instance, no one is deceived in the judgment: "This whole is greater than its part," just as no one is deceived in the judgment: "Every whole is greater than its part"—so, too, no conscience can err in the judgments: "I should not love God" or "Some evil should be done" (Aquinas 1953, Q. 17, art 2, Corpus).

Yet, even if an individual person's conscience is in error, that judgment is still morally binding, according to Aquinas. This idea is one which would make Arendt very uncomfortable, and indeed did during the Eichmann trial when she observed that Eichmann claimed to have followed his conscience when he executed thousands of Jews (Arendt 1994). Clearly, the judgment of Eichmann's conscience was wrong, but Aquinas argues that an erroneous conscience must be still be followed, which clearly shocked Arendt.[15] That is to say, even if the conclusion of one's conscience is wrong, that person is morally obliged to act in accordance with that judgment because his acting against it violates his moral integrity.

However, Aquinas's conclusion does not excuse an erring conscience. Even if a person acts in accordance with a false conscience, thus maintaining his or her moral integrity, he or she simultaneously violates it since the act would still be wrong. In both instances, acting against or in accordance with an erroneous conscience, a wrong is being committed against an individual and/or against the common good. How does Aquinas reconcile such a tension? He prioritizes the interior freedom and integrity of the individual human person, even when that freedom would threaten the good of the person and the community. In *De Veritate*, Aquinas gives a seemingly impenetrable argument: God's law always trumps false conscience; one must obey a higher authority (such as God's law) over a lower authority (such as an individual's conscience). The authority of conscience is lower than God. Thus a mistaken conscience could never be above the law of God, for surely the law of God has greater authority and import than the individual conscience. But for Aquinas, the authority of one's individual conscience takes priority over a divine command, for in not following one's conscience one violates one's own integrity with respect to what one considers intrinsically evil. However, Aquinas makes a very important remark, almost in passing: "Accordingly, although such a false conscience *can be changed*, nevertheless, as long as it remains, it is binding" [emphasis mine] (Aquinas 1953, Q. 17, art. 4, Corpus).

[15]And since Aquinas did not experience the Nazis as Arendt did, we don't know how he would have characterized ideological totalitarianism and its impact on conscience.

Aquinas believes that a person's conscientious judgment is an essential part of his or her moral freedom and integrity.[16] Yet, much like Arendt, he recognizes the very real possibility that any one person's sincere and conscientious judgment can be wrong. However, a faulty conscience can be changed, and indeed, for Aquinas, it *must* be changed since both to follow and not to follow a false conscience is damning. How does one change a false conscience? This question points us to the important *relational* aspect of conscience present in Aquinas's analysis and lacking in Arendt's. For Aquinas, conscience is individual, but is also relational, that is to say, dependent upon other human beings for the formation of its content and judgments.[17] A person with a false conscience can learn why his or her judgments of conscience are wrong and can change. It is this relational aspect of conscience that makes it relevant for citizenship. Let us consider this idea in more depth.

First, let us go back to the very content of *synderesis*, the natural inclinations that Aquinas identifies as being part of conscience itself. I want to focus on one particular natural inclination because I think it is within this context that Aquinas and Arendt resonate so well with one another. Aquinas states that we have a natural inclination to live in society, and therefore we have a responsibility to shun ignorance, and to avoid offending our fellows (Aquinas 1948, I-II, Q. 94, art. 2, Corpus). Aquinas explains this particular inclination as unique to man—and it refers to his specifically *relational* nature. Arendt might call this natural inclination 'human plurality,' but she does not explicitly connect this idea to conscience, as Aquinas does.

[16] This is not necessarily to argue that Aquinas advocates a kind of prototype of liberal toleration. For example, some may point to his saying that those who once accepted the Christian faith and then left it must be compelled, even physically, to return to it as an example of his not respecting the convictions of conscience. However, in this very same part of the *Summa Theologiae*, Aquinas does argue that those who never held the Christian faith must not be compelled to accept it (II-II, Q. 10, Art. 8). Moreover, later in the same question of the *Summa Theologiae* and in the third part, Aquinas argues that the children of Jews and other non-Christian parents should not be baptized against the will of the parents because to do so violates natural justice that entrusts children to their parents' judgment on their behalf (II-II, Q. 10, art. 12 and III, Q. 68, Art. 10). He even makes the case that the liturgical rites of other religions ought to be tolerated within a political regime (II-II, Q. 10, Art. 11). So, while Aquinas certainly seems to espouse some ideas (e.g. compelling apostates to return to their faith) that would disqualify him from being a model of liberal toleration, he also espouses ideas that show his respect for the judgment of a sincere conscience as a matter of justice. Another possible objection to my understanding of Aquinas is to say that he is against coercion. Again, Aquinas is very clear that he is not against coercion. Indeed, he calls law itself a kind of coercion and a necessary one (cf. *Summa Theologiae*, I-II, Q. 92 and Q. 95). However, law is based on reason and thus intelligible for the human person. Likewise, the conscience, also being a part of the rational faculty of the human person is essential for understanding the nature of law. Aquinas is adamantly against coercing a person's conscience, but he does believe that true and false convictions of conscience may exist and that false convictions must be changed, although not *necessarily* through violent coercion. Helping to form a conscience that can judge correctly is part of what I call the relational aspect of conscience. There are, to be sure, exceptions where Aquinas does allow for coercion (e.g., apostates) and so there is certainly tension in his thought, but he was much more radical on the topic than many of his contemporaries.

[17] And also, for Aquinas, the formation of one's conscience depends on the person's relationship with God, a point that I have not emphasized here but remains very important for Aquinas, who, as a Christian, understands God to be a person with whom one can have a relationship.

Aquinas also makes the case for conscience as relational in his commentary on the scriptural book of Paul's pastoral letter to the Romans. Here of course, Aquinas is not giving a philosophical explication, but rather considering conscience in terms of a scriptural letter in which Paul addresses theological issues to a particular community. The issue Paul addresses relates to the relationship between the Jews and the newly converted Gentiles and whether the Gentiles must follow the divinely prescribed law of the Jews. The example here is not purely political, but it does relate to a community and a moral conflict within that community, "for the Jews objected to the Gentiles that when they lived without God's law, they sacrificed to idols. The Gentiles on their part objected to the Jews that even though they received God's law, they did not keep it" (Aquinas 2012, Chapter 2, Lecture 1, §170). It is precisely this tension between the Jew and Gentiles that leads Paul and his commentator Aquinas to reflect on the natural knowledge of right order given to each human person. It is by emphasizing their natural (though partial) knowledge of God's law through *conscience* that Paul seeks to illustrate the participation of the Gentile converts in the life of God's law, "For when the Gentiles, who have not the law, do by nature those things that are of the law; they, having not the law, are a law to themselves, who show the work of the law written in their hearts, their conscience bearing witness to them" (Romans 2: 14–15). Thus, Paul points to something that the community shares in common, viz. conscience itself.

But Paul's advice gets more specific, in particular addressing the ways that members of the community should avoid offending one another. The issue in the commentary that points us toward the relational aspect of conscience may seem strange or incomprehensible to the contemporary reader. In the 14th chapter of the letter, Paul addresses a controversy regarding the Jewish dietary laws. Paul writes, "For if, because of food, your brother be grieved, you no longer walk according to charity. Destroy not him with your food" (Romans 14: 15). It is an issue related to the law of the Jews, and Aquinas explains the meaning of this passage:

> There were among the Romans some Jews converted to Christ, who distinguished among foods according to the law; but others, having a perfected faith, used all food without distinction, which of itself was lawful.... On this point it should be known...that the Jewish people, boasting that they are God's portion, call unclean the good which all men use, e.g. the flesh of swine, hares, and food of that sort. Furthermore, the nations which used such foods were not God's portion; consequently, such food was unclean. (Aquinas 2012, Chapter 14, Lecture 2, §1117)

Aquinas notes that Paul asks his readers not to scandalize or cause one another to sin by their actions; members of this new community of faith are responsible for one another and for the interior good of other members. If another member of the community in their conscience truly believes that eating a type of food violates the law of God, Paul advises his readers to abstain from engaging in such behavior, even though in truth it does not violate God's law, since the New Law as revealed in the person of Christ has perfected the Old Law as revealed to the Jews.

Aquinas agrees with Paul, but he adds more, in an attempt to reconcile the individual and relational aspects of conscience. Aquinas comments that if another's conscience is in error about a particular circumstance, such as the moral gravity of eating a particular food, then those other members of the community whose consciences guide them correctly are obligated not to engage in the offensive behavior, *at least until* they can explain that it is not wrong to the member who has an erroneous judgment, since an erroneous conscience does not have to be permanent and ought to be changed. For Aquinas, there is an obligation to inform the member of the community with an erroneous conscience, and after instructing that person, those with right judgment are also obliged to continue to act in accord with their conscience. Aquinas explains,

> [N]ot to discriminate among foods is a good work; therefore, it should not be avoided just because someone with an erroneous conscience makes a stumbling block of it. For according to this, Catholics would have to abstain from meat and marriage to prevent heretics from being offended according to their erroneous conscience". (Aquinas 2012, Chapter 14, Lecture 2, §1121)

We see, then, that for Aquinas, a person must *instruct* a person with an erroneous conscience but then *continue to act in accordance* with his own. Such an assertion has tremendous political implications as it points to an essential tension in a political community, viz. the tension between the individual and common good, or as we stated earlier, the tension between being a good person and a good citizen. Aquinas argues that the judgment of one's conscience is binding, be it erroneous or correct in its convictions. Yet, he must also be sensitive to the conscience of his neighbor, despite the rectitude or error of his neighbor's conscience. The obvious question is how do we know who has the erroneous conscience? The particular case given in St. Paul's letter to Romans, viz. the eating of certain foods, hardly seems to be a matter of moral consequence to anyone today; and those religious traditions that do distinguish certain foods to be in accord with or against the divine law no longer have much political or public debate on the matter. But Arendt gives one political example in Eichmann, and we may wonder whether his convictions could have been changed or prevented using Aquinas's criteria.

For Aquinas, consciences can and must be changed, but this ought not be accomplished through coercion: rather it is to be accomplished through relationship. To consider precisely what this means, I turn briefly to Alasdair MacIntyre's analysis in his *Dependent Rational Animals*, because MacIntyre develops and elaborates Aquinas's ideas. MacIntyre, like Aquinas, begins with an underlying vision of the human person's nature both rational and political. According to this view, human beings are ordered toward a particular end, and every person is endowed with *reason to judge* by what means to attain that end, and he lives in community with other human persons also seeking their end. This is what Aquinas calls the 'natural inclinations.' For MacIntyre, this describes the status of the human condition as dependent, rational animality. Human beings exist in a state of dependency on other human beings for the fulfillment of their needs and flourishing, and, in a particular way, they are dependent upon others to help them become "independent practical reasoners" (MacIntyre 1999). (Recall that for Aquinas, *synderesis* is the natural habit of practical reason, connecting conscience to practical reason). Aquinas and MacIntyre share a vision of the human person as existing in a state of dependency, that is, that man is by nature a rational and political animal and by means of this status he has need of relationship with other human persons (Aquinas 1949). This means that human beings need relationships to become persons of moral integrity.

What MacIntyre calls 'independent practical reasoning' is precisely the activity of conscience for Aquinas and very similar to the activity of thinking for Arendt. MacIntyre explains that it is the ability:

> to evaluate, modify, or reject our own practical judgments, to ask, that is, whether what we take to be good reasons for action really are sufficiently good reasons, and the ability to imagine realistically alternative possible futures, so as to be able to make rational choices between them, and the ability to stand back from our desires, so as to be able to enquire rationally what the pursuit of our good here and now requires and how our desires must be directed, and if necessary, reeducated, if we are to attain it. (MacIntyre 1999, 83)

Young children of course need to rely upon the guidance of parents and teachers to help them develop their capacities for independent practical reasoning as they grow and mature. However, since human judgment is always subject to error, even once a person has become 'an independent practical reasoner,' one still needs the help of others to help correct erroneous judgments. The social relationships that we have with families, friends, colleagues, and fellow citizens enable us to have either a confirmation or a challenge to our own judgments by those who know us well (MacIntyre 1999).

To put this in another way, the formation of an individual conscience does not happen in isolation—we live in communities with others with whom we have relationships, and these relationships form our conscience and our reason. According to MacIntyre,

> [P]ractical reasoning is by its nature, on the generally Aristotelian view...*reasoning together with others*, generally within some determinate set of social relationships. Those relationships are initially formed and then developed as the relationships through which each of us first achieves and is then supported in the status of an independent practical reasoner" [emphasis mine]. (MacIntyre 1999, 107)

Yet even this relational aspect of conscience is not the perfect bulwark against moral and political evil. MacIntyre certainly acknowledges that relationships can also cause erroneous consciences, as "defective systems of social relationships are apt to produce defective character" (MacIntyre 1999, 107). Relationships themselves must be good in order for the relational component of conscience to help change an erring judgment, especially without coercion. MacIntyre explains:

> It is because and insofar as my judgments about myself agree with the judgments about me made by others who know me well that I can generally have confidence in them.... There are of course certain kinds of social interaction and relationship that, far from preventing imprisonment by self-deceiving phantasy, produce or reinforce it. But genuine and extensive self-knowledge becomes possible only in consequence of those social relationships which on occasion provide badly needed correction for our own judgments. When adequate self-knowledge is achieved, it is always a shared achievement. (MacIntyre 1999, 95)

In short, on MacIntyre's view, we must recognize that our very dependency and responsibility toward one another in relationships enables us to become both good persons and good citizens. Arendt has an intimation of this but cannot quite integrate it into her thinking, whereas Aquinas can do so explicitly. There will likely always be tensions, problems, and even extreme political emergencies but in order to be a good citizen, one must first be a good person.

Conclusion

The questions we have considered in this paper, viz. the nature of conscience and its role in shaping the lives of individual persons and of citizens in a political community, is an increasingly pressing political problem. Through her philosophical interpretation of thinking, Arendt has emphasized the radical individuality of conscience and its being the locus of moral integrity and human dignity. Aquinas very much concurs with Arendt in recognizing the important relational component in the formation of conscience—and in the ability for thinking itself as Arendt understands it. Relationships serve to form conscience and to inform erroneous conscience and therefore can serve as a bulwark against political evil, although not always perfectly.

Human beings do not just make moral choices about private, individual matters. In our everyday, lived and shared political life, we are confronted with moral debates in the public square that call on citizens to reflect, to think, to reason, and to judge together. Conscience and moral convictions are not just politically relevant in the 'boundary situations' of political emergency that Arendt describes. Rather, we use our moral judgment in community when discerning the everyday doings of politics: the just distribution of goods and services, how to care for society's vulnerable and weak, how to restrain the most wealthy and powerful from coercing or exploiting their fellow citizens. These are the essential functions of any political society, and they cannot be fulfilled without a genuinely conscientious citizenry.

References

Aquinas T. (1948). *Summa Theologiae.* Trans. English Dominican Friars. New York: Benzinger. 3 Volumes.

Aquinas, T. (1949). *On kingship to the king of Cyprus.* Trans. G.B. Phelan. Toronto: Pontifical Institute of Medieval Studies.

Aquinas, T. (1953). *De Veritate (Disputed Questions on Truth).* Trans. J. V. McGlynn, S. J. Chicago: Regnery.

Aquinas, T. (2012). *Commentary on the letter of Saint Paul to the Romans.* Trans. F. R. Larcher, O.P. Eds. J. Mortensen and E. Alarcon. Lander: The Aquinas Institute for the Study of Sacred Doctrine. Volume 37.

Arendt, H. (1958). *The human condition.* Chicago: University of Chicago Press.

Arendt, H. (1971). Thinking and moral considerations: A lecture. *Social Research, 38*(3), 471–446.

Arendt, H. (1972). Civil disobedience. In*Crises of the republic* (pp. 51–102). San Diego: Harcourt, Brace, Jovanovich.
Arendt H. (1973). Remarks of Professor Hannah Arendt to the American Society of Christian Ethics. Hannah Arendt Papers at the Library of Congress. http://memory.loc.gov/ammem/arendthtml/mharendtFolderP05.html. Accessed 3 Feb 2016.
Arendt, H. (1978a). *Life of the mind: Thinking*. London: Secker and Warburg.
Arendt, H. (1978b). *Life of the mind: Willing*. London: Secker and Warburg.
Arendt, H. (1990). Philosophy and politics. *Social Research, 57*(1), 73–103.
Arendt, H. (1994). *Eichmann in Jerusalem: A report on the banality of evil*. New York: Penguin.
Brightman, C. (1995). *Between friends: The correspondence of Hannah Arendt and Mary McCarthy 1949–1975*. New York: Harcourt Brace.
Canovan, M. (1992). *Hannah Arendt: A reinterpretation of her political thought*. Cambridge: Cambridge University Press.
D'Arcy, E. (1961). *Conscience and its right to freedom*. New York: Sheed and Ward.
Hittinger, R. (2009). Examination of conscience. *First Things*, January 2009. http://www.firsthings/article/2008/12/004-examination-of-conscience-5. Accessed 1 February 2013.
Irvin, R. A., & Stansbury, J. (2004). Citizen participation in decision making: Is it worth the effort? *Public Administration Review, 64*(1), 55–65.
Kateb, G. (1983). *Hannah Arendt: Politics, conscience, evil*. Totowa: Rowman and Allenheld.
Kries, D. (2007). *The problem of natural law*. Lanham: Lexington Books.
Lebech, M. (2003). *Arendt and Aquinas: Two worlds or one?* https://core.ac.uk/download/files/374/11523124.pdf. Accessed 10 February 2016.
MacIntyre, A. (1999). *Dependent rational animals: Why human beings need the virtues*. Chicago: Open Court.
Strauss, L. (1953). *Natural right and history*. Chicago: University of Chicago Press.
Thunder, D. (2014). *Citizenship and the pursuit of the worthy life*. New York: Cambridge University Press.
Villa, D. (2001). *Socratic citizenship*. Princeton: Princeton University Press.
Winters, F. X. (1987). The banality of virtue: Reflections on Hannah Arendt's reinterpretation of political ethics. In J. W. Bernauer & S. J (Eds.), *Amor Mundi: Explorations of the faith and thought of Hannah Arendt* (pp. 187–218). Dordrecht: Martinus Nijhoff.
Wolin, S. (1960). *Politics and vision: Continuity and vision in western political thought*. Boston: Little, Brown and Company.

An Ethical Defense of Citizenship

David Thunder

I die the King's good servant, but God's first. (Thomas More's last words before his beheading on 6 July, 1535)

...it is necessary to a prince, if he wants to maintain himself, to learn to be able not to be good, and to use this and not use it according to necessity. (Niccolo Machiavelli, *The Prince* (1532))[1]

In many parts of the Western world, we have reached a low point in public confidence in the moral value and relevance of citizenship, in the integrity of our political institutions, and in the nobility of public office.[2] There appears to be a creeping cynicism about the very possibility of an ethically inspired and inspiring form of

[1] Machiavelli 1998, Chapter xv, p. 61.

[2] For example, according to annual Gallup polls conducted in the United States between 1973 and 2013, the proportion of the population who had either "quite a lot" or "a great deal" of confidence in the Supreme Court dropped from 45% to 34%; in Congress from 42% to 10%; in the presidency from 52% to 36%. The only public institutions for which a *majority* of respondent expressed "quite a lot" or "a great deal" of public confidence as of 2013 were the military (76% compared with 58% in 1975); small business (65% compared with 63% in 1997); and the police (57% compared with 52% in 1993), though in light of the latest rash of police scandals, that figure is likely to now be much lower. The results of these polls can be found at http://www.gallup.com/poll/1597/confidence-institutions.aspx#1 (accessed February 18, 2017). Significant declines in trust in national and European political institutions have been recorded in European countries over the past decade. For example, Eurobarometer polls showed that 32% of Europeans tended not to trust the EU in early 2007, compared with 60% in 2013. Interestingly, Eurobarometer polls also show that in most European countries the levels of distrust in *national* parliaments have also increased during this period, and have remained consistently higher than distrust in European Union institutions.

D. Thunder (✉)
Institute for Culture and Society, University of Navarra, Pamplona, Navarra, Spain
e-mail: dthunder@unav.es

D. Thunder (ed.), *The Ethics of Citizenship in the 21st Century*,
https://doi.org/10.1007/978-3-319-50415-5_6

participation in the public life of one's city and country. The cynicism I refer to is more than an acknowledgment of the corruptibility of the political community and its participants: it is a deep pessimism about their perfectibility. As such, it can be very destructive for political and social life, because it can demoralize citizens and sap them of energy and enthusiasm for putting their talents at the service of the community, especially the political community. The best persons in our society may not see the point of serving a community that is morally degenerate or on the brink of moral bankruptcy, leaving the political field wide open for the less scrupulous to enter where the virtuous dare not tread.

If we are to secure the political field for those among us brave enough to enter and virtuous enough to serve the common good, we need to restore public confidence in the ethical value of citizenship and public service. At a theoretical level, this would require the elaboration of an attractive ideal of citizenship capable of speaking to people's ethical concerns, and helping to combat widespread disillusionment over the perceived corruption of political life. But in this essay, rather than developing a full-fledged ideal of citizenship, I prepare the ground for such an ideal by defending the moral legitimacy of modern citizenship against some fairly influential objections. I hope that by pre-empting some serious ethical concerns about citizenship in the Western world, I can at least help pave the way for those brave enough to embark on the larger project of developing an ethical ideal of citizenship suitable for a postindustrialized, globalized society. The three objections I address are rooted in (i) the alleged complicity of ordinary citizens in a range of collective and institutional evils, (ii) the alleged necessity of ruthless utilitarian reasoning in political life, and (iii) the alleged incompatibility of modern citizenship with the Christian way of life.[3]

The Problem of Civic Complicity

It is frequently objected against citizenship that in spite of its manifest benefits (representation, protection, public order, and so on), it implicates us directly in grave wrongdoing, including the evils of deception and state-sponsored violence. The objection goes something like this:

> Nobody would dispute the fact that people do good and just things in their capacity as citizens, and that citizens are justly honored for brave and generous deeds. However, even the most well-intentioned and just people can find themselves thrust, in spite of their best intentions, into webs of complicity with evil. Insofar as I participate in a representative political system, I must take on at least *some* responsibility for the good and bad actions that are undertaken on my behalf, by my government and political representatives. In addition, insofar as I pay taxes into the public coffer, I must acknowledge that I am supporting, albeit indirectly, the good and bad activities being funded by my government. Thus, just by being a citizen, I automatically get implicated in evil or unjust projects.[4]

[3] This chapter reframes and reworks material scattered across my book, *Citizenship and the Pursuit of the Worthy Life* (Thunder 2014). In particular, the three objections fielded in this article are discussed on pp. 103–119, 123–131, and 176–180.

[4] Cf. Beerbohm 2012 for an in-depth discussion of this problem.

Of course, this objection would have no purchase if our governments happened to be consistently just or at least never seriously unjust, for then we could simply take credit for the good actions of our governments and never have to take responsibility for grave injustices. However, it seems hard to deny that many constitutional democratic governments, no matter how robust their commitment to domestic and international justice may appear on its face, can and do undertake deeply unjust projects on behalf of their citizens. For example, even if we happen to approve some military interventions, it would seem unreasonable to expect state military expeditions to be just *as a matter of course*, given the scale of violence and deprivation inflicted by war, and the complex mix of economic and political interests at stake.

Assuming that constitutional democratic governments do in fact inflict grave injustices, whether through war or through misguided domestic policies, and assuming that these injustices are carried out on behalf of citizens and with their financial contributions, what conclusions follow when assessing the degree of a citizen's complicity with evil? Some have argued, based on these sorts of assumptions, that citizens are inevitably complicit in wrongdoing, just by virtue of exercising their role as citizens.[5] However, it is not clear to me why a citizen who objects to his government's unjust policies in a democratic electoral system is necessarily complicit in those policies. When I elect someone to represent my interests and the interests of the nation, my agency does not get absorbed into his. In other words, when I elect him to represent me, I am not thereby endorsing every possible policy he might enact. What if all viable candidates are committed in advance of the election to what I take to be deeply unjust policies? Then I have the choice to abstain from voting and/or to voice my opposition to the injustice in question. Even if a questionable candidate is subsequently elected, and the real impact of my dissent is negligible, my decision not to vote, coupled with a good faith effort to voice my opposition publicly, may serve as a symbolic gesture of dissociation from the unjust policies that the available candidates intend to perpetrate.

A similar line of argument applies to the question of taxation. It is true that once my taxes are collected, they get allocated to a wide range of different government undertakings, and that unless I am an elected representative, I have little or no say over how exactly my tax contributions are spent. Even if I attempt to punish a government for misallocating taxpayers' money or using it for immoral purposes, there is no guarantee that my vote will be effective, or that the new government will be much better. Thus, nobody can guarantee that their tax contributions are used exclusively for noble purposes. A critic of citizenship might draw the rather disheartening conclusion that citizens are complicit in serious wrongdoing just by virtue of the fact that they pay taxes.

[5] For one version of this argument, see Kateb 2008, esp. 15: "How can one love such a mottled or hybrid entity as a country, particularly when, as in a democracy, the country's people are (always by imputation and sometimes in fact) directly and indirectly responsible for the country's wicked policies?" Beerbohm 2012 accepts that citizens have at least indirect responsibility for their country's unjust policies, but he suggests they can mitigate their personal complicity by taking certain measures to dissociate themselves from the policies in question, such as active resistance or protests against them.

This argument is not unreasonable. On its face, there is something ethically dubious about paying money into a giant fund in the certain knowledge that money is likely to be used, at least in part, for gravely unjust purposes. However, there are several considerations that significantly attenuate (even if they do not entirely eliminate) the responsibility of taxpayers for the misguided uses to which their money is put: first, paying taxes does not rise to the same level of voluntariness as, say, contributing to a charity of one's choice, given that failure to pay taxes incurs hefty penalties, including fines and imprisonment, while the only way to evade such punishments is either to conceal one's income or to stop earning income and thus expose oneself and one's dependents, if any, to poverty or at least significant economic insecurity.

Second, the social advantages of widespread tax compliance may override the objection that some of one's tax contributions are spent unwisely and unjustly. One might just bite one's lip and hand over one's taxes, not because every cent is well spent, but because the overall impact of tax compliance on the common good is positive: many public funds are indeed spent on infrastructure, public services, the arts, and other worthy and necessary projects. A government that cannot efficiently collect taxes cannot successfully perform its normal functions, while individual citizens' refusal to pay taxes is sure to foster feelings of mistrust and resentment among their peers, as they will frequently be perceived as free-riding the system under the cloak of moralistic justifications. In short, the withholding of taxes on moral grounds, if viewed as a universal right or accommodated through tax exemptions, would likely destabilize a political order and render government ineffective, unable to serve the public interest. These social costs significantly weaken the case for withholding taxes from partially unjust regimes, while the social benefits of tax compliance seem to provide strong reasons for participating in a taxation system even if one has reservations about how some of one's taxes are spent.

If one paid taxes precisely with the intention of supporting unjust causes, then the fact that there is a balance of good consequences would not let one off the hook. Tax compliance is expressive of human virtue (most obviously, the virtue of justice) only when it is *intentionally* directed to the common good and *not intentionally directed toward unjust projects*. It may seem puzzling to insist that a good intention can redeem an action that contributes causally to bad projects, but this is not so strange when we consider the role of intention in other contexts. To pay taxes is to channel resources into the hands of other people, whose decisions about how to use those resources we cannot directly control. In this respect, it is similar to many other actions that contribute to collective outcomes, such as the work of a civil servant or the purchases of a consumer. In cases where the good outcomes to which the action contributes are at least as significant as the bad outcomes to which it may causally (though not willingly) contribute, the agent may decide that the good effects of his action, which he *intends*, justify his *tolerance* of the bad effects to which he *unintentionally* or unwillingly contributes.[6] We should add one more proviso, namely

[6]This is an application of the doctrine of double effect. For an early formulation of this doctrine, see Aquinas 1981, II–IIae, q. 64, a. 7. For an overview of the doctrine, see the *Stanford Encyclopedia of Philosophy*, "Doctrine of Double Effect" (http://plato.stanford.edu/entries/double-effect, accessed January 6, 2017) and Mangan 1949. According to Mangan, the doctrine of double effect asserts that "[a] person may licitly perform an action that he foresees will produce a good effect

that citizens should take action to mitigate or eliminate serious injustices that they may be facilitating through their tax contributions, to the extent that this lies within their power, whether through political advocacy, public protest, or some other countervailing measure. Any complex system of human action raises these sorts of difficulties, and if we were unwilling to play a facilitating role within social and economic systems with mixed outcomes and some degree of waste and abuse along the way, a great deal of human collaboration, especially involving complex large-scale systems, would be impossible.

We could imagine our skeptical friend pressing his case further: "even if we err on the side of paying taxes," he might argue, "nevertheless, when a government intends to undertake gravely unjust actions on a large scale, such as a long-drawn-out war of conquest, surely this must tip the balance in favor of withholding taxes?" I am certainly willing to concede that in cases where a large portion of a government's budget is dedicated to unjust or immoral policies, a citizen may be justified in withholding taxes from such a government – the government in question may have simply forfeited its right to the citizen's financial support. However, it is less clear to me that a citizen would be ethically *obligated* under such circumstances to withhold taxes from the government, for the following reason: since taxes are allocated, in principle, to the whole machinery of government, one may contribute taxes with the intention of supporting a government's legitimate purposes, while *tolerating yet resisting* through other means such as lobbying and public protests, the financial empowerment of unjust actions as an unintended effect of one's contribution. Especially in cases where the costs of withholding taxes constitute a crippling burden (e.g., imprisonment or unemployment), which is what we would normally expect, a citizen may legitimately pay his taxes while seeking other ways to resist and mitigate the unintended bad effects of his contributions.[7]

The Alleged Ruthlessness of Political Life

Another fairly common objection against citizenship and in particular against the notion that public office is a morally ennobling calling is that it generates demands and responsibilities that simply cannot be met by a morally "scrupulous" or

---

and a bad effect provided that four conditions are verified at one and the same time: that the action in itself from its very object be good or at least indifferent; that the good effect and not the evil effect be intended; that the good effect be not produced by means of the evil effect; [and] that there be a proportionately grave reason for permitting the evil effect" (p. 43, as quoted in *Stanford Encyclopedia of Philosophy*, "Doctrine of Double Effect").

[7] Henry David Thoreau 1993 seems to constitute a conspicuous counter-example to this claim: he refused to pay at least a portion of his taxes because of what he perceived as the injustices of his government, and was willing to suffer imprisonment as a consequence. There is certainly something admirable about someone who suffers in defense of his principles. But it is less clear that all citizens are morally obliged to suffer in the same way, or that Thoreau was advocating that all citizens, no matter their circumstances, withhold taxes from unjust governments.

sensitive soul. Citizens who serve in public office should be willing to get their hands dirty, or even bloody if necessary to protect the security of their nation. Strict fidelity to ethical principles might be possible for ordinary citizens with little direct involvement in affairs of state, but it is not a luxury our statesmen and legislators can afford, if they hope to fulfill the demands of public office. Our legislators and political leaders must be willing to forge dubious alliances, authorize morally questionable military operations, and drag their country into all-out war when the public interest demands it, even if it keeps them up at night. This sort of argument has its fair share of defenders, most famously – or infamously – Niccolo Machiavelli.[8]

The force of this argument is difficult to resist, especially in a time when cynicism about political life is quite pervasive. Nevertheless, we should not concede the "dirtiness" of political office too quickly, because it has deeply disturbing implications: first, if the responsible exercise of political office requires the lowering of ethical standards of character and conduct, then those who care about their soul would do well to stay out of the affairs of state, leaving the field open to the less scrupulous. Second, if we endorse the exemption of politicians from standard ethical requirements in the name of political responsibility, we are providing a dangerous pretext for unscrupulous or self-serving politicians to rationalize their misconduct by appeal to political "necessity." Last but not least, the credibility of the regime as a whole may suffer a substantial blow if those at its helm are perceived to be exonerated from the ethical demands of everyday life on account of the "dirty work" they have to do on our behalf.

We have good reason, then, to put up a fight before conceding that holders of public office are condemned to immorality. Rather than addressing broad generalities, I would like to address three specific ways in which public office is alleged to require some sort of departure from ethical principles we feel bound by in ordinary life.[9] In the first case, an electoral candidate agrees to award a building contract to a dishonest ward boss to secure his own election; in the second, a political leader authorizes the torture of a political dissident to secure intelligence on the location of a bomb targeting innocent civilians; and in the third, a political leader authorizes a war to avert an imminent genocide. For each case, I consider to what extent, if at all, the agent in question finds himself under the necessity of acting unethically in virtue of his office.

[8] See Machiavelli 1998, esp. Chapter xv, p. 61: "…many have imagined republics and principalities that have never been seen or known to exist in truth; for it is so far from how one lives to how one should live that he who lets go of what is done for what should be done learns his ruin rather than his preservation. For a man who wants to make a profession of good in all regards must come to ruin among so many who are not good. Hence it is necessary to a prince, if he wants to maintain himself, to learn to be able not to be good, and to use this and not use it according to necessity." For other defenses of the courage to make ethical compromises in politics, cf. Weber 1946; and Walzer 1973.

[9] The first two of these cases are taken directly from Walzer's essay "Political Action: The Problem of Dirty Hands" (1973).

Let us begin with the building contract case. Walzer imagines a politician who wishes to "do good by only doing good" confronted by the choice to do a backroom deal with a dishonest ward boss:

> In order to win the election the candidate must make a deal with a dishonest ward boss, involving the granting of contracts for school construction over the next 4 years. Should he make the deal? Well, at least he shouldn't be surprised by the offer, most of us would probably say (a conventional piece of sarcasm). And he should accept it or not, depending on exactly what is at stake in the election. But that is not the candidate's view. He is extremely reluctant even to consider the deal, puts off his aides when they remind him of it, refuses to calculate its possible effects upon the campaign (Walzer 1973, 165–166).

Walzer goes on to make two judgments about this case: first, that because this man has scruples about making such a backroom deal, "we know him to be a good man"; and second, that if we estimate the importance of the campaign "in a certain way," we will "hope that he will overcome his scruples and make the deal…we don't want just anyone to make the deal; we want him to make it, precisely because he has scruples about it" (166). Presumably the reason we want him to make the deal with the ward boss is because that is the only realistic way for him to win office; and the reason we want a man of scruples to make the deal is because his scruples suggest that he will make ethically questionable deals only reluctantly and for the public interest rather than for his own selfish goals. Paradoxically, if Walzer is right, then the only way to ensure that principled people participate effectively in public office is by allowing them some leeway to cut questionable deals along the way.

The question whether or not political efficacy requires serious ethical compromises such as questionable backroom deals cannot be answered in abstraction from the details of particular cases. It certainly seems likely that winning certain elections, or securing the passage of certain laws, or winning support for certain policies, may require ethically questionable actions. For example, there are surely times when the only way an officeholder can gain the requisite votes for his favored law is by pledging his support for laws to which he has a principled objection. The popular perception, which I cannot verify based on philosophical arguments and casual observations, is that strict adherence to principles of honesty, fairness, truthfulness, etc. is generally or very often an obstacle to political efficacy. Whether or not this is in fact the case, however, is not dispositive for the normative question at issue, namely, whether or not politicians *ought to* give up or compromise their important ethical commitments for the sake of political efficacy. Nothing Walzer has said convinces me that they should.

The first problem with Walzer's argument is that he assumes that a person of principle can be prepared, albeit reluctantly, to cut questionable deals with dishonest ward bosses, and nonetheless remain loyal *in general* to the ethical principles for which his peers and constituents admire him. Even if we grant, arguendo, that a candidate in certain political contests must engage in unethical behavior in order to stand a realistic chance of success, the sort of pragmatic calculus that permits a candidate to secretly grant building contracts to a dishonest ward boss is not the mark of a person of integrity. While it is conceivable that someone might make one or two isolated deals of this sort and still retain a steadfast commitment to living a worthy life, in practice the sort of reasoning that justifies those deals gradually but steadily becomes entrenched as a habit of mind. If winning office can justify *this* questionable deal, then why not undertake *that other questionable deal* to get my policies passed once I've won office? In short, the frame of mind that justifies questionable backroom deals, even if accompanied initially by "scruples," cannot easily be restricted to one or two extreme situations. Rather, it is symptomatic of a significant shift in moral sensibility, and unavoidably impairs the wholeheartedness of a person's commitment to do what is right and avoid what is wrong.

The second problem with Walzer's argument is that it assumes too blithely that just because the stakes are high in an election, a candidate is well advised to put his electoral success above his ethical principles. But as St. Thomas Moore reminded his betrayor, Richard Rich, what good is it to win the whole world and suffer the loss of one's soul? It seems both unfair and unreasonable to expect political candidates or holders of public office to sacrifice their ethical principles for the sake of desirable political outcomes. As Bernard Williams famously argued, making people's ethical decisions wholly contingent on a consequentialist calculus blatantly violates their integrity by putting their choices at the mercy of events and choices completely beyond their own control. They become a cog in a "utility" machine, and all of their personal projects and commitments become instrumentalized to some external good to be maximized or protected no matter what (Williams 1973). If the ability to adopt and remain faithful to ethical principles is a crucial dimension of a worthwhile and dignified human life, then a common good that requires politicians to make dishonest deals does not seem like a common good worthy of our allegiance: indeed, it does not seem like a genuine *common good* at all!

Now, let us turn to a second case that allegedly illustrates the necessity of ethical compromise in politics. This case, also presented by Walzer, concerns the use of torture to avert a terrorist attack:

> [C]onsider a politician who has seized upon a national crisis – a prolonged colonial war – to reach for power. He and his friends win office pledged to decolonization and peace; they are honestly committed to both, though not without some sense of the advantages of the commitment. In any case, they have no responsibility for the war; they have steadfastly opposed it. Immediately, the politician goes off to the colonial capital to open negotiations with the rebels. But the capital is in the grip of a terrorist campaign, and the first decision the new leader faces is this: he is asked to authorize the torture of a captured rebel leader who knows or probably knows the location of a number of bombs hidden in apartment buildings around the city, set to go off within the next twenty-four hours. He orders the man tortured, convinced that he must do so for the sake of the people who might otherwise die in the explosions – even though he believes that torture is wrong, indeed abominable, not just sometimes, but always. He had expressed this belief often and angrily during his own campaign; the rest of us took it as a sign of his goodness. How should we regard him now? (How should he regard himself?) (166–167).

Two things are worth nothing about this second case: first, the stakes have been raised considerably higher than before – now, it is not simply a question of "making a difference" by being elected, but of preventing the callous murder of hundreds, perhaps even thousands, of innocent civilians. Second, the action required of the officeholder is deemed by him to be not only ethically questionable but also "wrong, indeed abominable." Walzer argues that the "good politician" in this case will authorize the torture but also acknowledge that he is thereby guilty of wrongdoing. "His willingness to acknowledge and bear (and perhaps to repent and do penance for) his guilt," Walzer suggests, "is evidence, and it is the only evidence he can offer us, both that he is not too good for politics and that he is good enough" (167–168).

The basic thrust of Walzer's argument concerning the torture case is that a responsible politician cannot afford to be "too good" to discharge his responsibilities, even if they require him to do something he believes to be "wrong, indeed abominable." Again, there is something quite appealing about this argument. After all, there is no denying that the goal of saving people from terrorist attacks is noble, urgent, and compelling; and if we have good reason to believe that *this* suspect has information to prevent the attacks, information he is refusing to disclose, then torturing him may well be the most efficient way, indeed the *only* realistic way, to secure the intelligence required in order to intercept the bombs in a timely manner. In this particular case, we can be reasonably certain of his complicity in the crime, so we are not torturing an innocent. Why not torture a guilty criminal to save thousands of innocents, even if we find torture morally objectionable? Is the sacrifice of a moral principle an unreasonably high price to pay for the protection of thousands of civilians, especially if we know it is a guilty party who is to be tortured?

A full examination of these arguments would require a comprehensive treatment of the morality of torture, including a close examination of the definition of torture and a distinction between torture and other forms of intimidation and violence. For our immediate purposes, I will just assume that torture is understood as the "[infliction of] severe or excruciating pain or suffering (of body or mind)"[10]; that the politician authorizing the torture considers torture "wrong, indeed abominable"; and that the form of coercion being contemplated is severe enough to fall squarely within the category of torture as opposed to mere intimidation or manipulation. I shall also assume that the politician is reasonably certain that this man knows where the bombs are located, and that torture is the only reliable method for obtaining that information from him. These may seem like generous concessions,[11] but they enable us to consider Walzer's argument in the most favorable light possible.

This case is structurally similar to the building contract case – a certain form of political efficacy is assumed to require an ethically dubious action. But in this case, the political success being contemplated is the protection of hundreds or perhaps thousands of innocent civilians against a terrorist attack. Thus, it might appear more

[10] "Torture, n.". OED Online. November 2010. Oxford University Press. http://www.oed.com (accessed March 14, 2011).

[11] Particularly the concession that torture is the only or indeed the most reliable method to obtain information from prisoners. For one argument against that position by a former interrogator at Guantanamo Bay, see http://www.thepublicdiscourse.com/2011/09/3934/ (accessed January 6, 2017).

self-indulgent in this case to forego political success in order to honor an ethical principle. However, I believe we should resist the conclusion that the torture should be authorized, for two reasons: first, I do not believe it is fair or reasonable to expect a politician to act in profoundly immoral ways, and in so doing, to defile his conscience, for the sake of achieving a desirable political outcome – even if that outcome is noble and vitally important. It might be fair to demand this sacrifice *if* politicians could be held responsible for all outcomes it is within their physical power to prevent. However, this is not a reasonable view of political responsibility. Nobody holds me responsible for the deaths of thousands of people because a mass murderer orders me to shoot my children "or else I will detonate the bomb," and I refuse to cooperate. Those deaths are morally attributable to the murderer, and are in no morally relevant sense attributable to my inaction, because I cannot be blamed for refusing to undertake actions that I reasonably judge to be egregiously wrong.[12] The same principle applies to the holder of political office: he is not responsible for outcomes that can be prevented only by his acting against his own conscience. Otherwise a person's ethical integrity, viz. his ability to guide his own life by his own ethical lights, is held hostage to a range of contingencies totally beyond his control, including the malice and wickedness of other agents.[13]

A second reason to resist Walzer's conclusion about the moral necessity of torture is that it would set a dangerous and easily manipulated precedent. The danger of the logic of "emergency exceptions" to weighty ethical principles is highlighted by Jeffrey Stout:

> When their dirty hands come to light, and there is no denying the bad things they have done, officials often plead necessity. They claim that they had to do bad things if they were to serve us well in dire circumstances. There was no choice. That, they say, is the way politics works in the real world. At one level, the problem of dirty hands is the question of how democratic citizens ought to respond when political officials make this excuse for admittedly bad acts. Often the excuse turns out to be phony – another bad act. The circumstances are not what the dirty politician says they were. Perhaps they were not dire at all […] In most cases where people plead necessity in ordinary life, there is more room for maneuver than they acknowledge. They say, "I had no choice," but what they really mean is that the alternatives they did consider seemed unacceptable at the time (Stout 2004, 186).

---

[12] Of course, this does not mean that someone will not feel deep regret and sorrow when he finds himself unable to prevent a tragedy or crime from occurring. However, this is not the same as guilt or culpability. If I am right, then in those cases where a person does feel guilty for a tragedy he cannot prevent in an ethical manner – assuming, of course, that he is not morally complicit in the chain of events leading to it – that feeling of guilt is not rationally warranted.

[13] The implausibility of the general principle that "if action x is necessary to avoid a horrible calamity, then action x is morally obligatory," is illustrated by Bernard Williams' imaginary case in which "Jim," a wandering botanist, is ordered by a "captain" in a remote village to shoot an innocent prisoner and thereby liberate nineteen other prisoners. The captain has told Jim that if he refuses to comply, he (the captain) will order all twenty prisoners shot. I do not believe Jim is under any obligation to comply with the captain's order. That is because we cannot reasonably be held responsible for outcomes that are caused by the evil actions of *other agents*, just because those outcomes could be prevented by our own abandonment of an important ethical commitment (in this particular case, the principle, "do not kill innocent persons"). As Williams puts it, "each of us is specially responsible for what *he* does, rather than for what other people do" (Williams 1973, 99).

If "wrong, indeed abominable" actions can be justified to save innocent civilians in order to secure intelligence on a bomb threat, why not undertake a series of morally dubious or even "abominable" actions in other instances where there are perceived or real threats to national security? Where do we draw the line if we permit politicians to set aside weighty ethical principles in order to address emergency situations? Walzer's justification of torture and other "abominable" actions, if accepted, provides an easy pretext for politicians to take convenient moral shortcuts rather than searching creatively for an ethically acceptable solution. What other sorts of conduct might be authorized in times of war, if we accept Walzer's rationale for torture in "extreme" situations? Illegal internments? Terror campaigns against innocent civilians? Nuclear holocausts?

Of course, Walzer might push back by insisting that I am underestimating the likely political backlash of acting with integrity, irrespective of the consequences. He might point out that a politician bound by the principle, "do no evil that good may come of it," would be considered reckless by his voters, who would understandably question why a man entrusted with matters of public security would not use every tool available to him to prevent terrorist attacks or other threats to public safety. The politician who "sticks to his guns" and refuses to bow to such public pressure for "results" may be forced by his voters or allies into early retirement. The politician whose decisions of conscience endanger national security or put soldiers in harms' way will have to face the political consequences of his decisions, sooner or later. Can we reasonably ask this sort of sacrifice of someone in public office? Clearly, the answer will depend on whether or not we believe their actions are justifiable. If one accepts that there are certain types of actions that are morally offensive irrespective of their alleged utility, then one naturally expects a person of integrity to refuse to either endorse or be complicit in such actions. In an ideal world this choice would not be politically suicidal or damaging. But in a fallen world, doing the right thing often comes at a price. It is the mark of a morally virtuous agent to be prepared to pay that price. We may have compassion for someone who succumbs to public pressure and acts unjustly but that is not the same as excusing or justifying their behaviour.

I would like to consider one more case that might be taken to illustrate the necessity of ethical compromise in the political arena: imagine that the President of the United States obtains reliable intelligence that a popular militia group, with the tacit support of its national government, is on the verge of committing genocide against all citizens belonging to a particular tribe or ethnicity. Diplomatic efforts have broken down and the perpetrators have publicly declared their intentions to "wipe out" their enemies, and show them "no mercy." The tribe under attack is in a minority, in many cases largely defenseless against the violent mobs, while government soldiers at best turn a blind eye. Unless the U.S. president authorizes the American army to intervene, he will almost certainly witness one of the worst atrocities of the century. What should he do?[14]

---

[14]The case I am describing is not entirely fanciful – it closely resembles the 1994 Rwandan genocide.

On the one hand, it might seem clear that he should authorize his troops to insert themselves between the marauding mobs and their intended victims. Naturally, war is a messy business: there will be deaths and injuries on both sides of the conflict. But the costs of inaction are too shocking to contemplate: if the use of military force is the only way to prevent the genocide, then so be it. After all, military might brings with it the responsibility to protect the defenseless against their would-be aggressors.[15]

On the other hand, upon closer inspection, there may be reasons to hesitate about engaging in war. Even if every effort is made to avoid or minimize civilian casualties, the ravages of war are nearly always visited on guilty and innocent parties alike. When food distribution, medical supplies, and infrastructure are crippled, innocent civilians are not only exposed to great personal inconvenience; they are also threatened with insecurity, poor health, hunger, and possibly even death from malnutrition or inadequate access to medicine and healthcare facilities. When military installations in close proximity to civilian populations are targeted, civilians may be killed in crossfire or because of inaccurate intelligence, or they may be used unscrupulously as human shields. In short, even if we set aside the *direct* targeting of civilian populations such as the infamous Dresden bombings, and insist on the minimization of civilian casualties, the *probable and foreseeable* effects of war include the impoverishment, heightened insecurity, ill health, psychological trauma, and death of innocent civilians.

Assuming that this is true of war in general, a responsible political leader would authorize a war only with a heavy heart, and when all other viable options have been exhausted. He would have to ensure that the likely ravages of war – the death and destruction it will visit on combatants and noncombatants alike – are proportionate to its likely benefits, in this particular case, the likelihood that it will be successful at averting the genocide. I say that he would authorize war only with a "heavy heart," because he would do so in the certain knowledge that innocents will either die or have their lives turned upside down as a direct or indirect result of his decision, and this is deeply regrettable and heart-wrenching. However, so long as the anticipated costs of war, tragic and regrettable as they are, are not disproportionate to its anticipated benefits, every reasonable effort is made to minimize harm to civilians, and those harms that are inflicted on noncombants are unintended, the war may be ethically permissible. After all, there is a great moral difference between directly targeting innocent civilians and tolerating their death or injury as an *unintended effect* of a military campaign.[16]

---

[15] The International Commission on Intervention and State Sovereignty, established by the Canadian government, issued a document in December 2000, entitled "The Responsibility to Protect," articulating the doctrine that the international community has a responsibility to intervene, if necessary with force, to prevent mass atrocities. A version of this doctrine was subsequently ratified by the United Nations at the 2005 World Summit (Outcome Document, pars 138 and 139).

[16] This is essentially an application of the doctrine of "double effect," discussed briefly in fn. 6 above.

The upshot of this argument is that a political leader might authorize a military attack, which will foreseeably result in grave harms to innocent parties, without foresaking his commitment to live a worthy life. In extreme situations a statesman may be required to undertake actions that rightly bring him great sorrow and regret, because none of the available choices is something to celebrate or be complacent about. Nonetheless, a person of integrity, when confronted with a difficult situation of this sort, continues to struggle to act according to the highest ethical standards, even in the face of ruthless and unscrupulous enemies. A decision to go to war to protect the innocent need not entail any betrayal of core ethical principles, so long as a serious effort is made to honor them to the best of one's ability. Nor need such a decision entail an abandonment of the principle, "evil may not be done that good may come of it."[17] For the toleration of evil as an *unintended effect* of one's actions, however regrettable and saddening, is not equivalent to directly performing an evil deed.

The Alleged Incompatibility of Citizenship with the Christian Way of Life

A third objection could be pressed by a citizen who also happens to be a deeply committed Christian.[18] Such a citizen could argue that modern political community is premised on secular ideas like freedom, equality, and economic growth, and as such cannot make room for the "folly" of the Christian way of life, whose model is the man-God who died a cruel death on a cross, and whose message is that we are called to live a life of faith and love against all human odds. If St. Augustine was even half right, then the gulf between the worldly purposes of the "city of man" and the heavenly purposes of the "city of God" cannot be collapsed in this life. We may of course build what Hauerwas calls "ecclesial communities" founded explicitly on faith, but large-scale religiously diverse democracies are a far cry from *that*. They are unified around ideas of national identity and self-interest rather than around Gospel ideals of faith, hope, and love. To dream of a full reconciliation between the values of "worldly" citizenship, and the values of a community of faith, is to dream of pie-in-the-sky.

---

[17] Such a principle is cited disapprovingly by St Paul in Romans 3:8.

[18] A similar inquiry could be undertaken concerning the compatibility of constitutional democratic citizenship with versions of other major religious faiths, in particular Judaism, Hinduism, and Islam. I have only pursued this inquiry in regard to Christianity because being a practising Christian with some acquaintance with the Christian tradition, I feel I can make an informed argument about the implications of constitutional democracy for Christian faith. Given my limited knowledge of other religious traditions, I leave a proper treatment of the implications of citizenship for Judaism, Hinduism, and Islam to scholars better positioned to address them than I am.

Our Christian critic would likely resist the notion that we ought to strive to excel as citizens, seeing in such an ideal a serious temptation to compromise the integrity of the Gospel, to scale back one's Christian commitments for the sake of being good citizens of the "city of man." Some theologians, such as Stanley Hauerwas, have argued that faith and the values of constitutional democracy are ultimately irreconcilable. That is because where communities of faith emphasize the value of submission to religious authority, humble service of the community, and renunciation of one's own interests for the good of others, constitutional democratic polities exalt individual freedom, self-assertion, loyalty to the nation-state, and liberation from traditions and authorities beyond the state. The church of God is called to stand for a very different model of justice and social order, premised on the divine authority of Revelation, mutual trust and love rather than on contingent human agreements, fear and coercion:

> The challenge is always for the church to be a "contrast model" for all polities that know not God. Unlike them, we [Christians] know that the story of God is the truthful account of our existence, and thus we can be a community formed on trust rather than distrust. The hallmark of such a community, unlike the power of the nation-states, is its refusal to resort to violence to secure its own existence or to insure internal obedience. For as a community convinced of the truth, we refuse to trust any other power to compel than the truth itself [...] Put starkly, the way the church must always respond to the challenge of our polity is to be herself. This does not involve a rejection of the world, or a withdrawal from the world; rather it is a reminder that the church must serve the world on her own terms. We must be faithful in our own way, even if the world understands such faithfulness as disloyalty (Hauerwas 1981, 84–85).

If the church is called to "be herself" and witness to the "scandal of the Cross," even on pain of being perceived as disloyal to the secular polity, then surely from the standpoint of the Christian, conformity to an ideal of citizenship tailored to the secular polity and its needs is either unrealistic or an invitation to political conformism and moral hypocrisy. If Christians were to sincerely strive to adapt themselves to their political roles, they would become moral hypocrites, embracing individualism, autonomy, and self-interest in certain circumscribed situations such as political advocacy; and love, service, and religious authority at church services on Sundays. To the extent that Christians become "good citizens," the distinctiveness of ecclesial communities and their power to witness to the Gospel is weakened, and the "adaptation" to citizenship may literally end in the death of the church to the values it originally stood for. Sooner or later, the embrace of worldly citizenship would convert churches into voluntary associations of autonomous individuals who happen to have shared religious interests, not divinely ordained sources of salvation.

Or so the Hauerwasian critique of citizenship might go. What is one to say in response to such a critique? One possible response would be simply to assert the priority of constitutional democratic culture and its associated values over all rival values, including Christian values. On this view, insofar as constitutional democracy presents problems for Christian integrity, there must be something wrong with Christian integrity – perhaps it is unreasonably dogmatic, fideistic, or blind to the values of political order. But that is not the response I would offer, because I think this is conceding far too much ground to the Hauerwasian critique, insofar as it significantly exaggerates the distance between Christian faith and constitutional democratic citizenship. Furthermore, this exaggeration makes the prospects of a rapprochement between Christianity (at least of the sort described by Hauerwas) and constitutional democracy very dismal indeed. Hauerwas's characterization of constitutional democracy effectively renders citizenship completely unacceptable to a significant portion of the inhabitants of Western democratic polities, at least those who share Hauerwas's counter-cultural Christian faith.

The Hauerwasian critique of modern democratic citizenship as I have presented it can be greatly softened by two considerations: first, Hauerwas's critique of the modern nation-state derives an unfair advantage from his tendency to identify the objects of civic allegiance in an undiscriminating way with the values of the surrounding culture. But in fact, what citizens are asked to support *as citizens* is something much less ambitious than the whole ensemble of values associated with a secular liberal culture. Few would deny that many aspects of the Christian way of life, including the submission to ecclesial authority in matters of dogma and moral practice, the sense of sin, and belief in the redemptive value of suffering, are baffling to many citizens of constitutional democracies, and it is clear enough that the lifestyles, motivations, and commitments of many citizens of constititutional democracies are incompatible with the teachings of many Christian churches. However, none of this demonstrates any principled opposition between constitutional democratic *citizenship* and Christianity.

Where Hauerwas and other radical critics of democracy go wrong is in their move to equate constitutional democracy and constitutional democratic citizenship with Enlightenment ideals of individual autonomy or with the predominant values of a secular liberal culture.[19] The values that happen to be socially dominant and institutionally reinforced within the jurisdiction of a polity, whether narcissism, individualism, or materialism, are not what citizens give their allegiance to *as citizens*. Their ultimate allegiance as citizens is to the fundamental animating values of their polity and to the good of its people, not the perpetuation of its regnant institutions and its dominant cultural values. Citizens can be critical of their nation and of its dominant cultural values and engage in and support radical reform of their shared

[19] For example, in a chapter entitled "Why Justice Is a Bad Idea for Christians," Hauerwas observes that "[g]eneral appeals to justice too often result in contradictory social strategies that offer little evidence of the integrity of Christian witness on such matters" (Hauerwas 1999, 47). He then points out that we hear appeals for women's liberation, which rest on the value of autonomy, along with egalitarian appeals for humanitarian assistance, which rest on values of equality, while egalitarian and libertarian values cannot be fully reconciled. But the way in which some, or even many, citizens happen to appeal to the idea of justice, while it may be a feature of the political culture of constitutional democracy, is not necessarily what defines the content of the principles that citizens pledge their allegiance to as citizens. Clearly, any plausible understanding of constitutional democracy must affirm a more moderate and nuanced view of liberty and equality than one in which equal welfare systematically overrides liberty or liberty overrides all claims of individual need.

institutions, even abolition of those institutions in extreme circumstances, where they conscientiously judge that this is the only responsible way to serve the common good of the people. Thus, citizenship properly understood, while it requires an acceptance of the equal dignity of all, rule of law, and other basic constitutional democratic values, does not require one to be an uncritical patriot, or to subscribe to the dominant values of a secular liberal culture.

A second point that should greatly soften the force of the Hauerwasian critique is that the moral legitimacy and value of citizenship does not entail that political life can be preserved from all ethical tensions, or that civic roles do not pose serious ethical challenges from time to time. Any sensible and honest person should recognize that a certain degree of tension is the price of living a human life in community with others, something we need to learn to manage as effectively as we can, rather than to suppress at all costs. For example, certain public roles may expose Christians to temptations to greed and corruption, yet they may undertake them for the common good, and do their best to resist the associated temptations with the grace of God. To completely avoid all circumstances unfavorable to Christian integrity, or to insist that all roles be entirely supportive of Christian faith, would be utterly unrealistic and probably self-indulgent. There will always be opportunities in this world for brave Christian witness, and this is something the defender of modern citizenship can acknowledge just as much as Hauerwas.

The probability of conflicts between Christian faith and public roles appears to be borne out by the historical record: Christians have had their fair share of conflicts with the authorities of constitutional democracies, and have not always been well received in secular liberal cultures. Even if citizenship in a constitutional democracy is in principle compatible with the Christian way of life, clearly this does not guarantee that the institutions and practices of constitutional democracy will *in practice* accommodate the integrity of Christian citizens in all times and places. For example, there have been times when Christians were victimized or punished for living up to the demands of their highest principles, even when those principles represented humanly noble and admirable ideals. Think of Martin Luther King's struggle to recognize the equal dignity of blacks and whites, a struggle that was profoundly motivated by a biblical vision of justice for all of God's children. More controversially, Catholic hospitals and businesses in the United States that refuse to provide their employees with insurance coverage for contraceptives (including abortifacients) were confronted with the threat of heavy legal sanctions, including hefty fines, under President Obama's Affordable Care Act (specifically, the "HSS mandate").[20] These sorts of political conflicts arise from the choices of political

[20] I give this example simply to illustrate the fact that church–state conflict is not something we are likely to put behind us anytime soon. This point can be appreciated independently of one's opinion concerning the rights and wrongs of this particular dispute. The mandate has been challenged in the courts on grounds that it constitutes an unconstitutional attack on religious freedom. Some of these challenges have been successful. For a statement by American bishops condemning the mandate on grounds that it attacks the religious freedom of Catholics, see http://www.usccb.org/issues-and-action/religious-liberty/our-first-most-cherished-liberty.cfm (issued on April 12, 2012, last accessed February 18, 2017).

actors, whether legislators, executives, or judges, at particular times and places. While such policies are typically implemented through constitutional democratic institutions and *in the name of* constitutional democratic values, they do not necessarily represent a correct application of the values and demands proper to constitutional democracy. As such, they do not prove that citizenship in a constitutional democracy is inherently opposed to the wholehearted practice of Christian faith.

* * *

I opened this discussion by remarking that in many parts of the Western world, public confidence in the moral values and relevance of citizenship, in the integrity of our political institutions, and in the nobility of public office, have dropped to alarmingly low levels. The notion that citizenship is a natural expression of high-minded commitment to the common good rings hollow in the face of the rot of corruption, populism, and sectarianism that we see eroding our political culture and institutions in many Western countries. Yet if we are too zealous in our condemnation of politics, we run the risk of discouraging our best and brightest young citizens from investing their energies in the common good, and serving their countries in political careers. To the extent that virtuous citizens defect from the political process, they unwittingly leave the political field wide open to calculating, unscrupulous, and careerist politicians who are more committed to their own prestige and bank account than to the common good of their polity. Political philosophers can do their part in averting this disastrous outcome by developing ideals of citizenship and public service that can resonate with decent, ordinary people. I hope to have removed some of the obstacles that stand in the way of such a project, by refuting or at least heavily blunting three powerful objections that a skeptic might bring against the ethical value of citizenship and public office.

References

Aquinas, T. (1981). *The Summa Theologica of St. Thomas Aquinas (Five Volumes).* Christian Classics.

Beerbohm, E. (2012). *In our name: The ethics of democracy.* Princeton: Princeton University Press.

Hauerwas, S. (1981). *A community of character: Toward a constructive Christian social ethic.* Notre Dame/London: University of Notre Dame Press.

Hauerwas, S. (1999). *After Christendom? How the Church is to behave if freedom, justice, and a Christian nation are bad ideas.* Nashville: Abington Press.

Kateb, G. (2008). Is patriotism a mistake? In*Patriotism and other mistakes* (pp. 3–20). New Haven: Yale University Press.

Machiavelli, N. (1998). *The prince.* Chicago/London: University of Chicago Press.

Mangan, J. (1949). An historical analysis of the principle of double effect. *Theological Studies, 10,* 41–61.

Stout, J. (2004). *Democracy and tradition.* Princeton: Princeton University Press.

Thoreau, D. H. (1993). On the duty of civil disobedience. In*Civil disobedience and other essays.* New York: Dover Publications.

Thunder, D. (2014). *Citizenship and the pursuit of the worthy life*. New York: Cambridge University Press.
Walzer, M. (1973). Political action: The problem of dirty hands. *Philosophy & Public Affairs, 2*, 160–180.
Weber, M. (1946). Politics as a vocation [1918]. *From Max Weber: Essays in sociology* (pp. 77–128).
Williams, B. (1973). A critique of utilitarianism. In*Utilitarianism: For and against* (pp. 77–150). Cambridge: Cambridge University Press.

Part IV
The Ethics of Citizenship in a Multicultural Society

Confucian Citizenship of Shared Virtue

David Elstein

Originating in the ancient Mediterranean world, citizenship is a concept foreign to traditional Confucian thought. Of course, this is true not only of citizenship but of many more concepts that are incorporated into modern political theory, and hence in the early twentieth century many intellectuals felt the entire tradition of Chinese thought was backward and had to be rejected. In response, modern Confucians have adapted Confucian thought for new social conditions, arguing for modifying it to include aspects of modern political thought such as rights and democracy. In this chapter, I argue that citizenship is one such concept. I will try to demonstrate that although classical Confucian thought did not have room for an account of citizenship, this was primarily due to the conditions of the time. Modern Confucianism needs its own theory of citizenship.

Liberal accounts of citizenship will not suffice. Confucians work with a more substantive account of virtues than liberals do, which are not strictly political. As in other classical philosophies, political order and moral goodness are intertwined, not separate endeavors. A Confucian theory of citizenship supposes that there are some virtues fundamental to being a good citizen and leading a good life. If one is persuaded that divorcing ethical and political goods is unachievable and that Confucianism offers an attractive and relatively inclusive picture of a good human life, a Confucian theory of citizenship may advance beyond liberalism.

The biggest obstacle to developing a Confucian theory of citizenship is that classical Confucian thought sees the public as political patients, not agents. Rulers are supposed to consider the people's interests and rule for their benefit, but aside from occasional consultation the people were passive recipients, not active determiners of political action. Chinese political thought had no category for those who participate in politics but are not rulers or government officials. There was a distinct divide between those with political or administrative power and those who were merely

D. Elstein (✉)
State University of New York at New Paltz, New Paltz, NY, USA
e-mail: elsteind@newpaltz.edu

D. Thunder (ed.), *The Ethics of Citizenship in the 21st Century*,
DOI 10.1007/978-3-319-50415-5_7

political patients. Any Confucian account of citizenship will need to address this divide and explain why it must be reconsidered.

The approach adopted in this chapter is to consider the conditions conducive to realizing fundamental goals of Confucian ethics; to wit, developing individuals' moral capacity which is understood as actualizing human nature. In doing so I follow the branch of modern Confucianism generally called New Confucianism which developed primarily in Hong Kong and Taiwan in the decades after the Communist takeover of mainland China.[1] This approach is by no means universally accepted by all contemporary Confucians. Some prefer to focus on the meritocratic tradition in Chinese political thought.[2]

A complete defense for adopting the method of New Confucianism is not possible here and indeed I do not believe the interpretive question can be settled by textual evidence. My reasons for preferring the New Confucian democratic approach over Confucian meritocracy are not strictly textual. Rather, I think New Confucianism has a more attractive and realistic goal and is more likely to be broadly accepted by contemporary Confucians, as well as having more relevance to non-Confucian ways of thought.

An Outline of Classical Confucian Political Thought

To understand the starting point for adapting Confucian thought to modern conditions, we first need to look at classical Confucian political philosophy and then we can understand the difficulties posed to a Confucian theory of citizenship. I will focus here on the two main obstacles that I perceive: the passive role given to the public in a Confucian polity and the absence of a defined political space between the local community and the world as a whole.

Classical Confucian philosophers—I focus specifically on Kongzi (Confucius) and Mengzi (Mencius)—explicitly emphasize that the ruler's character and virtue decisively determine the quality of the government. Implicitly, they describe the relationship between governors and governed in hierarchical and unidirectional terms. That is, the ruler has a great deal of influence both to determine the extent to which people can attain their interests and on their moral character. The converse, however, is not true. Moral transformation flows from the ruling class to the people, who are frequently characterized as passive recipients of this influence (Gan 2012, 15–16). In one anecdote Ji Kangzi, an influential minister in Kongzi's home state, suggested executing those who did not follow the proper Way. Kongzi responded, "Why must you use executions in your governing? If you yourself want goodness,

[1] Confucianism was largely suppressed in mainland China from the 1949 revolution until the 1980s. Confucian philosophers who remained in China were prohibited from publishing works on Confucian thought and pressured to support Marxism publicly. Confucian thought continued to develop outside China.

[2] Prominent examples are Bai Tongdong (2013), Joseph Chan (2013), and Jiang Qing (2012).

the people will be good. The virtue of the gentleman is like the wind; that of the people is like the grass. When the wind blows over it, the grass is sure to bend" (*Analects* 12.19). This illustrates the point precisely: the grass bends before the wind without will or choice, and without substantive power to affect the wind. This is typical of how the ruler's virtue is described (*Analects* 2.1). The influence is not reciprocal; the public does not have similar power to affect the rulers.

We find the same idea in Mengzi when we pay attention to the metaphors he uses to describe political relations. One very common metaphor is that the ruler is parent to the people (*Mengzi* 1A4, 1B7, 3A3). Rather than implying that rulers have unconditional power, I think the point of this metaphor is to encourage rulers to act in the people's interests. As parents act in the best interests of their children, so should the ruler (Chang 1998, 129–30). It also establishes a clear hierarchy that is incompatible with citizenship in the sense of exercising political agency, an understanding going back to Aristotle (Collins 2006, 120). In ancient (and modern) China children did not determine the direction of the household, and I believe Mengzi and other Chinese thinkers feel it would be equally unnatural for the people to take an active role in politics. They accepted that rulers were determined through inheritance and conquest when necessary, and that most people would never exercise any political power. A ruler should absolutely govern for the benefit of the people. In their ideal, the ruler and government officials act as trustees, acting on behalf of the people's interests better than the people themselves could.

Their explicit accounts of the people provide additional support for these metaphorical descriptions. Both Mengzi and Kongzi are similar to Plato in that they think of governing as a kind of craft in which it is possible to have expertise in an objective sense. Governing is a specialized kind of activity which demands rigorous training. While in theory anyone with the ability might acquire the relevant techniques, the reality is that most people simply cannot dedicate their time to this. Hence it is much better for all concerned to leave government to the experts. In one passage Mengzi compares the art of governing to building a house or carving a valuable piece of jade. Just as one would ruin a precious piece of jade by entrusting it to an untrained carver, letting amateurs (here Mengzi is talking about hereditary rulers, not the public, but the point applies *mutatis mutandis*) make policy risks the ruin of the state (*Mengzi* 1B9).

To be sure, there are times when rulers ought to consult the people. Yet this is precisely consultation, not letting them make the final decision. In certain instances, Mengzi cautions the ruler not to listen just to those around him, but gather opinions more broadly. But we must be cautious not to read too much into this. Cheng Chung-ying says that in this passage, "It is the people's judgment that should be decisive" (C. Cheng 1998, 151). This is simply not how the text reads. Mengzi does not say to hire whomever the people say is worthy; he says that when they say someone is worthy, the ruler should "investigate, and only hire him if he really is worthy" (*Mengzi* 1B7). After hearing public opinion, the ruler must still investigate and judge for himself whether public opinion is right before acting. The ruler should listen to public opinion, but he still makes the final decision (Bai 2009, 46; Murthy 2000, 37). The public may offer opinions but do not exercise power.

The other main obstacle to citizenship is that Confucian thought does not define a category in between the local community and the world as such (or as they knew it). As Danielle Allen put it using Aristotelian language, citizenship is a kind of political friendship (2006, 140). Because friendship with everyone in the world would be essentially meaningless, a solely cosmopolitan kind of citizenship (such as in Stoicism, arguably) undermines the concept of citizens as a group who share a particular bond and have some degree of common political and social culture. While Confucians distinguish different types of relationship with distinct obligations, the most fundamental division is "family" and "everyone else." Bonds of shared community are rarely discussed and seem adventitious. Free movement is assumed; their arguments to rulers about the value of practicing good government are substantially predicated on it encouraging people to move to well-governed states and thus increasing the ruler's power (*Analects* 16.1, *Mengzi* 2A3, 2A5). There is virtually no suggestion that people are or ought to be loyal to a specific political community. Friendship is discussed many times in the *Analects*, but it is a friendship of shared pursuit of the Way and a commitment to moral perfection (bearing many similarities to Aristotle's account of the best kind of friendship). There is nothing like political friendship to bond those in a political community who are not actually personally acquainted.

The main source of bonding capital or something like it is cultural identification, not political identification. Confucians, especially Xunzi who emphasized this the most, felt that a shared ritual system was the best guarantor of social bonds. But Xunzi implies strongly that there is *one* ritual system which everyone ought to share, the Way of the Zhou dynasty which achieved ritual perfection. Instead of different communities with their own ritual norms, he envisions one ritual standard to rule them all. This universalized way of thinking is reflected politically in a cosmopolitan ideal which jumps from the family and locality directly to the world as known (typically called *tianxia* "all under heaven" or *sihai* "[within] the four seas"). At the time when the writings now known as the *Analects* and *Mengzi* were taking shape, China was divided into a number of states contending for supremacy. Mengzi especially lamented this circumstance, but instead of diverse polities co-existing peacefully, he instead imagined that the known world would be unified under the rule of a single true king who brought the various territories together through the power of his virtue.

This established the model for the majority of Chinese history: division is aberrant, unity is the norm. And so we find a yearning for a past state of political unity and hope for it in the future (*Mengzi* 2A5, 3B5). The most influential ideal of unity in Chinese political thought, still appealed to today, is the "Grand Union" from the *Records of Ritual*:

> When the great Way was practiced, a public spirit ruled all under heaven. [Those in power] employed men of virtue and ability. Their words were sincere, and they cultivated harmony. And so people did not love their parents only, nor treat as children only their own sons. The elderly were provided for, the able-bodied had employment, and the young were nurtured.…This was called the Grand Union. ("Li Yun" 2013, slightly modified)

This concept of the Grand Union has influenced contemporary cosmopolitan accounts of Chinese political thought. The best examples are the work of Gan Chunsong and Zhao Tingyang. Both argue for the importance of going beyond the nation-state to international and transnational political institutions. In some of Zhao's work, he wants a world government to take the place of current state structures, which would become more akin to local governments (Zhao 2009, 2012).

While a cosmopolitan conception of citizenship is possible (as the Stoics illustrated), it is at best a highly attenuated form. Gan, Zhao, and other contemporary Confucians are of course correct that the current structure of nation-states obscures the considerable impact that states have on their neighbors, who have no say in internal matters of sovereignty. Environmental effects, notably, are extremely difficult to contain within state boundaries. No one would deny an increase in global connectivity, which raises political issues that cannot be dealt with effectively solely within the model of national sovereignty (Held 1999). Yet at the individual level, the vast majority of people everywhere have most of their interactions with fellow nationals. It is difficult to imagine that real connections of citizenship can exist between people on opposite sides of the world, who not only are not personally acquainted but do not share a culture, language, or history (Kymlicka 1999).[3] This is not to say that there can be no cosmopolitan institutions, but only that national citizenship cannot be entirely replaced by cosmopolitan citizenship. Such a kind of citizenship, if it can be called that at all, lacks most of the basis for shared goods and a sense of identity that citizenship is supposed to be.

Nor is it reasonable to suppose that the entire world can share a set of ritual or cultural standards as classical Confucians desired. There is unquestionably a certain ethnocentrism in the assumption that Chinese rituals are superior to others, supported by frequent pejorative references to the norms and rituals of other peoples (*Analects* 9.14, *Mengzi* 3A4). Gan Chunsong reads such comments on the inferiority of non-Chinese peoples not as claims of ethnic superiority, but higher cultural advancement (2012, 48). I do not think cultural superiority supports equality any more than ethnic superiority would. It still does not treat other cultures as worthy of respect. The ideal is not only cosmopolitan, but cosmopolitanism by cultural assimilation. I believe this is not a tenable proposition today.

Developing Citizenship

A Confucian account of citizenship must deal with these two problems: it must articulate the value of the citizen's role in politics and it must provide some rationale for an intermediate category between the local community and the world, some understanding of how citizens are connected in ways that people who merely occupy the same planet are not, while accepting some cultural pluralism.

[3] In my view, Kymlicka focuses on language as a criterion for shared identity too exclusively: most Canadians and Americans share a native language but there is no move to merge politically.

I develop an argument for the importance of citizenship based on the democratic thought of New Confucians, particularly Mou Zongsan and Xu Fuguan, who articulated their democratic views in opposition to Communist rule on the mainland and the one-party dictatorship of the Nationalists (GMD) in Taiwan in the 1950s and 1960s. They wanted to uphold the relevance of Confucian thought against those who attacked it as hopelessly anti-modern, while also rejecting the connection conservatives drew between Confucian politics and authoritarian rule. Although not their precise intent at the time, their interpretation of Confucianism points toward a form of citizenship with more specific content than liberal thought.

From Mou Zongsan I draw the idea of an indirect or dialectical connection between Confucian ethical thought and democracy. Mou describes how modern Western political thought distinguishes morality and politics, focusing on developing political institutions which would be efficacious regardless of who occupied them. This was due to the development of theoretical reason. Traditional Chinese philosophy, on the other hand, emphasized moral reason and offered a moral solution to politics. The character of government depends on the character of the leader. And so the political goal was "sagely rulers and worthy ministers" (*shengjun xianxiang* 聖君賢相) (Mou 1988, 184). Politics focused on encouraging moral character, not developing effective institutions.

In Mou's view Confucianism is not fundamentally antithetical to democracy, but the Chinese mode of reasoning was not conducive to developing democratic practices. Democracy is a natural extension of the ideas in Confucian political thought, specifically, the ideas of equality, freedom, and respect for the individual as a moral subject.[4] The ideas were there, but not the means to realize them effectively.

Mou discusses the relationship between ethics and politics in terms of the connection between inner sageliness and outer kingliness (*neisheng waiwang* 內聖外王), calling democracy "the new outer kingliness." He distinguishes two types of connections: direct and indirect. Developing democracy requires an indirect connection (Mou 1991, 55–56). The problem with traditional Confucianism was the attempt to make a direct connection between inner sageliness and outer kingliness, and this is what led to the focus on sagely rulers and wise ministers, not democracy.

We must understand the contrast between direct and indirect connection. The paradigm of "direct connection" is deductive inference (Mou 1991, 56). In politics, this is the belief that a morally good ruler is necessary and sufficient for good government: the direct connection is between a virtuous leader and moral politics. Hence, the emphasis on the ruler's character in classical Confucianism. But historically this did not work. This is why he argues for an indirect or dialectical connection, what he terms "self-restriction" (*ziwo kanxian* 自我坎陷) (Mou 1991, 58).

[4] Mou was talking about political equality specifically, arguing that equality of basic human nature is worthy of a certain kind of respect. Certain kinds of social hierarchy (based on age or moral achievement, for example) require an extra level of respect, but this is personal respect, not something to be recognized with distinct political status.

What Mou means is that the moral reasoning at the foundation of Confucian thought restricts itself to allow for the development of democratic institutions.

Democracy is not essentially a moral system. People can vote as they choose and are not required to evaluate candidates morally—elections are not limited to the virtuous. This is why there can be no direct connection between Confucian morality and democracy. In the ideal of sagely rulers and worthy ministers, government is not independent from morality, as the possibility of good government depends on moral rulers and officials. However, traditional Confucian thought had no way to guarantee that only sages and worthies will have power, so could not consistently realize its own goal of a moral politics. Only democracy can achieve that (Mou 1991, 59). Realizing morality in politics thus demands that moral reasoning restrict itself so theoretical reason can develop to produce value-neutral democratic institutions (Mou 1991, 59, 136–37). He argues that democracy is in fact necessary to realize the goal of Confucian morality, to allow each person to realize his or her moral nature. And democracy requires citizen involvement.

The requirements of citizenship are developed further in Xu Fuguan's thought. Mou focuses mainly on how democracy defines and limits the power of the rulers, not on the role of citizens. In Xu's account, the unique contribution of Confucian thought in Chinese intellectual history is its focus on the development of moral subjectivity and realizing universal moral nature (Xu 1990, 69–70, 86–89). His political thought is founded on this, and much like Mou he concludes that democracy is the form of government that gives people the political agency necessary to make possible the realization of aspects of moral subjectivity that require being exercised in public. It also better satisfies the people's interests. He leaves the virtues necessary for citizenship mostly implicit, but his thought provides a direction for the further development of Confucian citizenship theory.

In Xu's view, the critical value in Confucianism is protecting life. Most fundamentally, this means caring for the people's physical needs, but is not limited to this (Elstein 2014, 69). It does mean that preserving the physical well-being of the people is the first priority, so he strongly opposed violence and coercion to attempt to force people to adopt certain moral values (Xu 1988a, 198). This is one reason he opposed authoritarian governments that tried to enforce a moral code. As I described above, classical Confucian political thought makes the rulers the trustees of the people's interests, making political decisions for their benefit. Xu's objection to this is that this was simply a hope: there was no structure to make sure this is what rulers would do. Democracy is less dependent on rulers' desire to rule in the people's interests. It gives people mechanisms for ensuring that they do (Elstein 2014, 72). People exercise their agency in democracy and in a properly functioning democracy, their choices determine political decisions.

A key feature of democracy for Xu is that everyone can express their opinions and exercise political agency. He implicitly rejected the analogy between government and crafts mentioned above. In one discussion, he distinguished fields where expertise ought to be decisive (such as academia) and politics: politics must be open to all, even those who are not experts (Xu 1985, 169). For one thing, this can help limit the tendency of governments to become totalitarian and suppress dissent. Even more importantly, however, participation in political matters is an important aspect of developing political and moral agency. To limit political involvement to the experts would be to prevent most people from fully developing their moral and political capacities (Xu 1985, 37–38, 169–70; 1988a, 190), which are crucial for a flourishing life.

Another crucial contribution of Xu's thought is his emphasis on freedom as a condition for virtue and the importance of practice and realization. Like many New Confucians, Xu was deeply impressed by Kant and his idea that morality must be autonomous. True virtue must be chosen by the self, not imposed from outside. Real virtue must be freely chosen; external forces such as punishments or even submitting to a teacher can only produce a semblance of virtue, not the real thing. And virtue is not a theoretical endeavor; it must be realized in active practice (Xu 1988b, 249). Political virtues thus require political practice, for example, developing tolerance of opposing views and refining capacities of judgment. So not only does democracy require a level of participation, but if there are virtues that pertain to public life as Xu contended (see below), then a full individual moral life also must involve activity in the public realm.

The nature of this activity need not be strictly political in the narrower sense of the word. The *Analects* itself defends the relatively private activities of being a filial son and good brother as a form of participating in politics (2.21). What Xu has in mind goes beyond that into more public activities, but "public" does not strictly mean "political." Coming from a Chinese tradition (and present) where people faced imprisonment or execution for expressing the wrong political views, he argued that part of political freedom is the freedom not to get involved in politics (Xu 1985, 98–99). However, he also advocated a more expansive set of possibilities for acting in society and having a public role, pointing to the need for something of a civil society (Xu 1985, 56; 1988a, 76). His proposals lack specifics, but it is evident that he did support avenues for social action that are not necessarily political activities.[5] These too could be channels for developing and practicing public virtues. What Xu's account leaves out is a more complete articulation of the role of the citizen and its virtues.

The Role of the Citizen

In order to develop a Confucian account of citizenship, we must consider how to describe the role of the citizen in Confucian terms. One approach is to stick closer to the texts, which use family relations as a basis for describing other relationships.

[5] What he was wanted to argue is that some kind of public role and opportunity for social recognition is important, but that historically in China the fact that the only opportunity for that was serving in government led to Confucians compromising their values in order to have that opportunity. Politics should be one option, but not the only one. See Elstein 2014, 75–75 for additional discussion of this point in Xu's thought.

It is true that familial metaphors have been common in traditional Confucian thought and occasionally contemporary Confucians argue for treating the state as an extended family (Kim 2014, 147–53). For reasons described earlier, unlike in Greece and Rome there was no discussion of citizenship as such and essentially no conception of it in ancient China. However, rather than continuing to attempt to force citizenship into the family analogy which fits poorly, I propose instead to recognize the historical factors that led to ignoring citizenship and argue that this lacuna needs to be rectified for a viable modern Confucian political theory. Citizenship is a distinct role with distinct demands.

The focus on family in Confucian thought makes sense. No infant can survive without extended, focused care from adults, most commonly its biological parents. Familial relationships are not only necessary for survival, they have lasting psychological and emotional effects. While it may have been too much to think, as classical Confucians occasionally implied, that someone who cares for family properly will always care for others as well, there is some truth to the notion that someone who does not have good models in early childhood will find it hard to develop trust in others generally. In addition, the population of the time was overwhelmingly rural and clan-based, so people would associate with relatives and neighbors most frequently and there were fewer opportunities to interact with strangers. Naturally, technology for mass communication with distant people was unimaginable. Furthermore, as described above, the public was thought of as entirely passive, ready to be acted upon by the rulers and officials. Under these circumstances, it is understandable that the role of citizen was never articulated.

Obviously, this is not the case in any developed nation now, democratic or not. Population in developed and developing nations is increasingly urban, technology is making communication ever easier, and the scope of government has vastly increased. Everyone has more contact with non-familial actors today than in ancient times (Thunder 2014, 143). The possibility for concerted public action is also much greater, and hence citizen unrest concerns the Chinese government. Even a non-democratic government cannot entirely ignore how the people feel and what they want. Certainly in a democracy, as most Confucians today advocate to some degree, citizens have a role in politics and people relate to each other as participants in shared government (among other things). This is a different type of role.

This completely different political, social, and technological situation demands a re-thinking of the roles in a Confucian society. Arguably, the most important challenge in a polity is establishing a presumption of trust between strangers, so that people feel they are stakeholders in a common enterprise. Inevitably some interests will have to be sacrificed for others, but when this becomes too extreme or one-sided, trust is lost (Allen 2006, 38–48). This is a precarious situation. Group identity as fellow citizens gives people a reason to trust each other. This is founded on shared history, shared language, and common rituals.[6] Yet this cannot be the same as family identity, even an extended family. The bonds of citizenship simply are not the same as kinship. Length and depth of acquaintance matter. I believe it is not psychologically

[6] For a challenge to this claim, see Pogge 1992, n. 39.

possible to care for strangers in the same way, nor would it be desirable. Citizens relate to each other in a more limited sphere. Yet the commonality of sharing a political culture is worth something. It is not surprising that people tend to care more about the welfare of their fellow citizens than strangers in foreign countries.

All this indicates that Confucians need to provide space for citizenship as something *sui generis* between family identity and identification with *tianxia* or the entire world. Perhaps at some point in the future cosmopolitan identity will become a reality. There is definitely need for greater international cooperation on issues that are not restricted to national boundaries. However, the reality at present is that national identity is a significant factor in most people's lives. National governments have more power than transnational organizations and people have greater ability to influence them. The role of the citizen is mainly focused within the nation-state, and this intermediate level needs to be recognized.

Separating public and private virtue entirely, as some liberals do, is not an option for Confucianism. Taking a cue from Rawls, some contemporary Confucians distinguish Confucian civic virtue from Confucianism as a comprehensive morality. I believe this is an untenable position, both as an interpretation of Confucian philosophy and as a philosophical position generally. Since a number of authors have remarked on why liberal neutrality is not attainable, I will not say much more. I will only point out that as virtues are thought to be habits or dispositions, it is difficult to understand how dispositions can be strictly segregated between public and private life. Habits of thought and affect developed in one domain inevitably will carry over into others.

In any case, Confucianism can hardly endorse liberal neutrality while remaining recognizable as Confucianism. As illustrated above, the early Confucians saw the family as the critical site for developing virtues that would then apply more broadly. It is characteristic of Confucian thought not to separate the ethical and political realms entirely (Angle 2009, 179–90; Tan 2003, 128–32), an idea which caused problems in Chinese political history.[7] The New Confucians of the twentieth century indeed realized the downsides of this, arguing for greater independence. Mou Zongsan wrote that moral reason had to be restricted in order to allow for the development of independent political theory, and then politics "naturally becomes an independent domain temporarily distinct from and seemingly unrelated to morality." However, this is merely a linguistic convenience, to allow talking about politics as a distinct field. The reality is that "it is obvious that [political] freedom must connect to moral reasoning and self-awareness; there is nothing abstract or abstruse here, nor is there any metaphysical theory likely to incite controversy" (Mou 2014, 391). Complete independence is neither possible nor desirable.

The desire to make political virtues a wholly distinct set of course owes much to liberalism and expresses a reasonable desire to avoid excessive interference with personal morality from both the government and fellow citizens. However, behind it is an assumption that if political virtue and personal or familial virtue are analogous, then benevolence toward fellow citizens must be basically the same as

[7] See El Amine 2015, 9–15 for a slightly different take on this question.

benevolence toward one's own family. Given the way Confucians recognized differences in level of concern based on the closeness of the relationship, there is no reason to draw this conclusion. I will argue that Confucians recognize different ways of manifesting the same general virtues in specific contexts. One can think of the public virtues as different species but sharing a genus with the familial virtues. Both are thus subsets of the broadest virtues. This avoids the concern about managing two independent sets of virtues, yet does not demand an unattainable goal of liberal neutrality. Public virtues can be related to private ones, with a narrower scope.

The Virtues of the Citizen

Mou Zongsan and Xu Fuguan can take us partway down the path of a Confucian account of citizenship, but neither do enough to specify the virtues demanded by public life, nor how they relate to the fundamental Confucian virtues. Mou provides a list of the basic virtues, what he believes are the fundamental characteristics of universal human nature: filiality, brotherly respect, conscientiousness, trustworthiness, propriety, righteousness, integrity, and a sense of shame (Mou 1991, 126). Some are applicable to public life, but still generally assume continuity between familial relations and relations between citizens. I believe Confucians need to go beyond this to consider public virtues in themselves and how public virtues relate to the basic virtues, rather than assuming that familial virtue can easily transfer to public life.

Any list of fundamental virtues in Confucian thought must start with Mengzi, who listed benevolence, righteousness, ritual propriety, and wisdom as the cardinal virtues. Of these, benevolence and righteousness are the most important, with ritual propriety and wisdom defined derivatively. Most later Confucians followed Mengzi; the most significant change in later Confucianism was that benevolence became the comprehensive virtue as well as a particular virtue of concern for the well-being of others.[8] Mengzi himself suggested that the family was the initial site for developing virtue, which ideally one would extend to others. Virtue was rooted in familial virtue generally, with suggestions that someone who did not treat family members properly could not be virtuous otherwise (e.g. *Analects* 1.2, *Mengzi* 4A19, 4A27, 7A15).[9] Perhaps as a result, Confucians historically did not pay close attention to how these virtues could extend to public situations, or whether there were distinctly public virtues.

The four fundamental virtues in Mengzi certainly have some application to citizenship. Benevolence refers to an attitude of sincere interest in and concern for

[8] For example, the Song dynasty Neo-Confucian Cheng Hao said, "Righteousness, propriety, wisdom, and faithfulness all are manifestations of benevolence" (H. Cheng 2014, 140).

[9] Exactly how extension works is left vague and it may well be that Confucians were historically too optimistic that familial virtue would transfer to other situations readily.

others' well-being. The paradigm Mengzi gives is parent-child relations, and this was extended to politics in the metaphor of a ruler being a parent to the people. However, benevolence need not and did not always have that hierarchical dimension. Later Neo-Confucians frequently said the benevolent person forms one body with all things, even feeling regret for broken tiles and stones (Wang 2014, 242). The questions surrounding the breadth of benevolence need not detain us. What does require examining, however, is the scope of benevolence toward fellow citizens.[10] A general Confucian principle is that the closer the relationship, the greater the obligation to care for the needs of the other party, so family takes priority over neighbors, who in turn take priority over strangers.

What earlier Confucians did not explicitly articulate, however, is that one's benevolence must also have a different scope with regard to different classes of recipients. It is not just that I should care for my wife over a stranger if I have to choose between them. It is appropriate for me to have a much greater scope of concern for my wife than it would be for a stranger. A deeper level of acquaintance, such as in family relationships, naturally translates to a wider scope of benevolence than would be possible or desirable with acquaintances or strangers.[11] When considering what benevolence requires for fellow citizens, it is not helpful to say that a nation is modeled after the family. It is surely psychologically impossible to care about the well-being of millions of strangers the same way one cares about one's own family (Kim 2014, 171). Moreover, most people would experience such concern as intrusive and probably offensive.

This is where the virtue of righteousness comes into play. An approximate definition of righteousness would be the virtue of showing proper respect according to someone's social role. The examples Mengzi gives are mainly about proper treatment of older brothers or elders generally, no doubt due to the cultural context in which age demanded greater respect. However, I believe the virtue of righteousness is more general in application than merely age differences. It is often contrasted with gain or profit and linked with a sense of shame; that is, to feel shame at not doing what is right (*Analects* 4.16, 7.16; *Mengzi* 2A6). Construed more broadly then, righteousness means acting according to the standards of the particular relationship. It can moderate benevolence appropriately, meaning one's concern for fellow citizens is not identical in scope to concern for family or friends.

Ritual propriety also has direct applications to citizen relations. "Ritual" in classical Chinese subsumes much more than the English term, including what we could call customs and etiquette: norms governing all sorts of interactions. A key characteristic of rituals is their role-specific nature: rituals are a way of defining and marking the distinctions of respect that belong to righteousness and which distinguish the

[10] For purposes of this essay, I will use "breadth" to mean the set of potential objects of benevolence and "scope" to refer to how comprehensive an agent's benevolence is with regard to one particular class of objects.

[11] This is reflected in occasional comments about how friends should hold each other to a higher moral standard (*Analects* 12.23, 12.24). Mou Zongsan as well notes that friends can be more demanding of each other than is appropriate for a government to be toward its citizens.

varying scopes of benevolence. Hence, Mengzi said that the core of ritual is "the adornment of [benevolence and righteousness]" (4A27).

The reliance on ritual as opposed to law is frequently pointed out by scholars who describe how Confucian political thought differs from liberalism (Hall and Ames 1999, 214–20; Rosemont 1998; Tan 2003, 183–85). While I believe that it is naïve to hope that rituals can replace law entirely as a method for resolving or avoiding conflicts, I also agree with Steve Angle and Joseph Chan when they suggest that law should not be the first resort, either (Angle 2009, 216–21; Chan 2013, 120–25). Adjudication is invariably antagonistic: for one side to win a lawsuit the other must lose. This does not develop bonds of trust and civic friendship. Hence Confucians hoped to reduce reliance of law (*Analects* 12.13). Participation in common rituals, in contrast, does help reinforce the sense of communal purpose and interests that are at the heart of citizenship. As other relationships have their particular ritual expressions, citizenship needs its own. Building trust requires more than just talking. Participation in a shared activity, as rituals are, improves trust and cooperation (Kramer 1999, 579–80; Rappaport 1999; Sosis and Bressler 2003). In increasingly fractured communities, this is a point that needs emphasis.

What must be added to these general virtues is an account of virtues specific to the role of citizen. Much as filiality is specific to the parent-child relationship, we may expect that the citizen role has its own species of the more general virtues. It seems clear that toleration of other views and respect for some norms governing public debate should be among the virtues of citizenship.[12] Trust in the political process is also important, though of course this also depends on the government demonstrating concern for the public interest. A degree of humility is desirable. If one is sure one's own values and moral convictions are correct, there is little need to listen to other people with different views (Metzger 2005, 23ff; Schneewind 1990, 62). Even Kongzi denied he was a sage and was willing to learn from others (*Analects* 7.33, 7.34, 9.8). The contemporary Confucian Xu Fuguan emphasized what he called "concern consciousness": an awareness of unlimited responsibility to others (Xu 1990, 20–21, 91). Part of this responsibility is a willingness to listen and understand others' positions. This is another way the citizen relation differs from certain others (parent-child relations, notably): equal recognition and consideration of each other's interests is critical in a democratic system.

The model of family will almost invariably import some untenable assumptions. Extended family still has greater personal acquaintance than can be expected of citizens in modern states. Crucially, even more egalitarian family relations than were assumed in Confucian texts are surely going to have some hierarchy. Children do not have equal decision-making power in major family matters. Citizenship requires treating others as equal, recognizing that they have equal say in political matters *qua* citizens and usually sharing fundamental rights. It is a different type of relation, but

[12] I have in mind something analogous to public reason as Rawls uses the term, but given the Confucian emphasis on ritual and developing affects rather than strict rationality, "reason" may not be the most appropriate term. For one example of this (which I do not entirely endorse), see Kim 2014, chap. 5.

that does not mean the virtues appropriate to citizenship are entirely separate from others. Rather than making public virtues a wholly separate category, the concern for autonomy and privacy can be better addressed by recognizing differences in the scope of virtues, and limiting the scope for the political domain and the relation of citizens.

Citizenship of Shared Virtue

To sum up so far, I am arguing that a Confucian political community must have a conception of a good citizen, and a good citizen will instantiate many of the virtues that are part of the Confucian conception of the good person generally, in a more restricted fashion. This obviously supposes a good deal of agreement on what these virtues are, agreement that it might be thought is impossible to attain given what Rawls called the "fact of pluralism" and his belief that agreement on comprehensive doctrines can only be attained by coercion. Confucians will certainly oppose using coercion, since they believe that it cannot produce true virtue. Yet this overlooks that there is a wide continuum between complete agreement on all aspects of morality, and only trying to attain agreement on the barest virtues necessary for political life. Partial agreement may well be attainable without coercion, as William Galston describes (1991, 88–89). That is to say, agreement on Confucianism as a totalistic philosophy of life is not necessary, nor does accepting the general account of the virtues in Confucianism entail accepting their specific expressions (many of which seem dated if not offensive by modern standards). It would require accepting the general scheme of the main virtues, but there is little reason to think that agreement on broad virtues or conceptions of flourishing is impossible (Thunder 2014, 102).

Contemporary Confucians have addressed the question of pluralism and diverse understandings of virtue. Most recognize the need for accepting a greater degree of pluralism than was traditional. Whereas Xunzi implies that one ritual system can be judged superior in general, I doubt any modern Confucian would make this claim. They recognize the importance of a shared ritual system, but also that there can be diverse systems which may all serve the intended function. Many modern Confucians adopt the formula "pattern is one but its manifestations are diverse" to explain how the set of virtues that are the core of human nature can have different expressions in different communities (Liu 1993). Others use a Hegelian framework to allow for the recognition that there can be different historical expressions of an absolute principle (Lee 2013, 165). The key point for them is that within a given community, there is significant agreement on how the universal virtues are expressed and understood. Indeed, it might be said that this agreement is one of the constituents of a community.

While Confucians will agree with the criticisms of liberal neutrality and accept that a substantive view of the good is inevitably part of a cohesive political society, they should not, I believe, accept either communitarianism or liberal pluralism. Although some Western scholars have argued that Confucianism is like communitarianism in insisting that values have to be rooted in communal tradition (Ames 2011; Rosemont 2004; Tan 2003), if this means that all standards of value are historical and community-based, most contemporary East Asian Confucians would reject this. There can be different ways of manifesting universal values, but they are committed to a universal human nature. According to New Confucians, there is a transcendent moral subject that is ontologically prior to the person-in-society, "a moral subject that transcends historical and social contexts" (Lee 2005, 255–57). They agree that human nature can only be realized in society and there will necessarily be particular ways of expressing this nature, but any good society expresses universal human values.

This description will undoubtedly sound similar to one type of liberal philosophy, namely, the liberal pluralism of William Galston. He, too, rejects complete localism of morality and argues there are certain minimal boundaries on any acceptable moral code (Galston 1991, 38–39). The significant distinction is found when considering Galston's list of goods: life, development of basic capacities, fulfillment of interests, freedom, rationality, society, and subjective satisfaction (Galston 1991, 174–77). I doubt Confucians would quarrel with any of these. Although the emphasis on rationality might raise questions Galston is clear that this is not rationality as opposed to inclination. The problem is rather that these goods are too vague and not strictly moral.

Let me make the last point clearer: I am not suggesting that Confucians recognize only moral goods as worthwhile. Although the texts can sometimes give that impression by contrasting what is right and what is profitable (in one's interest), this is only to insist that what is right has to have priority (*Analects* 16.10). A reasonable desire for personal interests is not condemned. As Mengzi said, "What person does not want wealth and prestige? But to be concerned solely with wealth and prestige is to take a selfish 'vantage point' " (2B10). Galston's view of heterogeneity means there is no single scale for weighing these different goods. While he is quick to note that that does not mean there is never any principled way of making trade-offs when goods conflict (Galston 1991, 180–81), I doubt this is sufficient for Confucians. Moral goods *always* have to trump non-moral goods in relatively comparable circumstances.[13] Non-moral goods definitely are a lower priority (*Analects* 4.16, 7.16; *Mengzi* 1A1).[14]

In addition, Galston gives a higher priority to developing capacities related to individual choice, following the liberal tradition of Mill. For Confucians, choice *itself* is not a good, though their conception of virtue suggests that choice on some level is still necessary for true virtue (Xu 1990, 20–21).[15] Rather, as I outlined above, Confucians will give priority to more substantive virtues while still allowing for diverse cultural manifestations of these virtues. Galston's goods are largely

[13] Which is not to say there are hard and fast rules for making these decisions. In my view, the best interpretation is that it is a matter of what Mengzi called "weighing" (*quan* 權); that is, deciding based on the particulars of the situation.

[14] Additional discussion of the relation between right and profit is in (Elstein and Tian 2017).

[15] I develop this point further in work in progress.

subjective. While of course certain social conditions will be required for their realization, the way he defines most of the goods implies that the basic measure is the individual and there do not seem to be any limits in principle of what an individual can define as his interests or sources of subjective satisfaction, for example.

Confucians will similarly disagree with David Thunder's proposal to make integrity the primary standard of a worthy life. According to Thunder, one of the benefits of integrity is that it is a structural value and can bypass controversies about what constitutes a worthy life. What is valuable is integrating one's character, goals, and so on into what the agent reflectively takes to be a worthy life (Thunder 2014, 27–34). For Confucians, this is still too subjective and individual. Subjective recognition is important, but the goods are objective. Furthermore, Confucian virtues are understood relationally for the most part: one cannot have a good life without being benevolent, which requires people to be benevolent *to*. Sociality constitutes an indispensable part of a good human life, where it is just one of the possible goods in Galston's list.

Since there is more specific content in the virtues of the citizen than in liberal pluralism, there is a correspondingly greater role for the government to encourage a particular kind of life. Any government that provides education will encourage some sorts of values. Exactly how and to what degree a government should do so is probably a matter to be determined through the political process rather than determined in the abstract. Observing the coercive practices of the regimes in China and Taiwan, many modern Confucians have been concerned about excessive government interference. Yet they realized that governments cannot be completely neutral. Any society can take steps to try to ensure its continuation, which includes encouraging commitment to the political system. This might take the form of compulsory voting (as in Australia) or merely encouraging participation in any number of ways. Complete freedom from government interference is clearly impossible, but the concern about coercive pressure is reason for caution.

Another difference with liberalism is the focus on *how* citizen virtue is encouraged and developed, particularly with shared rituals. Again, we need to understand "ritual" more broadly than it usually is in English, meaning norms for interaction generally. These both develop and express the virtues, and so rituals of citizenship both develop the dispositions of appropriate care and respect for fellow citizens, and also express them in recognizable ways. For Confucians, it is not enough to have shared values or virtues articulated; they need to be performed and expressed. When actions do not coincide with what is professed, the actions carry more weight (*Analects* 4.24, 5.10). Paying lip service to equality, for example, does little when people are treated manifestly unequally. Habituated actions—rituals—enact the virtues of citizenship.

Challenges

The account of citizenship I have offered, particularly government involvement in encouraging the virtues of the citizen, will naturally raise questions from a liberal perspective. In East Asia, governmental involvement in individual ethical life is less controversial than in most Western countries since religion was historically not the divisive issue that it was in Europe and America, which was a major factor in the formation of liberal philosophy. Still, it is fair to say that there is some concern to respect individual autonomy and limit government involvement in personal virtue appropriately. The theory of citizenship I have outlined could be challenged on this dimension.

For example, one challenge is whether encouraging substantive virtues of the kind I have described respects what Rawls called "the fact of pluralism." It certainly does influence individual pursuits more than liberalism, even Galston's liberal pluralism, which emphasizes virtues directed to individual choice such as developing capacities and refining one's judgment. Appealing to a divide between public and private virtues as liberals do is not a real option since I have denied that such a split is realistic. The scope of the virtues as civic is different than when considered as private virtues, but the fundamental character of many of them is related. If this is correct, then pluralism is always limited and complete neutrality is not possible, as many political philosophers have argued. So this is not a problem specific to Confucian philosophy, although one might still reasonably argue that liberalism preserves *greater* room for pluralism, as in fact Galston does.

Here one might appeal to the reality that Confucian societies are less pluralistic than Western liberal societies. I do not know if there is a systematic way to measure this—to my knowledge, no one has attempted to quantify pluralism—but it seems obvious to anyone who has spent time in both. This may mean that citizens will continue to accept a greater government role in determining and encouraging the virtues of a good life. Insofar as they do not, it may be that that society is becoming less Confucian and needs a different public philosophy.

Still, even accepting less pluralism and more government involvement, the question remains about where the acceptable limits are. How much diversity can a Confucian society accept? What kind of government involvement is acceptable? Contemporary Confucians have had various answers to this. On the more conservative side, the mainland Confucian Jiang Qing argues for a Confucian state religion, but allowing unrestricted private practice, comparable to the status of Anglicanism in the UK. One branch of the legislature is reserved for Confucian scholars and their considerable power in his structure means Confucian values will probably dominate government (Elstein 2014, chap. 7). A more moderate position was taken by Mou Zongsan, who thought that government should not represent a specific moral position, but that education had to have a basic ethical content, much as I have described here (Mou 2014, 393–95). Then there is Xu Fuguan, who insisted that the democratic process always has to take precedence and adoption of any ideology or doctrine had to be decided democratically and with provision for future revision (Elstein 2014, 75–77).

I agree with Xu Fuguan: if democracy is indeed an implication of Confucian ethical thought and necessary to make the realization of human nature possible, then it must be protected. Even if the government attempts to enforce the correct view of human life in the name of Confucian values, this still must be opposed. And of course, the history of the twentieth century taught that governments were much more likely to twist Confucian values for their own purposes than be sincerely committed to them. At the same time, citizen or public virtue is just one aspect of many. As Confucians recognize role-specific virtues as well as a variety of ways of manifesting them, there should be little problem with recognizing diverse expressions of private virtue within general boundaries established by the view of human nature (whether and how these should be politically enforced is another question). Commitment to shared public rituals of citizenship, for example, can coexist with a variety of personal ritual practices. Celebrating the 4th of July as a commitment to public identity as an American citizen does not interfere with a variety of private moral doctrines.

The more difficult question comes when the demands of private roles conflict with the demands of citizenship. For example, as described above participation in the public sphere is an important part of Confucian democracy. Confucianism is analogous to civic republicanism in the way public involvement is necessary to a good life. But what happens when some people have private beliefs that are incompatible with functioning as citizens in this way, such as certain religious groups for whom involvement in mainstream society and politics is forbidden (Hutterites, for example)? Does a Confucian society need to accept this? A group like this would not be free riders completely, as they would have to pay taxes and comply with other passive requirements of citizenship. Yet clearly a democratic polity cannot tolerate *everyone* refusing to take part in government. From a Confucian perspective, I cannot see a compelling argument for allowing groups with a principled refusal to participate to enjoy the benefits provided by the society. As a practical matter, they might be tolerated if they are relatively few and well-established. But for immigration purposes, for example, there are grounds for requiring commitment to the basic requirements of citizenship as a condition for admission and naturalization.

Public education is an especially sensitive area. The particular realities of East Asian societies place great emphasis on education, especially public education. Public high schools and universities are almost invariably considered the best and there is tremendous competition for spots at the best schools. Of course, the government is heavily involved in curricula at public schools, which typically have much less local autonomy than in the United States, for example. Thus, while in theory parents have alternatives to government-run education, in reality they are not equal. Hence the values that are encouraged in public education are particularly important. The lesser degree of pluralism noted above and the very different role of religion in society mean that this is likely less of a problem than it is in the US. There have never been controversies about teaching evolution, for example, as far as I know. Some political and historical content has been controversial, however, such as how World War II is covered in history textbooks in Japan or the actions of the Nationalist Party during the period of martial law in Taiwan.

The advantage of a democratic society with free media is that these issues can be confronted and discussed. While education cannot be entirely neutral, citizens can exercise some measure of control over the content of education and there is nothing to prevent parents or children from accessing alternative sources of information, in marked contrast to the much more restricted access in China, for example. The fact that decisions about curricula arouse controversy is an indication that government officials cannot completely control the process and simply make whatever decisions they feel benefit their party or ideology. Given the reality that education has to have some specific content and will invariably communicate some values, I do not think much more can be done than to make the process relatively transparent and preserve the possibility for change.

Conclusion

In this chapter, I have outlined why Confucianism has not had a theory of citizenship and why it needs one. Even Confucian opponents of liberal democracy understand that there have to be channels for the public to be involved in government. Proponents of Confucian democracy obviously agree, and so Confucians need to think about what it means to be a citizen in a modern Confucian society. I argue that modeling the state on the family, as classical Confucians did, is not a helpful way of thinking about the role of the citizen. It should be considered on its own terms. Citizens relate to each other in more limited ways and in a democratic society at least, without the hierarchy that is usually present in family relations. However, Confucians cannot endorse a complete separation of civic and private values, as some liberals do.

Instead, I suggest that civic virtues be considered species to the genus of the basic virtues of human nature. This genus/species analogy allows for different cultural expressions of the virtues, while preserving the universality of human nature that is the hallmark of the Mengzian line of Confucian thought and which dominated most of Chinese history. Universality at the general level is compatible with cultural variation at the specific level. Yet within a given community, Confucians think there has to be more agreement on substantive values than liberals do. Government neutrality is not an option, and attempts to restrict common virtues to more structural ones, as William Galston and David Thunder recommend, is not enough for Confucians. This is where Confucians depart from liberalism. How much agreement is needed and how it should be encouraged (or enforced, if necessary) are difficult questions contemporary Confucians need to ponder as they develop a Confucian theory of citizenship.

References

Allen, D. S. (2006). *Talking to strangers: Anxieties of citizenship since Brown v. Board of education*. Chicago: University of Chicago Press.

Ames, R. (2011). *Confucian role ethics: A vocabulary, Ch'ien Mu Lecture Series*. Honolulu: University of Hawaii Press.

Analects. (2003). Trans. by E. Slingerland. Indianapolis: Hackett.

Angle, S. C. (2009). *Sagehood: The contemporary significance of neo-confucian philosophy*. Oxford: Oxford University Press.

Bai, T. (2009). *New mission of an old state: Classical Confucian political philosophy in a contemporary and comparative relevance context* 旧邦新命:古今中西参照下的古典儒家政治哲学. Beijing: Peking University Press.

Bai, T. (2013). A Confucian version of hybrid regime: How does it work, and why is it superior? In D. A. Bell & C. Li (Eds.), *The East Asian challenge for democracy: Political meritocracy in comparative perspective* (pp. 55–87). New York: Cambridge University Press.

Chan, J. (2013). *Confucian perfectionism: A political philosophy for modern times*. Princeton: Princeton University Press.

Chang, W. (1998). Confucian theory of norms and human rights. In W. T. de Bary & W.-m. Tu (Eds.), *Confucianism and human rights* (pp. 117–141). New York: Columbia University Press.

Cheng, C.-y. (1998). Transforming Confucian virtues into human rights: A study of human agency and potency in Confucian ethics. In W. T. de Bary & W.-m. Tu (Eds.), *Confucianism and human rights* (pp. 142–153). New York: Columbia University Press.

Cheng, H. (2014). On understanding benevolence. In J. Tiwald, & B. W. Van Norden (Eds.), P. J. Ivanhoe (Trans.), *Readings in later Chinese philosophy: Han to the 20th century* (pp. 140–141). Indianapolis: Hackett.

Collins, S. D. (2006). *Aristotle and the rediscovery of citizenship*. New York: Cambridge University Press.

El Amine, L. (2015). *Classical Confucian political thought: A new interpretation*. Oxford: Princeton University Press.

Elstein, D. (2014). *Democracy in contemporary Confucian philosophy* (Routledge studies in contemporary philosophy). New York: Routledge.

Elstein, D., & Tian, Q. (2017). Confucian business ethics: Possibilities and challenges. In B. Kaldis & F. Eugene Heath (Eds.), *Wealth, commerce, and philosophy: Foundational thinkers and business ethics*. Chicago: University of Chicago Press.

Galston, W. A. (1991). *Liberal purposes: Goods, virtues, and diversity in the liberal state* (Cambridge studies in philosophy and public policy). Cambridge/New York: Cambridge University Press.

Gan, C. (2012). *Back to Wangdao: Confucianism and the world order* 重回王道—儒家與世界秩序. Shanghai: East China Normal University Press.

Hall, D., & Ames, R. (1999). *The democracy of the dead*. Chicago: Open Court.

Held, D. (1999). The transformation of political community: Rethinking democracy in the context of globalization. In I. Shapiro & C. Hacker-Cordón (Eds.), *Democracy's edges* (pp. 84–111). London/New York: Cambridge University Press.

Jiang, Q. (2012). In D. Bell & R. Fan (Eds.), *A Confucian constitutional order*. Princeton: Princeton University Press.

Kim, S. (2014). *Confucian democracy in East Asia: Theory and practice*. New York: Cambridge University Press.

Kramer, R. M. (1999). Trust and distrust in organizations: Emerging perspectives, enduring questions. *Annual Review of Psychology, 50*(1), 569–598.

Kymlicka, W. (1999). Citizenship in an era of globalization: Commentary on held. In I. Shapiro & C. Hacker-Cordón (Eds.), *Democracy's edges* (pp. 112–126). London/New York: Cambridge University Press.

Lee, M. -h. (2005). *Political thought from a Confucian perspective* 儒家視野下的政治思想. Taibei: Taiwan University Press.

Lee, M. -h. (2013). *The self-transformation of contemporary Confucianism* 當代儒學的自我轉化 (Rev. ed.). Taibei: Academia Sinica Institute of Chinese Literature and Philosophy.

"Li Yun." (2013). *Chinese text project*. http://ctext.org/liji/zhong-yong. Accessed 23 July.

Liu, S. (1993). The contemporary explanation of 'pattern is one, Its manifestations are many' 「理一分殊」的現代解釋." In *The tension between ideals and reality* 理想與現實的糾結 (pp. 157–88). Taibei: Student Books.

Mengzi. (2008). Trans. by B. W. Van Norden. *Mengzi*. Indianapolis: Hackett.
Metzger, T. (2005). *A cloud across the Pacific: Essays on the clash between Chinese and western political theories today*. Hong Kong: Chinese University Press.
Mou, Z. (1988). *Philosophy of history* 歷史哲學 (Rev. ed.). Taibei: Student Books.
Mou, Z. (1991). The principle of authority and governance 政道與治道 (Rev. edn.). Taibei: Student Books.
Mou, Z. (2014). The principles of authority and governance. In J. Tiwald, & B. W. Van Norden (Eds.), D. Elstein (Trans.), *Readings in later Chinese philosophy: Han to the 20th century*. Indianapolis: Hackett.
Murthy, V. (2000). The democratic potential of Confucian *minben* thought. *Asian Philosophy, 10*(1), 33–47.
Pogge, T. W. (1992). Cosmopolitanism and sovereignty. *Ethics, 103*(1), 48–75.
Rappaport, R. A. (1999). *Ritual and religion in the making of humanity, Cambridge studies in social and cultural anthropology 110*. Cambridge: Cambridge University Press.
Rosemont, H. (1998). Human rights: A bill of worries. In W. T. de Bary & W.-m. Tu (Eds.), *Confucianism and human rights* (pp. 54–66). New York: Columbia University Press.
Rosemont, H. (2004). Whose democracy? which rights? A Confucian critique of modern western liberalism. In K.-l. Shun & D. B. Wong (Eds.), *Confucian ethics: A comparative study of self, autonomy, and community* (pp. 49–71). Cambridge: Cambridge University Press.
Schneewind, J. B. (1990). The misfortunes of virtue. *Ethics, 101*(1), 42–63. doi:10.1086/293259.
Sosis, R., & Bressler, E. R. (2003). Cooperation and commune longevity: A test of the costly signaling theory of religion. *Cross-Cultural Research, 37*(2), 211–239.
Tan, S.-h. (2003). *Confucian democracy: A Deweyan reconstruction*. Albany: SUNY Press.
Thunder, D. (2014). *Citizenship and the pursuit of the worthy life*. New York: Cambridge University Press.
Wang, Y. (2014). Questions on the great learning. In J. Tiwald, & B. W. Van Norden (Eds.), P. J. Ivanhoe (Trans.), *Readings in later chinese philosophy: Han to the 20th century* (pp. 238–250). Indianapolis: Hackett.
Xu, F. (1985). *Between academia and politics* 學術與政治之間. Taibei: Student Books.
Xu, F. (1988a). In X. Xiao (Ed.), *Confucian political thought and democracy, freedom and human rights* 儒家政治思想與民主自由人權 (Rev. ed.). Taibei: Student Books.
Xu, F. (1988b). The culture of the heart-mind 心的文化." In *Collected essays on Chinese thought* 中國思想史論集. Taibei: Student Books.
Xu, F. (1990). *A history of Chinese theories of human nature: The pre-Qin period* 中國人性論史: 先秦篇. Taibei: Commercial Press.
Zhao, T. (2009). A political world philosophy in terms of all-under-heaven (Tian-Xia). *Diogenes, 56*(1), 5–18.
Zhao, T. (2012). All-under-heaven and methodological relationism: An old story and new world peace. In F. Dallmayr & T. Zhao (Eds.), *Contemporary Chinese political thought: Debates and perspectives* (pp. 46–66). Lexington: University Press of Kentucky.

From Social Practices to Reflective Agency: A Postsecular Ethics of Citizenship

Paolo Monti

Introduction: Citizens as Co-practitioners

From a democratic perspective, few things are more disconcerting than considering the actions of people who radically estrange themselves from the civic texture of their own societies, to the point of methodically and violently pursuing the harm of other citizens and liberal institutions. We cannot but wonder what went wrong when we consider that the Madrid train bombers of March 2004, the London terrorists of July 2005, the Norwegian assassin of the Utøya island massacre in 2011 or the Charlie Hebdo and Bataclan attackers in 2015 were in fact, during their everyday life, students, workers and apparently quite decent members of their metropolitan neighborhood. For the most part, they were born, raised and educated in that country. There is no doubt that this kind of event is always quite complex and every serious assessment of it has to delve into multiple social, historical and political layers to find something approaching a plausible understanding of the causes. Moreover, behind such violent and tragic acts even the most insightful inquiry at some point meets a thick area of opacity and irrationality that cannot be entirely driven away. However, there is little doubt that, among other issues these phenomena raise, a significant share of concern goes to questions about the sense and scope of what it means to be a citizen: is citizenship adequately understood when defined as a mere legal status? What moves citizens to active and respectful public engagement? What grounds the relationship between the everyday activity of people in the field of civil society and their self-understanding as responsible citizens? Which reasons can support a normative view of what a citizen should be within the increasingly globalized and pluralistic landscape of contemporary societies? And what kind of motivation can drive people from different cultures, religions and origins to act cooperatively towards common goals even beyond their short-term self-interest?

P. Monti (✉)
Università Cattolica del Sacro Cuore, Milan, Italy
e-mail: Paolo.Monti@unicatt.it

D. Thunder (ed.), *The Ethics of Citizenship in the 21st Century*,
DOI 10.1007/978-3-319-50415-5_8

These ethical features of citizenship in democratic societies can be explored from several different perspectives, including the normative principles of the discursive public sphere, the requirements entailed by political agreements, the obligations that come from membership in a specific political entity. The account articulated here is grounded on the analysis of our condition of *co-practitioners* in civil society. I am going to argue that this kind of approach offers a conceptual contribution to the clarification of several ongoing debates over the problem of persisting disagreements in plural societies, the role and boundaries of religion in the public square and the limits and possibilities of democratic political representation. I also argue that this perspective can ground an ethics of citizenship sensitive to the situation of contemporary postsecular societies where the processes of secularization transformed, but did not remove, the public relevance of religions.

Social Practices and Civil Society

As active members of society – as workers, activists, consumers, players, etc. – we find ourselves constantly participating in numerous social practices and these practices come with different sets of embedded beliefs, rules and values. Our participation in this web of evolving, diverse and often interconnected practices places us within a texture of diffused social cooperation that constitutes the body of civil society.

By social practices I understand here, roughly, complex cooperative human activities, persistent in time and aiming at the achievement and progressive realization of their internal ends, in the light of shared cognitive representations.[1] The organic nature of practices and their duration and evolution in time is explained through the role played within them by linguistic repertoires and shared narratives. These define a constantly active repository of shared cognitive pictures within which the actions of different subjects are intentionally planned, reciprocally interpreted and collaboratively realized in the light of some shared beliefs, based on some shared reasons for acting, from some shared motivations and towards some ends determined within a set of relevant values. Education, research, medicine, and professions in general, are all definable as distinct fields of practice. The same can be said, though, of arts, sports and games. In some cases, the notion of practices serves to describe broad fields of agency, like cooking or caretaking, while in other cases it is applied to specific activities, like literary critique or growing bonsai trees. No matter how broadly or narrowly we look at social practices, when we think of our participation in the life of civil society we constantly refer to a set of practices whose inner workings are appropriately captured by this conceptual frame.

[1] The account of social practices sketched here draws from different sources, namely MacIntyre (1981), Schatzki (1996), Audi (2001), Tuomela (2002). For a more specific account of social practices and their epistemological implications, see also Monti (2012).

Particularly relevant to our purpose here, is the fact that the internal cohesion of a practice is not based exclusively on the practitioners opting for similar rational choices or on the application of common rules, but also on some shared understandings about their beliefs and the sense of their agency. As T.R. Schatzki notes:

> People's lives hang together not only through cooperation and rationality as well as conformity to ends, norms and rules, but also through understanding and intelligibility. Think for instance of how people brought up in the same culture typically understand objects in settings alike. No matter how ubiquitous and decisive normative regulation and cooperation-rationality-knowledge may be for human coexistence, this additional medium of coexistence accompanies and/or underlies their contribution to sociality and social order.[2]

Those who participate in a practice are thus embedded within a network of understanding and intelligibility that identifies the relevant meanings of the objects of their experience and the sense of their personal agency in that context. The activity of an art critic, for example, is not just a matter of specific means employed towards specific ends. The practice also encompasses an especially rich experience of the works of art, a certain understanding of what separates a good critic from a bad one, some sense of how art and its evaluation matter in the broader social context, standards of integrity required by the profession and so on. It is especially because of this that we always come to articulate some understanding of the relationship between our role within the specific practices we participate in – at work, in our free time, while taking care of someone or something we hold dear – and our sense of identity as a whole – which generally includes some broad moral, religious and political outlook. Even the most specific areas of cooperative activity we engage in bring into play some normative ideal of personal agency and some ethical requirements coming from the relationship with a broader circle of co-practitioners, interlocutors and competitors. For this reason, the social practices people join in civil society are an area of "permeability", where the self-understanding of the person as a practitioner has an influence over the self-understanding of the person as a whole, but also where deep personal convictions affect the way that person participates in the practice and interacts with her co-practitioners. From a social point of view, this is particularly apparent if we look at communities of practice, where the standards, beliefs and values relative to the practice are constantly developed and transmitted to new generations of practitioners. Workplaces, schools, universities, and hospitals are places where multiple practices are perfected and taught, but also where people are exposed to each other's personal beliefs, beyond the scope of the practice itself.[3] At this level, the forms of cooperation that are

---

[2] Schatzki (1996), 16.

[3] On this topic, see Raz (2003: 34–36). Joseph Raz argues that most values are dependent on a practice that sustains them. Some values, however, do not. Most notably, the value of people. As valuers, people are capable of appreciating and respecting values: they are indirectly dependent on the practices that make possible the existence of those values, but not for their value as persons. Even if we adopt a view that heavily links values to practices, by considering most values to be practice-relative, the person's value is not necessarily limited to the role of the person as a practitioner. On the other hand, though, the person will still come to experience and appreciate many identity-defining values only as an active participant in certain practices.

typical of civil society interact with the more general sets of personal representations and beliefs that characterize the moral, religious and political spheres. This cross-contamination is strikingly evidenced by the fact that most actors of civil society bring with them some kind of ideological or religious baggage and, conversely, many political and religious movements are born and developed from the grounds of civil activism.

It is primarily in this cooperative and practical fashion that, by inhabiting a public space with our diverse beliefs – moral and technical, religious and secular, etc. –, we also find ourselves implicated with others and their beliefs. The objects, standards and purposes of our practices are to some extent shaped by the presence of beliefs that differ from our own, since those beliefs are held by people who are, directly or indirectly, our co-practitioners at various levels of social life. It is often in this way that our beliefs are challenged and re-adjusted: through the constant interaction with the beliefs of our co-practitioners.

The different ways our personal beliefs come to interact with those of others we cooperate with is determined by the specific self-understanding that those co-practitioners entertain about the relationship between their personal beliefs and their social agency. The nature of this self-understanding, which articulates how personal beliefs and social agency are mutually related, is crucial when it comes to the kind of interaction that citizens have among themselves and to the way their beliefs become reciprocally influential and relevant. Let us explore this point in greater detail to determine how it can be relevant for the subject of citizenship.

Making Sense of Public Agency

In recent decades, the wide-ranging debate on the scope of public reason and the boundaries of liberal democracy has frequently focused on the place of certain beliefs and reasons – notably, but not exclusively, the religious ones – in public discourse and formal political deliberation. However, the challenge of pluralism is a more pervasive issue and often exceeds the way beliefs and reasons enter the arguments of our discursive public sphere (Salvatore 2010). Besides the extreme phenomena of terrorism and social conflict, this also appears when dealing with our everyday co-practitioners as agents that hold certain fundamental beliefs and act from different self-understandings of their sense of public agency. Most of us are familiar with experiences like the uneasiness of meeting someone that is apparently being generous, sincere and just while, at the same time, publicly holding fundamental beliefs that are divergent from ours. Or consider the difficulty of interacting with someone that holds convictions very different from ours but that, at the same time, is a colleague we have to work with. The crucial point in these situations is the tension that each person has to articulate between her most important personal beliefs and moral convictions on one side and her self-understanding as an agent involved in public cooperative practices on the other.

What are the implications of this self-understanding of the relationship between cooperative social agency and identity-defining beliefs? While cooperating, the agents share their actions, literally their operations, within the field of some social practice. On the one hand, their actions are based on the specific assumptions of each practice – like its rules, standards and know-how's. In this sense, the practitioner's actions are shaped by practice-relative criteria. Additionally, when performing a specific role in a practice, the agents are under the influence of beliefs that constitute their sense of personal identity, such as their moral values and standards of personal integrity, fairness, honesty. The practitioner's actions represent a way of to meet the standards of the practice as well as to work out a more general moral self-understanding. Regardless of the limited scope of the practice at hand, the realm of deep, personal commitments comes into play and shapes the self-understanding that people bring into the social space. It is evident when this self-understanding is dissonant among practitioners of the same area, but even when it is not particularly apparent, say because a certain kind of understanding is positively shared among most co-practitioners, it is nonetheless at work. A shared self-understanding confers a high degree of like-mindedness between people who are not just pursuing the same kind of activity oriented towards a certain end, but who are also enacting a certain sense of what it means to be good agents, both in general and within that field of practice. When different self-understandings of what it means to be a good agent come into conflict in the same field of practice, though, people become seriously aware of the presence of different identity-defining beliefs. The fact of pluralism becomes all of a sudden extremely relevant as we stumble into it in the realm of social cooperation.

Our liberal and democratic settings largely rely on a traditionally modern self-understanding of the public agent that tends to separate comprehensive agent identities from public agency to minimize the clash of beliefs. The functionalist outlook that underpins the organization of our workplaces and the bureaucratic rationality of our public administrations contribute to this attempt of separating as much as possible these two sides, to allow for a smoother flow of cooperation between the diverse actors of our plural societies. An abundance of potential conflicts is addressed this way but, under some circumstances, this separation is problematic. The debate here is vast and, for the purposes of the present account, I will just mention two critical points.

First, the boundaries between the private and the public are mobile and sometimes fuzzy: the symbols and garments people wear, the kind of food they give to their children, the medications they receive are all examples of how deeply personal and intimate some issues of public concern may be. Some of the most heated controversies on the place of religion in the public square have stemmed from these uncertain boundaries: the ban of the Islamic veil in the French classroom, the compatibility of the Sikh turban with positions as officers of the law, the demand for kosher and halal food in public canteens and so on.

Second, our self-understanding and our other-understanding are connected and, thus, constantly challenged: as sharp and deep as our separation of public roles and personal convictions may be, the need to cooperate with people who articulate that relationship differently pushes us to deal with their resulting agency and to reframe our own understanding accordingly. How our religious beliefs should influence our dealings with colleagues or how our personal moral principles should come into play when dealing with customers coming from different backgrounds are, in fact, quite basic questions in our social life and our effort to respond appropriately is not bereft of consequences for how we understand the balance between our personal convictions and our public agency.

On this approach, our fundamental beliefs are not just mere pieces of content placed in the pluralistic space of public communication and debate. The way those beliefs impact our life is also constantly mediated through the understanding of our role as public agents, particularly as co-practitioners with others that may, or may not, share our beliefs and their implications over the boundaries of the public setting we inevitably share. Civil society mirrors this geography of diverse self-understandings with its pluralistic and varied composition. Social enterprises, different forms of associative life, churches and religious organization, humanitarian groups, advocacy groups, cultural and artistic movements, trade unions, charities, sport and gaming clubs: these entities express different levels of connection between a certain form of social agency and a more or less defined moral, religious and cultural identity. Within this diverse landscape, each individual is often involved in more than one community of practice at the same time, thus holding different kinds of membership, dealing with different kinds of co-practitioners, acting in different fields and always trying to make sense of his or her self-understanding as both agent and believer. This is not always an easy relationship and the arrangements individuals and groups achieve are often temporary and precarious. Sometimes the deepest identity-defining beliefs work positively as a source of justification and commitment for forms of fruitful civil engagement that aim at various collective goods. Other times, though, the clash between strong identities within the field of social practices may be disruptive, to the point of harming or even halting the flow of cooperative effort. Inasmuch as civil life proves crucial to the overall conservation and development of our increasingly complex and plural societies, we are pushed to consider the relevance of this subject in the realm of the political, and particularly the normative entailments of the condition of being a citizen and participating in political discourse and the life of democratic institutions.

From Civil Society to Active Citizenship

Understanding civil society as a web of practices enacted by individuals whose condition as both believers and co-practitioners is shaped and challenged by their cooperative interaction has important implications for how we describe and design the processes of public deliberation and political representation. These processes largely rely, in fact, on that civil ground of diffused social cooperation and engage the members of civil society in specific sets of political practices that aim to preserve and develop the conditions of that cooperation. By engaging in public discussion, deliberation and advocacy, the individuals, as citizens, express, negotiate and re-asses many of their own beliefs. The participation in these structured forms of discursive and cooperative deliberation constantly puts in question the sets of beliefs people hold about what is just, what kinds of needs are a priority and how their own personal claims should be reconciled with the claims of others. A significant amount of empirical research conducted through deliberative exercises shows a correlation between the engagement in cooperative practices aimed at establishing the allocation of scarce resources and a shift in the conception of just distribution and the assessment of the priority of needs among co-practitioners.[4] This should not come as a surprise as long as we assume, as I have suggested so far, that it is mostly by being compelled to cooperate with someone else in a public setting that we are in fact also substantially exposed to his or her beliefs.

As I mentioned earlier, however, most debates on the boundaries of public reason in the past few decades have revolved around the preemptive definition of subsets of beliefs and reasons that should be allowed in the public square, in light of a concept of universally acceptable reasons that are deemed appropriate for a transparent political discourse equally accessible to all citizens. This is especailly true of the large debate on public reason, in particular for or against the Rawlsian "principle of restraint". The principle is intended both as a *proviso* and as a duty of civility. As a proviso, it requires politicians and officials to express their comprehensive views – religious or secular – in formal political settings only as long as they also provide political reasons that can be understood and agreed upon by all citizens. As a duty of civility, it requires citizens to vote on the basis of political reasons that can be understood and agreed upon by their fellow citizens regardless of their comprehensive doctrines.[5] The public reason approach grasps, indeed, a normative ideal that we should treasure when facing the issue of being co-implicated with others in pluralistic settings. In particular, when it comes to citizenship, it articulates in contemporary terms the fundamental democratic ideal of citizens as both subjects and co-authors of the law, insofar as their political conduct is justified based on universally accessible reasons. On the other hand, the focus on the formal political settings and on the procedures of representative democracy is certainly not the whole picture of what is at stake in the complex and far from ideal setting of our social life. Developing the debate on public reason with a privileged attention towards these areas of political life is misleading, since the understandings and motivations that citizens enact in those circumstances are generally conceived and developed in much more basic and less formalized contexts of social cooperation. As we have seen, in dealing with others

[4] See Danis et al. (2004, 2007, 2010). These studies, in particular, are related to the development of an interesting deliberative tool, CHAT – "Choosing Healthplans All Together" – used to determine public opinion about what should be included in basic health insurance packages for the uninsured. CHAT has been adapted and applied in several different cultural and economic settings, from the United States to developing countries. One of the most noteworthy results is the shift in the attitudes of the participants that after engaging in the cooperative exercise become more inclined to assume community-oriented priorities over strictly individual ones, which usually prevailed at the beginning of the process. Similar interesting findings come from other cases of structured deliberation and civic participation, such as in instances of participatory budgeting and citizens' juries.

[5] Rawls (1993: 444–466).

as co-practitioners we are dealing also with their different understanding of the relationship between their identity-defining beliefs and their public agency. This general insight becomes especially relevant when representative claims arising from the cooperative texture of civil society become explicitly political.

The democratic system, which creates and nurtures the conditions of this widespread pluralism, is challenged by the need to integrate the diversity of self-understandings that its citizens express and to provide them with fair and effective conditions of access to the space of public deliberation, where their representative claims can be expressed and debated. As Robert Talisse noted, pluralism is often construed as a diversity of views and values that leads to disagreements among citizens on relevant issues. Democratic procedures would offer the adequate framework for these disagreements to be negotiated. This perspective, however, overlooks the fact that this assumption of negotiability is the source of the most profound disagreements. The negotiability of disagreements needs constantly to be arranged, by defining a form of self-understanding that allows for it:

> There is a good reason to think that citizens cannot adopt such a self-understanding without transforming and thus violating the values they hold most dear; for, according to many citizens, their moral commitments – along with their particular understandings of justice, liberty, dignity, equality, and the right and the good – are prior to their democratic commitments.[6]

If these conflicting self-understandings, and the scope of their possible transformations, are crucial to any serious attempt to deal with what has been called by Talisse the problem of 'deep politics',[7] the critical implications of pluralism in our societies cannot be truly faced through the mere exercise of formalized and regulated negotiations within the pre-defined boundaries of a public reason. The possibility of democratic deliberation and negotiation is in fact based in the first place on the development of shared attitudes and understandings that citizens develop and adjust in their everyday experiences of cooperation at least as much as in their formal participation in democratic procedures. On the view I am articulating here, these self-understandings are seen as largely mediated by the roles actively undertaken by the citizens at a pre-political level, as members of civil society, and especially by the reflective understanding of how their personal moral and possibly religious commitments are to be related to the larger cooperative context they are embedded in.

This awareness of the implications of social cooperation for one's self-understanding in pluralistic contexts sheds useful light on recent debates on the concepts of postsecular society and political representation. Below, I will explain how this is so, and then suggest how, on the basis of such awareness, it may be possible, or even morally required, to question or shift one's own self-understanding in relation with the condition of being discursively and practically co-implicated with others as citizens in a democratic setting.

---

[6] Talisse (2009: 35).

[7] See Talisse (2009: 11–41).

On Religious Commitment and Political Representation

This conceptual frame focused on our condition as co-practitioners in civil society is especially useful in clarifying both (a) the ongoing debate on the role and limits of religion in the public square and (b) the renewed interest in the problem of how the representative claim is justified, formulated and democratically institutionalized in modern democracies.

On one hand, (a) the debate over the unexpected upsurge in the relevance of religion in political affairs has attracted a good share of attention in several fields, ranging from political theory and sociology of religion to law and political science. The crisis of the standard theories of secularization, that expected the disappearance, or at least extreme privatization, of religious beliefs, prepared the ground for a new set of views. Among these, the postsecular stance, as defined by Habermas (2006), Taylor (2007) and others (Gorski et al. 2012; Nynäs et al. 2012), has provided a substantial contribution to the understanding of the consequences of religious pluralism in contexts of late secularization. The Habermasian perspective builds on Habermas's analysis of the processes of modernizations and the setbacks of the discursive public sphere, acknowledging the persisting role of religions in articulating and sustaining crucial forms of social cooperation:

> The balance between the three principal media of societal integration achieved over the course of modernity is being jeopardized because markets and administrative power are displacing social solidarity – i.e. the coordination of action through values, norms, and language use oriented to reaching understanding – from ever more domains of social life. Thus, it is also in the interest of the constitutional state to conserve all cultural sources that nurture citizens' solidarity and their normative awareness. This conservative turn finds expression in talk of the "postsecular society".
>
> By this is meant not only the fact that religion must maintain its position in an increasingly secular environment and that society must anticipate that religious communities will continue to exist. […] The public consciousness of a postsecular society reflects, rather, a normative insight that has implications for political interactions between religious and non-religious citizens (Habermas 2008, 111).

The notion of postsecularity in Habermas captures some descriptive aspects of the transformation of democratic societies in recent decades, but also points to some interesting normative implications that come from the increasing awareness of that prolonged co-existence of secular and religious outlooks within the same contexts. I argue that this transformation of the public conscience is mostly due to how the persisting co-implication of religious and secular cooperative actors within the same public space affects their self-understanding as religious and secular citizens that share a setting whose political boundaries and symbolic resources are not defined exclusively by one side or the other. A large chunk of the scholarly discussion about the crisis of the standard theory of secularization (see Martin 2005; Berger 1999, 2010; Casanova 1994, 2006; Calhoun et al. 2011) has focused on how the definition of secular perspectives is in fact internally and dialectically indebted to the on-going transformation of religious worldviews and vice versa. This transformative process mutually binds the diverse self-understandings that the social actors bring into the public sphere to the point that neither the secular nor the religious perspective can claim an exclusive ownership over the pre-political foundations of our social and political life, ranging from the standards of rational discourse to the resources of public justification and motivation.

On the other hand, (b) the debate over the nature and limits of political representation in democratic national societies – and, more and more, in a global civil society – has increasingly focused on the multiple meanings of representation beyond the formalized procedures of voting and electing[8] and on a constructivist perspective about the formation of the representative claim (Saward 2005). This approach construes the processes of political representation as made up of distinct practices that generate, communicate and empower original representations rather than processes that merely express pre-existing cultural or religious identities. As Michael Saward explains:

> The view presented here suggests that the political science sense of representation – someone standing for or acting for someone else – requires that attention be paid to representation in the cultural studies sense: the making of depictions or portrayals of others. To act for someone is unavoidably to portray them in a certain way as well. [...] To represent is to do much more than see just what a constituency wants and to replicate what they want. Invariably, there will not be clear 'want', but rather a mixed and shifting set of preferences, half preferences and apathy that a would-be representative must shape, mould, quite possibly 'create' and try to sell back to the relevant constituency (Saward 2005, 189).

By shaping beliefs and images that are subsequently resold to the represented, the representatives engage in the practices of political representation as a struggle to build new cognitive and symbolic pictures that the represented can in turn come to buy and accept as their own to make sense of their political relationship with others (Barnett 2004). On this view, as Saward notes, "political representation is a process that involves the constitution of the identity of the representative and the represented" (Saward 2005, 183). I argue that, in this sense, the representative processes are not effective primarily because they express pre-existing identities and beliefs but rather because they successfully shape a certain self-understanding of what it means to be a political agent that fosters new possibilities and directions of social cooperation in the light of certain beliefs. The content of certain traditional identity-defining beliefs may be left unchanged, but the transformation of the self-understandings of the actors at stake effectively shifts their sense of identity in different ways. At this level there is also an essential role for political leadership, a role that is generally mistrusted by deliberative democrats, due to their noble but dangerously abstract ideal of argumentative debate and rational deliberation.[9]

[8] On this perspective, see the seminal works by Urbinati and Warren (2008) and Castiglione and Warren (2006).

[9] See Szakolczai (2013). Arpad Szakolczai argues that the modern idealization of the public sphere as the space of rational argumentation and reasonable agreements has in fact disguised the reality of a public arena where theatrical repertoires of comical representation and ridiculing of the interlocutor occupy the main stages of public visibility and play a crucial role in directing public opinion. Even without sharing all his conclusions and the sharp critique of the Habermasian project, his analysis is quite effective in showing how far some of the main lines of political theory have wandered from the reality of everyday public discourse and political practice.

While political leadership must always be guarded against the temptations of autocracy, it can also play a decisive role in embodying and publicly representing certain understandings of how some identity-defining beliefs and some forms of public agency can be positively interpreted, re-interpreted and articulated in a pluralistic setting.

Both debates, on the role and limits of religion in the public square and on the formulation of representative claims, deserve a more in-depth discussion that we cannot pursue here. My concern for now is to show how both these lines of argument take seriously the political implications of the shifting self-understandings of citizens. In this context, I suggest that some basic normative features of democratic citizenship may find adequate ground in the reflective consideration of the cooperative relationships that ordinarily substantiate citizens' agency in civil society. With this purpose in mind, we can now turn to consider which kind of ethical implications can be drawn from the premises laid out so far.

A First Sketch of an Ethics of Citizenship

If the picture we have drawn is plausible, the reflective reconsideration of our constitutive co-implication with others as co-practitioners brings to light how this co-implication also defines, more or less directly, our beliefs and our sense of identity as members of a pluralist civil society that hold and justify certain beliefs by being exposed to the beliefs of others. I argue that this, in turn, grounds a moral duty of responsibility towards the integrity and development of that society and that one's own self-understanding of the relationship between identity-defining beliefs and public cooperative roles is brought into question and transformed by this duty. Rather than insisting on the separation between identity-defining beliefs and social cooperation, this view suggests to focus on the implications of our involvement in social cooperation for our identity-defining beliefs and the way we hold them.

Since the development of one's own fundamental beliefs is tested and shaped through the interaction with one's own co-practitioners, every citizen should act responsibly towards the preservation and development of that basic web of cooperation, as a pre-condition not only of their own social agency, but also of their own personal beliefs and reasons for action. This responsibility is primarily carried out through the discursive involvement of citizens in the institutional processes of public deliberation and political representation, but is also constantly developed in the informal public sphere. This discursive involvement requires the citizens to keep a 'conversational' attitude (Rorty 2003), upon the reflective awareness that by belonging to the web of civil society they are already belonging to a communicative sphere where the beliefs of others are inseparable from their participation in the cooperative body of civil society.

This conversational attitude may be essentially defined as a commitment to positively foster, and negatively not to stop, the civil conversation among citizens as co-practitioners. The responsibility to hold such an attitude can be expressed by two interconnected normative claims:

(i) The involvement in a cooperative web of social practices demands an attitude open to the discursive and critical public assessment of one's own beliefs based on a reflective awareness that one's own involvement in that cooperative web of relationships with others, and their beliefs, is already in some way internal to the formation of one's own beliefs. Denying this practical and cognitive co-implication with others contradicts the resources of one's own self-understanding as a holder of beliefs who inhabits a certain public sphere, since those resources are always to some extent the result of a cooperative interaction. Consequently, refusing to assume a discursive and critical public attitude contradicts the conditions of one's own participation in social practices at large and the processes of justification of one's own beliefs.
(ii) The reflective awareness of the co-implication between the actors of civil society requires a cognitive disposition to also eventually re-arrange and re-formulate one's own arguments and beliefs to deal cooperatively with the arguments and beliefs of others. The practical involvement in a web of civil cooperation, and the enjoyment of the social goods that come from it, requires, as a condition for its own preservation and development, a similar cooperative disposition when it comes to the public formation, communication and mutual justification of beliefs.

All citizens should equally enter into a shared conversation with their own beliefs[10] and with their own self-understandings, provided that in time they become reflectively aware of the fact that, by doing so, they expose their beliefs to the cooperative nature of a shared conversation and are thus expected to cooperatively join a process of reformulation, justification, enrichment and even falsification of their own views. The awareness of this essential co-implication of one's own personal beliefs with those of others who share the same public square establishes the grounds of an ethics of citizenship where the cooperative aspects of civil society are reflectively transferred to the realm of political engagement.

This approach to an ethics of citizenship articulates the notion of a reflectively responsible self-understanding of the relationship between one's own identity-defining beliefs and public social agency: everyone is dependent on social cooperation and is in some way responsible for it but, at the same time, nobody owns entirely its constitutive cognitive and motivational resources. The ramifications of the responsibility of citizens for the preservation of the basic web of cooperation of civil society extend both to their ordinary conduct as members of their community and to their active involvement in the processes of formal political representation. In particular, within this normative perspective the enactment of public representative claims – about a certain identity or cause or conviction – should always preserve the integrity of the basic cooperative fabric of civil society against the potential

[10] For a different take on this attempt of sketching an ethics of citizenship that allows citizens to bring their own comprehensive beliefs as justifications into the public debate, see Clanton (2008).

overriding force of specific identity claims, whether of a political, religious, cultural or ethnic nature. In this sense, social conversation and cooperation are the most elementary common good of society, as they are an essential condition for the pursuit of every other good.

Disagreement and Conflict

Society is not just a place of diffused cooperation. Struggles for the balance of power and redistribution of wealth are pervasive. Injustice and mistrust, quite often built upon long histories of conflict and separation, constantly undermine the grounds of peaceful social co-existence. In some ways, modern political thought was born with Machiavelli and Hobbes precisely by putting the phenomenon of conflict and violence on the central stage of political theory. This account grounds a normative perspective on citizenship focused on the interaction of citizens in the field of social practices, and as such accords primacy to cooperation over conflict in the grounding of politics. That does not mean, though, that phenomena of extreme disagreement and conflict should be disregarded. Ethical perspectives are not meant to eliminate the possibility of evil, but to properly makes sense of it and articulate reasons to oppose it that any relevant actor should be able to understand and act upon.

In any society, full-fledged positions of estrangement and open conflict remain a live possibility that exceeds the boundaries of ordinary disagreement. I argue, though, that in pluralistic democratic societies the citizens who take that kind of extreme stance reveal, in some way, how deeply their own beliefs are intertwined with ‘foreign’ beliefs and with those who hold them. It is striking to consider the level of internal dissonance and manipulation that shapes the self-understanding of many inside our contemporary liberal societies, sometimes to the point of leading them to the deepest forms of estrangement, revolt and terrorism on religious and ideological grounds. From an ethical perspective, we can argue that such dissonance and manipulation is not only unacceptable from the point of view of the majorities – presumably western, democratic and maybe secular or Christian –, but it is also performatively self-defeating under the perspective of those who enact it. The recent episodes of terrorism in London, Madrid or Paris from which we started our reflections are quite telling. The individuals who enacted those attacks were all in a sense fighting against themselves, insofar as they were violently against the very social resources of cooperative origin that defined their defensive self-understanding, in a twisted way, as enemies of that pluralist, liberal and cooperative setting they were born and educated in. The suicidal attacks that mark the sad epilogue of many of these episodes are the tragic metaphor of a self-contradictory stance they had taken against their own identity as cooperative agents of a certain society. It is not by chance that contemporary religious fundamentalisms are, in many ways, not a heritage of the past, but a by-product of modernity, a way of thinking what being a faithful religious believer implies that was conceived within a secular horizon, mostly as a form of reaction and defense of it. A reflective awareness of one's own conditions of belief within a pluralistic public square can lead to a self-critical re-assessment and, consequently, enable an enduring conversation precisely because it grasps how the conversation with others is already in some way internal to one's own beliefs, as estranged as they may appear from the beliefs of others. The reflective reconsideration of the essentially social pre-conditions of one's own point of view require one to reshape accordingly one's self-understanding as a member of that society.

Not all situations of estrangement end in violence. However, a condition of persisting detachment, skepticism and opposition towards the sphere of democratic discourse and civic engagement can still be damaging for the life of political institutions and, ultimately, for the condition of a flourishing society. In dealing with the issue of persisting disagreements, it is important to distinguish between absolute conversation stops and relative conversation halts. Violence and suppression of the interlocutors are the most obvious cases of absolute conversation stops, but strong insulation and indifference may count as well. Established disagreements on normative issues, electoral outcomes or the promulgation of a certain piece of legislation are typical instances of relative conversation halts.[11] The latter category, the relative conversation halts, still falls within the conversational requirements we enunciated above: it is a form of punctuation that articulates the conversation but does not end it. In a situation of relative halt, the citizens can keep the conversation going. They are still in a conversational relationship, even if they might have to slightly readjust the terms of the discursive process from that point on. A controversial political decision on ethically sensitive issues like, say, stem cell research or assisted suicide, may create a situation in between a relative halt and a full stop to the conversation. In these troubled times for public discourse, a reflective framework that focuses on the ethical self-understandings of citizens rather than on the negotiation of the interests at stake may prove useful to keep the conversation going. The requirement (i) to assume an attitude open to the discursive and critical public assessment of one's own beliefs does not entail an expectation that one's interlocutors drop their religious or secular standpoint about matters of deepest concern. It serves, though, to avoid the shift from a situation of halt to one of full conversational stop. As long as the conversation is not closed, but only temporarily paused, the requirement (ii) to eventually re-arrange and re-formulate one's own arguments and beliefs to deal cooperatively with the arguments and beliefs of others can effectively direct conflicting citizens to pursue a further discursive evolution of the state of affairs, or at least to allow others to do it. The only self-understanding that is strictly un-conversational is one that actively rejects any co-implication with the beliefs of others and consequently undermines the possibility of a discursive mediation of social conflicts.

[11] Stout (2003), Wolterstorff (2012: 47–49).

Conclusion: A Postsecular Ethics of Citizenship

The account articulated here sketches the fundamentals of an ethics of citizenship based on a reflective take on the conditions of cooperative agency in pluralist societies. This sketch is grounded in a distinct characterization of (a) citizenship, (b) ethical normativity, and (c) the postsecular. I will conclude by summarizing this triple characterization, thus providing a tentative summary of the implications of my proposal and pointing to its possible further development.

As a view of (a) citizenship, it is multi-layered, reflecting our multi-layered belonging and participation in several levels of civil society, whether locally, nationally, or globally. This notion of citizenship is in fact not bound to membership in a specific kind of institutional, political entity. Rather, it emerges from the participation, which may be more or less active, in a body of social practices that may extend to different kinds of communal practices. In contemporary societies, we are simultaneously participating in multiple webs of cooperation that, through internet and social media, connect local communities and worldwide ones around either very specific fields of agency or very broad public causes. Our participation in public deliberation and democratic representation still happen for the most part through geographically and historically defined political institutions, but the sovereignty of these institutions is increasingly challenged and the result of this struggle is unclear, even unsettling to some extent. On the other hand, representative claims often develop beyond the boundaries of national states, to the point that on several global issues it has become more and more frequent to refer to a transnational public sphere whose actors range from formal international organizations to NGOs and social movements. Being an active citizen in this context may or may not involve some formal belongings to political entities, but it is always grounded in a communal practice.

As an (b) ethical view, it is normative by pointing to a reflective and conversational style of public agency rather than to the requirements of formalized membership. It suggests the articulation of a habitus of social responsibility more than the establishment of a set of rules and procedures. In other words, the kind of normative stance this approach suggest is, in fact, not rule-like, but rather virtue-like. It suggests a certain style of citizen agency grounded on a reflective self-understanding of the citizens as co-practitioners. The notion of style points to the connection between personal identity and public agency that is at stake in the self-understanding of people as co-practitioners.[12] The co-existence of citizens within a shared public sphere cannot be regulated only by transferring the conflict into a fixed set of procedural boundaries for the negotiation of individual beliefs and collective interests. The reflective attitude over our essential co-implication as social agents that I have illustrated is embedded within a wider, more substantial ethical picture. Citizenship

[12] In arts and literature, a style is generally something personal, which belongs to an author or a group, but also clearly public and recognizable. For a compelling account of the notion of style along these normative lines, a major reference is the theological work of C. Theobald (2007).

is always practically interpreted in different ways by different individuals, based on their different self-understandings as public agents. There will always be different ways of being a citizen, since people will always be Catholic, Atheist, Agnostic, Islamic, Protestant, Buddhist citizens. The two sides cannot be entirely severed, regardless of what our modern imaginaries tried to suggest with the sharp dichotomy between public and private (Taylor 2004, 83–107). At the same time, though, it is reflectively reasonable to expect that those citizens should attune their personal style of citizenship to their condition of structural co-implication with others, because of the reflective acknowledgement that their own identity is based on the inextricable cooperative interaction of their differences. The role of traits like hospitality, openness to conversation, and disposition to self-critical re-assessment are variously enacted as traits of different styles of citizenship, but also need to be attuned to the awareness of being defined and meaningful within a texture of social cooperation inhabited by others, which demands to be conversationally maintained and developed. Every religious and secular tradition is thus pushed, to a certain extent, from the focus on external conflicts back into its internal debate, where the definition of its plausible self-understandings is debated and where the viability of different public styles is forged. Attempts of radically refuting and denying that kind of structural co-implication will probably always happen, as they have happened in recent decades. However, the emphasis on un-conversational, partisan attitudes did not lead to the victory of either side, but rather to an increasing lack of confidence in the discursive resources of society as a whole and to the consequent risk of a post-democratic condition[13] that sees the rise of technocratic and economic paradigms as the dominating normative horizons of social life.

As a (c) postsecular perspective, the framework presented here aims to offer a normative stance that takes into account the resilience of secular and religious traditions in the contemporary political landscape. Those traditions were not dissolved by the crisis of grand narratives typical of the postmodern frame, but they were internally unsettled when it comes to their epistemic and practical claims. The consequences of the long historical processes of secularization brought about conservative reactions, religious and secular alike, but also fostered unexpected transformative processes of self-critique, translation, and cooperation.[14] The ethical outlook I have articulated here, like the postsecular, focuses on the plurality of self-understandings that citizens carry into the public sphere rather than on the diversity of contents that characterizes their beliefs. In this sense, an ethics of citizenship offers normative guidance for navigating shifting interpretations and self-reassessments, where religious and secular identities are co-implicated and need to arrange their inevitable co-implication in a discursive way rather than by engaging in self-defeating, radically adversarial strategies.

On this kind of account, the boundaries of public discourse are, to some extent, always the outcome of a cooperative process. Even controversies, as deep as they can be, are grounded in a situation of co-implication where each side defines its own

[13] See Crouch (2004).

[14] See Casanova (1994, 2006).

stances while exposed to those of others and defined by involvement within the same public space. As I have argued, everyone, as a member of civil society, is dependent on social cooperation but, at the same time, nobody can claim exclusive ownership over it. The reflexive assumption of this co-implication with the interlocutors should lead to develop and constantly adjust a consistent self-understanding as a citizen. From this perspective, acting as a citizen goes well beyond meeting certain formal requirements of membership. It is rather a way of joining the public conversation that reflects the ability to distinguish between personal and public narratives, individual commitments and public bonds, but also to cooperatively build new forms of self-understanding that foster the possibility of building, searching, educating, playing and reflecting together.

References

Audi, R. (2001). *The architecture of reason*. Oxford: Oxford University Press.

Barnett, C. (2004) Media, democracy and representation: Disembodying the public, in C. Barnett–M. Low (ed.), Spaces of democracy: Geographical perspectives on citizenship, participation and representation, London: SAGE.

Berger, P. (1999). *The desecularization of the world. A global overview*. Grand Rapids: W.B. Eerdmans.

Berger, P. (2010). Between relativism and fundamentalism. In P. Berger (Ed.), *Between relativism and fundamentalism: Religious resources for a middle position*. Eerdmans: Grand Rapids.

Calhoun, C., Juergensmeyer, M., & VanAntwerpen, J. (Eds.). (2011). *Rethinking secularism*. Oxford: Oxford University Press.

Casanova, J. (1994). *Public religions in the modern world*. Chicago/London: The University of Chicago Press.

Casanova, J. (2006). Religion, European secular identities, and European integration. In T. Byrnes & P. Katzenstein (Eds.), *Religion in an expanding Europe*. Cambridge: Cambridge University Press.

Castiglione, D., & Warren, M. E. (2006). *Rethinking democratic representation: Eight theoretical issues*. Prepared for delivery to "Rethinking Democratic Representation. Centre for the Study of Democratic Institutions University of British Columbia, 18–19 May, 2006.

Clanton, J. C. (2008). *Religion and democratic citizenship: Inquiry and conviction in the American public square*. Lanham: Lexington Books.

Crouch, C. (2004). *Post-democracy*. New York: Wiley.

Danis, M., Biddle, A. K., & Goold, S. D. (2004). Enrollees choose priorities for medicare. *The Gerontologist, 44*(1), 58–67.

Danis, M., Binnendijk, E., Vellakkal, S., Ost, A., Koren, R., & Dror, D. M. (2007). Eliciting health insurance benefit choices of low income groups. *Economic and Political Weekly, 42*(32), 3331–3339.

Danis, M., Ginsburg, M., & Goold, S. (2010). Experience in the United States with public deliberation about health insurance benefits using the small group decision exercise, CHAT. *The Journal of Ambulatory Care Management, 33*(3), 205–214.

Gorski, P. S., Kyuman Kim, D., Torpey, J., & VanAntwerpen, J. (Eds.). (2012). *The postsecular in question*. New York: New York University Press.

Habermas, J. (2006). Religion in the public sphere. *European Journal of Philosophy, 14*(1), 1–25.

Habermas, J. (2008). *'Prepolitical foundations of the constitutional state?' in between naturalism and religion* (C. Cronin, Trans.). Cambridge: Polity Press.

MacIntyre, A. (1981). *After virtue*. Notre Dame: Notre Dame University Press.
Martin, D. (2005). *On secularization: Towards a revised general theory*. Farnham: Ashgate.
Monti, P. (2012). On the rationality of social practices. In F. Botturi (Ed.), *Understanding human experience: Reason and faith* (pp. 103–120). Bern: Peter Lang.
Nynäs, P., Lassander, M., & Utriainen, T. (Eds.). (2012). *Post-secular society*. New Brunswick: Transaction Publishers.
Rawls, J. (1993). *Political liberalism*. New York: Columbia University Press.
Raz, J. (2003). *The practice of value*. Oxford: Clarendon Press.
Rorty, R. (2003). Religion in the public square: A reconsideration. *Journal of Religious Ethics, 31*(1), 141–149.
Salvatore, A. (2010). *The public sphere: Liberal modernity Catholicism, Islam*. New York: Palgrave MacMillan.
Saward, M. (2005). Governance and the transformation of political representation. In J. Newman (Ed.), *Remaking governance: People, politics and the public sphere*. Bristol: Policy Press.
Schatzki, T. R. (1996). *Social practices: A Wittgenstenian approach to human activity and the social*. New York: Cambridge University Press.
Stout, J. (2003). *Democracy and tradition*. Princeton: Princeton University Press.
Szakolczai, A. (2013). *Comedy and the public sphere*. New York/London: Routledge.
Talisse, R. (2009). *Democracy and moral conflict*. Cambridge: Cambridge University Press.
Taylor, C. (2004). *Modern social imaginaries*. Durham/London: Duke University Press.
Taylor, C. (2007). *A secular age*. Cambridge, MA: Harvard University Press.
Theobald, C. (2007). *Le Christianisme comme style* (Vol. I–II). Paris: Éditions du Cerf.
Tuomela, R. (2002). *The philosophy of social practice: A collective acceptance view*. Cambridge: Cambridge University Press.
Urbinati, N., & Warren, M. E. (2008). The concept of representation in contemporary democratic theory. *Annual Review of Political Science, 11*, 387–412.
Wolterstorff, N. (2012). In T. Cuneo (Ed.), *Understanding liberal democracy: Essays in political philosophy*. Oxford: Oxford University Press.

Liberal Citizenship and the Search for an Overlapping Consensus: The Case of Muslim Minorities

Andrew F. March

In this article I seek to establish what political liberalism demands of Muslim citizens living as minorities in liberal states by way of a *doctrinal affirmation of citizenship*. This is an inquiry of a special nature. My interests are not directly in what *policies* a liberal state should have, nor in what *practices* on the part of citizens are compatible with justice and equality, but rather in what *views* emerging from a comprehensive doctrine are reasonable responses to the liberal terms of social cooperation. My aim is to establish with as much precision as possible when it can be said that there is a consensus on the terms of social cooperation in a liberal society and thus that the comprehensive doctrine in question is providing its adherents with moral reasons for endorsing those terms. Thus, this is an inquiry into liberal political theory, but one inspired by the special concerns, misgivings and anxieties of a particular comprehensive doctrine.

In the case of Islamic legal, political and ethical doctrines the potential concerns and misgivings about citizenship in a non-Muslim liberal society are wide-ranging. For "normative Islam," embodied traditionally in Islamic jurisprudence, membership in such societies presents two broad sets of problems: one, in their being liberal, and, two, in their simply being non-Muslim. Islam, like most religions and many secular conservative traditions, is not traditionally inclined toward endorsing many of the institutions and policies that arise from a commitment to basic liberal values such as individual autonomy and civic equality. Islamic political ethics have not traditionally recognized the rights to revise one's conception of the good (such as through apostasy, conversion or the neglect of religious duties), to the unrestricted choice of one's spouse, or to blasphemous, scandalous or offensive speech. Furthermore, there are doctrinal challenges related to the very fact of living as minorities in a non-Muslim state. Islamic political and legal doctrines have

---

(slightly modified from version published in *Philosophy & Public Affairs* 34.4 (Fall 2006))

A.F. March (✉)
Political Science, Yale University, New Haven, CT, USA
e-mail: andrew.march@yale.edu

D. Thunder (ed.), *The Ethics of Citizenship in the 21st Century*,
DOI 10.1007/978-3-319-50415-5_9

traditionally opposed the subordination of Muslims to any form of non-Islamic political authority and the formation of bonds of loyalty and solidarity with non-Muslims. Although some traditional views, such as the prohibition on mere residence in non-Muslim states pronounced by some legal scholars, appear today to be medieval anachronisms ignored by many Muslims, there nonetheless persists a general antipathy in Islamic doctrine to such aspects of citizenship as serving in non-Muslim armies, contributing to the strength or welfare of non-Muslim states, and participating in non-Muslim political systems.

Thus, my inquiry into what an Islamic doctrinal affirmation of citizenship in a non-Muslim liberal democracy would consist of proceeds from the observation that grounds exist within Islamic ethics for rejecting most, if not all, aspects of such citizenship and that *some* Muslim citizens may be swayed by these views towards a principled opposition to liberal citizenship.[1] Given our knowledge of this background, we may ask what an Islamic affirmation of citizenship would look like. The crucial features of such an affirmation are that it be both acceptable from a liberal standpoint (i.e., that it is, in fact, an *affirmation* of the liberal terms of citizenship) and sufficiently Islamic to be plausible to believers (i.e., to help *solve* the basic problem of the rejectionist doctrine). Asking what Islamic doctrine would have to affirm for it to be said that it is providing believers with both authentic and principled reasons for endorsing liberal citizenship is best perceived as the search for a certain kind of *equilibrium*, namely, for that fully reasonable account of the minimal demands of liberal citizenship *least in conflict* with the aims and spirit of Islamic political ethics. An Islamic doctrine of citizenship in non-Muslim liberal democracies can be said to reflect equilibrium when it is as inclusive as possible of believing Muslims without violating any essential features or aims of a well-ordered liberal society.[2] Identifying this equilibrium is the aim of this article: we do not know

[1] Although here I am focusing specifically on the relationship between Islamic doctrine and liberal citizenship, the inquiry itself is a generic one. All comprehensive doctrines or, indeed, noncomprehensive collections of beliefs and preferences can be presumed to provide their bearers with a wide set of motivations for action, some of which may conflict with liberal terms of social cooperation. These questions would be of interest even without the more public examples of recent value conflicts in Western societies, simply because Islam is an important comprehensive doctrine that has achieved a critical presence in existing liberal democracies recently enough for there not to exist a significant philosophical literature on its relationship to liberalism and citizenship. Lest it be thought that asking these questions suggests a background suspicion or mistrust of Islamic political ethics, it should be borne in mind that these very questions are the subject of earnest, and constant, internal debate amongst Muslim religious scholars and intellectuals.

[2] I am not here committing myself to the view that a minimalist conception of citizenship is the correct one, nor that a minimal consensus on values or institutions is the best we can hope for. Rather, I am merely suggesting that if we take the fact of moral disagreement seriously as a political problem, then efforts to explore possible solutions to that problem should seek to maximize their *plausibility*, which I define as the likelihood of being persuasive to those who are compelled by the views at the root of the initial moral disagreement. That is, a consensus needs to sway those skeptical of it, not those already so inclined. In any event, it will become clear that readers should not be alarmed by my use of the term "minimalist": I am not interested in a doctrine of citizenship as mere law-abidingness or as a modus vivendi, but rather as an affirmation of civic commitments on moral grounds.

before engaging dialectically with Islamic ethics just what the minimal demands of liberalism are, and thus just how traditional or conservative a formulation of Islamic doctrine can be included in an overlapping consensus.

But why do we need an Islamic doctrine of citizenship in liberal democracies, any more than we need a Catholic, Mormon, Amish or hedonist doctrine of citizenship? Why is it not enough to determine through public reason what is reasonable for the state or political community to demand of its citizens and leave it at that? If citizens comply with just laws and act in a way that allows a well-ordered democratic society to enjoy stability, is it proper for political theorists to be inquiring into what comprehensive beliefs citizens should hold?

The interest in whether citizens hold comprehensive doctrines that are compatible with public conceptions of justice or citizenship derives foremost from the belief that support for liberal principles from comprehensive doctrines is of manifest importance for political and social *stability*. Whatever the strength of rational arguments for liberal principles, we can easily recognize that actual agents often require additional motivations for action, without thinking that those motivations provide independent philosophical justification.[3] On an aggregate level, we can acknowledge that liberal institutions are more stable when a persistent majority of citizens does not hold comprehensive views that declare those institutions to be illegitimate. Thus, to be interested in whether the comprehensive doctrines in a society are part of an overlapping consensus does not require taking sides in the debate on the philosophical or justificatory role of an overlapping consensus; it is more than enough that the existence of an overlapping consensus may contribute to a range of social goods about which liberals care, such as stability, social order, trust, harmony, efficient decision making, social integration, political legitimacy and respect for rights.[4] One may feel that the appeal to religious beliefs for such support is an unfortunate, perhaps even cynical, tactic for achieving social stability,[5] or one may argue in principle that *all beliefs* are ultimately derived from controversial metaphysical commitments and that the appeal to another's value commitments in moral argumentation is all we have.[6] However, unless one believes that religious doctrines *never* provide

[3] "A philosophic justification is not to be confused with popular acceptance, rough consensus, or even probable acceptance by all reasonable parties. [But] this is not to belittle the goal of popular consensus. In the sociological sense of the word, the *legitimacy* of a liberal regime depends on widespread acceptance of its justification" (Gerald F. Gaus, *Justificatory Liberalism: An Essay on Epistemology and Political Theory* [Oxford: Oxford University Press, 1996], p. 10).

[4] See Joshua Cohen, "Moral Pluralism and Political Consensus," in *The Idea of Democracy*, ed. David Copp, Jean Hampton, and John E. Roemer (Cambridge: Cambridge University Press, 1993), pp. 274–75.

[5] Gaus argues that this is the case only when you seek to persuade and motivate a person by appealing to values or beliefs that you not only do not hold but consider to be irrational or unreasonable, i.e., views that persist not because of the burdens of reason but in spite of them. (See Gerald F. Gaus, "The Rational, the Reasonable and Justification," *Journal of Political Philosophy*, Vol. 3, No. 3: 234–58, at p. 255.)

[6] Akeel Bilgrami has argued that the liberal aspiration of justification through purely external reasons (i.e., reasons that all rational subjects should endorse *in virtue of their own rationality* regardless of their substantive moral commitments) fails not only in practice but logically, and therefore

their adherents with motivations for action, or that they *ought not* be indulged by appealing to them to endorse the reasonableness of liberal terms of social cooperation, one has no reason to be indifferent to an investigation of their capacity to support or oppose liberal conceptions of justice or citizenship.

Justice and Citizenship

The crucial feature of a liberal regime usually regarded as the primary focus of non-liberal opposition is its political conception of individual autonomy and the set of policies arising to protect individual liberties and uphold state neutrality between conceptions of the good. However, the right to revise one's conception of the good is neither the first, nor perhaps even the most salient, ideological challenge liberal citizenship poses to Muslim citizens. While one possible Muslim response to life as a minority is to demand that internal Muslim affairs (especially family law and education) be managed along *shari'a* lines, or even that the non-Muslim state enact certain illiberal policies (such as restrictions on offensive speech or immoral behavior), we assume, by positing that we are dealing with a community that is a minority, that using the state to impose a conception of the good is not generally part of the political imagination of the community in question.[7] However, there does exist a wide range of questions about the permissibility of residing in non-Muslim states, being subject to their laws, being loyal to them, and forming bonds of solidarity with their other residents. The challenge of citizenship in liberal democracies for some minority communities is, thus, not only the recognition of neutrality and secularism as constraints upon the use of both state and non-state coercion, but also the recognition of the legitimacy of the political community in which they live and of

---

that "the task of achieving secular ideals in a world in which there are strong religious and cultural identities [requires] look[ing] for reasons that will appeal even to those with these identities" (Akeel Bilgrami, "Secularism and Relativism," *boundary 2*, 31 [2004], p. 175). John Kekes: "Reasonable conflict-resolution is made possible by the traditions and conceptions of a good life to which people who face the conflicts adhere" (John Kekes, *The Morality of Pluralism* (Princeton, N.J.: Princeton University Press, 1993), p. 76). And, of course, Richard Rorty: "The fact that we may belong to several communities and thus have conflicting *moral* obligations, as well as conflicts between moral obligations and private commitments generates dilemmas. Such dilemmas … are never going to be resolved by appeal to some further, higher set of obligations which a philosophical tribunal might discover and apply. All we can do is work with the final vocabulary we have, while keeping our ears open for hints about how it might be expanded or revised" (Richard Rorty, *Contingency, Irony, and Solidarity* [Cambridge: Cambridge University Press, 1989], p. 197).

[7] This is not to say, of course, that, because Muslim minorities do not expect a non-Muslim state to impose Islamic law or advantage Islam, they have positive Islamic reasons for supporting the individual freedoms that are protected by state neutrality or that they will refrain from demands for the state to limit such freedom generally. Demonstrating the *stability* of an overlapping consensus requires demonstrating that those supporting liberal institutions as a minority would continue to support them as a majority. A comprehensive overlapping consensus would require positive Islamic reasons for accepting the constraints placed on communal authority.

their own membership in it. The idiosyncratic concerns and aims of Islam thus make it necessary to complement our interest in justice with the concerns of what I will refer to broadly as *citizenship*.

Similarly, the requirement to endorse a political conception of individual autonomy obscures the ways in which doctrines might enjoin different standards of behavior for those who are seen to belong to a given community of shared ends and for outsiders. The liberal requirement that religious groups not seek to use the state to force others – those not sharing their comprehensive commitments – to comply with the moral precepts flowing from those commitments, and the liberal requirement that religious groups not use nonstate coercion to prevent members from leaving the group (from "revising their conception of the good") or flouting its rules, both flow from the same conception of the person as free and equal. This is consistent and coherent from a secular perspective, but not necessarily so from religious ones. In Islamic ethical and legal theories, it is largely Muslims, not non-Muslims, who are seen as objects of compulsion on moral or religious grounds. Nonetheless, Islam does generally permit non-Muslims to be marginalized and discriminated against, and generally regarded as unequal to Muslims or outside the relationship of solidarity.[8] What all this means for our purposes is that one implication of the liberal conception of individual liberty – that we should not seek to force fellow-citizens to adopt our conception of the good – is not complete to Muslims unless we specify whether those fellow-citizens are Muslims or non-Muslims. From the Islamic perspective, the moral challenge regarding non-Muslims is not recognizing their right not to be Muslim (this is widely acknowledged), but rather recognizing them as equals and as part of a relationship of solidarity.

Thus, it is significant that this article concerns itself explicitly with Islamic thought related to Muslims living as minorities in non-Muslim states and societies – their status, their rights, their loyalties, their duties and their well-being – and how Islamic doctrine on these questions corresponds to liberal conceptions of citizenship. In the rest of this article I present what I believe to be the most reasonable liberal demands of membership, belonging, loyalty, recognition and solidarity in light of the specific concerns of Islamic doctrine.

I begin by emphasizing two distinctions. The first is (to restate) between requirements of justice and requirements of citizenship. There are many ways in which an individual or a community can at the same time adhere to requirements of justice without actually fulfilling any duties of citizenship. One meets requirements of justice merely by not breaking just laws, but one can do this, and even give principled reasons for doing so, without expressing certain further beliefs about the political community. Such beliefs relate to the legitimacy of the political community as it is constituted, of one's contribution to its welfare and that of fellow citizens as a result of social cooperation, and of one's willingness to participate politically. This is an understanding of citizenship, whatever disagreements persist about its precise minimum requirements, as a moral choice rather than a legal status.

[8] See Patricia Crone, *God's Rule: Government and Islam* (New York: Columbia University Press, 2004), chap. 21, "Muslims and Non-Muslims."

There is thus a second distinction that will be crucial for this article, that between a citizen and a resident alien. The notion of a resident alien, or an "alienated citizen," refers to someone who lives within a state, accepts some benefits of social cooperation and renders the legal duties required of him, but does not seek to share political sovereignty with his compatriots, does not identify with the political system, and resents or is indifferent to the contribution he makes to society's welfare and security.[9] Many of the goals and values of political liberalism – a well-ordered society, fairness, shared political sovereignty, democracy, distributive justice, stability arising from an overlapping consensus – point beyond citizenship as law-abidingness to a morally motivated commitment to a political community, the rights of fellow citizens and a political system. A doctrine of resident alienage – political quietism mixed with alienation from the community and its political system – is precisely what political liberalism seeks to avoid through its philosophy of public justification.

This article will seek to identify the requirements of an Islamic affirmation of liberal citizenship – of an Islamic social contract with a non-Muslim liberal democracy – in three parts: residence, loyalty, and recognition/solidarity. I emphasize these aspects of citizenship based on my reading of Islamic responses to citizenship in non-Muslim democracies and will cite Islamic sources to justify this selection and to illustrate with precision what is required for a positive Islamic affirmation of citizenship.[10]

Residence in a Non-Muslim State

The affirmation of citizenship in a non-Muslim liberal democracy faces in classical Islamic doctrine a challenge at a very basic level. Classical Islamic law has dealt at length with the problem of Muslims residing in non-Muslim states, both in the sense of states with non-Muslim majority populations and states run by non-Muslim law. The question in the Islamic sources takes the form of whether it is lawful for a Muslim to reside in the non-Muslim world (what is often referred to as *dar al-harb* [the "abode of war"] or *dar al-kufr* [the "abode of unbelief"]) or whether a Muslim is obligated to migrate (perform *hijra*) to the "Abode of Islam" (*dar al-Islam*). Thus, when speaking of Muslim citizens of liberal democracies, the debate over

[9]This distinction is ubiquitous in Western political theory. See, in particular, Michael Walzer: "The alienated citizen receives whatever protection the state provides and lives every day with his fellows in the shadow of that protection. But he does not participate at all in political life; he chooses not to participate. He thinks of the state as an alien though not necessarily as a hostile force, and he wants only to live in peace under its jurisdiction" (*Obligations: Essays on Disobedience, War, and Citizenship* [Cambridge, Mass.: Harvard University Press, 1970], pp. 226–27.)

[10]Although there are mainstream Islamic sources that affirm all of the demands of citizenship as I characterize them in the following sections, I will not refer to them in the present work. As noted above, I present and discuss these sources in March, "Islamic Foundations for a Social Contract in Non-Muslim Liberal Democracies."

citizenship begins with whether a Muslim may even regard a non-Muslim majority society run by non-Islamic law as a place where she may reside.[11]

There is a tradition in Islamic law of regarding such residence as impermissible. In classical jurisprudence, this position was advanced mostly by the Maliki school of law[12] (predominant in North Africa) but in the modern period it has been advanced by Saudi adherents of the Wahhabi doctrine,[13] as well as some fundamentalist thinkers not adhering to any single school, such as the Egyptian Sayyid Qutb.[14] Although these authorities often claim that there is a categorical divine command to migrate from spheres of non-Muslim rule based on two Qur'anic verses[15] and a number of reports of Prophetic speech (*hadith*),[16] more interesting for comparative political theory are the substantive arguments in favor of, or explanations of, this divine command. Muslim thinkers who regard residence in a non-Muslim polity as unlawful generally advance six types of rational arguments: (1) that Muslims must not be subject to non-Muslim laws or authority; (2) that Islam and Muslims must not be put in a position of inferiority to non-Muslims; (3) that Muslims must avoid aiding

---

[11] See Yusuf al-Qaradawi, *Fi fiqh al-aqalliyyat al-muslima* (Cairo: Dar al-Shuruq, 2001), p. 25, where he lists the question of the legality of residing in a non-Muslim state as the first of the "juridical" problems facing Muslim minorities. For the best existing survey of the treatment of this problem in Islamic law, see Khaled Abou El Fadl, "Islamic Law and Muslim Minorities: The Juristic Discourse on Muslim Minorities from the Second/Eighth to the Eleventh/Seventeenth Centuries," *Islamic Law and Society* 1:2 (1994): 141–87.

[12] One of the most famous treatments of this problem is found in Ahmad ibn Yahya al-Wansharisi, *al-Mi'yar al-Mu'rib wa al jami' al-mughrib 'an fatawa ahl Ifiiqiya wa'l-Andalus wa'l-Maghrib*, ed., Muhammad Hajji (Rabat: Ministry of Religious Endowments and Islamic Affairs, 1981), v. 2, pp. 121–38.

[13] E.g., Salih ibn Muhammad al-Shithri, *Hukm al-luju' wa'l-iqama fi bilad al-kuffar* (Riyad: Dar al-Habib, n.d.).

[14] See Sayyid Qutb, *In the Shade of the Qur'an*, Adil Salahi and Ashur Shamis, trans. and eds., (Leicester: The Islamic Foundation, 2001), v. III, p. 286.

[15] Q. 4:97–100: "Those whom the angels gather in death while in a state of sin against themselves they will ask: 'What was your plight?' They reply: 'We were oppressed on earth.' The [angels] will say: 'Was not God's earth vast enough for you to migrate within it?' They will have their refuge in hell and how evil is such a destiny, except for those truly oppressed, those men, women and children who cannot find any means and have not been shown the way. For these there is hope that God will forgive them, for God is Forgiving and Merciful. Anyone who migrates in the path of God will find in the Earth many an abundant refuge. Whoever leaves his home in migration towards God and his Messenger, and death overtakes him, his reward with God is guaranteed, for God is Forgiving and Merciful." And, Q. 8:72: "Those who believed and migrated and struggled in the path of God with their property and their souls and those who sheltered and supported them, and friends and supporters of one another. Those who believed and did not migrate, you have no duty of protection towards them until they migrate. But if they seek your support in religion, you owe them this support, except against a people with whom you have a treaty. God sees all that you do."

[16] For example, "The *hijra* will not come to an end until repentance comes to an end and repentance will not come to an end until the sun shall rise from its place of setting." "I am innocent of [I disown] any Muslim who lives with the polytheists. For you will not be able to tell them apart." "Do not live with and associate with the polytheists. Whosoever lives with them and associates with them is like them." These are found in the various authoritative collections of *hadith*, the reported sayings and doings of the Prophet Muhammad.

or increasing the strength of non-Muslims; (4) that Muslims are forbidden from forming bonds of friendship or solidarity with non-Muslims; (5) that Muslims are required to avoid environments of sin or indecency; and (6) that in non-Muslim environments it will be more difficult to prevent the loss of religiosity in subsequent generations.

What is important for our purposes is that the reasons given for prohibiting residence are precisely objections to relationships with non-Muslims characteristic of bonds of citizenship. Thus, there is something crucial to emphasize for anyone wishing to explore the possibility of an overlapping consensus: that it is not only necessary to find Muslim scholars disagreeing with the idea of a prohibition on residence in a non-Muslim state, but the justifications and conditions for such residence must also address the above underlying objections in a way consistent with liberal terms of social cooperation; we are interested in residence in a society to which one can *belong*. To be sure, liberalism clearly does not preclude the forming of subnational communities (based on religion, culture, national origins, class, occupation, ideology, region, lifestyle, and so on.). Indeed, these substate communities may even legitimately claim a more profound or sublime sense of loyalty than the state or wider society. However, liberalism would insist that they should not claim predominance in the political sphere to the extent of denying the legitimacy of political arrangements that seek to protect the rights of all individuals constituting the political community, and by asserting a parallel political authority. The response of "internal retreat" violates liberal requirements of citizenship once it includes the claim to communal political-legal authority over members at the expense of the generally binding legal system. Although liberal pluralism is committed to providing certain conditions for the survival of minority groups and protecting the right to association, these conditions cannot exclude general exemptions from all basic duties that apply to all citizens equally, including the duty to pay taxes and obey the same laws.

A natural demand for the Islamic political imagination is for some such form of Muslim communal autonomy within individual non-Muslim states characterized, in the first order, by the application of Islamic family law for Muslims, and perhaps any other areas of the Islamic social code[17] that concern purely internal Muslim relations. For example, classical Muslim jurists who permitted Muslim residence in non-Muslim states were adamant that this was only under the condition that Muslims were secure in their persons, faith and property and that they had the freedom to "manifest their religion." However, there is an inherent ambiguity here as to whether "manifesting one's religion" refers to something like the religious liberties protected by a liberal state or to communal autonomy. Some jurists argue for the more demanding condition of communal autonomy, although some are clearly content with private religious liberties. The role of the theorist in this case is to rigorously examine the arguments advanced (usually advanced in a very different context than

[17] Islamic law is divided between the *'ibadat* (matters pertaining to individual worship and rituals) and *mu'amalat* (matters pertaining to interpersonal and social relations).

that of a modern liberal state) and seek to test whether the nature of the conditions for accepting a certain demand are compatible with political liberalism.

A further question relates to the realm of ends that communities seek to advance within liberal democracies. The crucial example here is the emphasis placed by Muslim thinkers on the duty of proselytizing (*da'wa*, or "calling," in Arabic). Muslim jurists from the Middle Ages to the present have seen residence in non-Muslim lands as a desideratum precisely because of the opportunities it gives for spreading the Islamic message. The prominent eleventh century Sunni jurist and political theorist al-Mawardi argued that, far from being prohibited, "residing in [one of the unbeliever's countries] is better than migrating because it is hoped that others will convert to Islam through him."[18] The influential contemporary Egyptian-Qatari cleric, Yusuf al-Qaradawi echoes this view: "There can be no questioning of the permissibility of residing in a non-Muslim country, or in 'the abode of disbelief' as it is referred to by the jurists, for if we were to forbid it, as some scholars imagine, we would close the door to the call to Islam and its spread throughout the world."[19]

Clearly, liberalism cannot object to a group's wish to win adherents through peaceful missionary activities. There is no question of a violation of justice here. In fact, there is an element to this justification that is *deeply affirmative* of a liberal social order, insofar as it refers to a benefit accruing to Muslims that is a core value in liberal societies, namely religious freedom (both to proselytize and to convert). However, the political theorist may see in this a motivation that in fact violates the spirit of citizenship if a doctrine justifies residence and belonging in a society *merely* on the grounds that it helps advance the group's communal aims. The concerns liberals have about such a justification are that: one, it risks seeing non-Muslims only as potential converts and not as free and equal citizens; two, it does not preclude the Islamization of the state if the group someday finds itself a majority[20]; and, thus, three, it may reveal a shallow commitment to the society and state as (potentially permanently) pluralistic and secular. The general concern is that any acceptance of liberal institutions or constraints will be purely tactical, rather than grounded in a principled acknowledgment of the fact of reasonable pluralism. Contrast the justification of residence from *da'wa* with a justification that points to a benefit accruing to Muslims from core liberal policies that is not merely a potential *consequence* of those policies but *intrinsic* to them, say the inherent goodness of living in a society where one is unafraid of the arbitrary exercise of power.

---

[18] In Abu Zakariyya' al-Nawawi, *al-Majmu' Sharh al-Muhadhdhab* (Beirut: Dar al-Fikr, 2000), v. 21, p. 7.

[19] Qaradawi, *Fi fiqh al-aqalliyat al-muslima*, p. 33–4.

[20] The notion that residence and integration in Western societies is desirable primarily as a means of influencing these societies to the political benefit of Muslims or in order to transform them into "Islamic societies" is not rare in Islamic discourses about the Muslim minorities in the West. See also Muhammad Husayn Fadlallah, *al-Hijra wa al-ightirab: ta'sis fiqhi li mushkilat al-luju' wa al-hijra* (Beirut: Mu'assasat al-'Arif lil-Matbu'at, 1999), p. 86, where he discusses Muslim immigration to the West in terms of the "control over Western society in its entirety achieved by the Jews through their immigration and residence there."

Thus, there is another way in addition to seeking to assert parallel or contradictory political authority in which a minority community could fail to affirm its citizenship within a political community, and that is by passively accepting a state's political authority but seeking to avoid any meaningful contribution to it. Loyal resident alienage is a very plausible Islamic response to living in a non-Muslim society. The response would consist in justifying residence and basic political obligation, but would call for no meaningful engagement with the society, contribution to its self-defense or welfare, or participation in its political system. It would also place a great emphasis on the conversion of non-Muslims and eventual transformation of the society and political system. There would be no call for breaking existing laws, but certainly for their ultimate Islamization. The inevitable insistence that such doctrines would result in "law-abiding citizens" is irrelevant; the underlying reasons and comprehensive beliefs are not contributing to support for social cooperation on liberal terms.

To be clear: groups that choose not to integrate themselves culturally, economically, socially or politically into the wider society in order to pursue a collective vision of the good (such as the Amish, Dukhobors, or Haredim ubiquitous in the multicultural liberalism literature) are not, by virtue of their rejection of the wider society and its public sphere, violating any particular requirement of justice. Although I am required as a citizen to regard my share of collective sovereignty as *no more* than equal to everyone else's, I am not required (by justice) to regard my own share with any great sentimentality. I am not in most liberal democracies required to vote. I am not required to regard my political community (nation) as my most *precious* loyalty or even one that trumps others in *all* contexts. I am not required to cultivate a range of specific and demanding civic virtues. This is not to suggest that ghettoization might not be a political problem or something to be addressed by liberal governments. It is also not to suggest that the desire to enhance social solidarity, integration or a civic ethos is an inappropriate object of political action or education, merely that it is difficult to assert that a group consciously turning its back on modern society and choosing to live solely in pursuit of the good is, *in this alone*, violating a requirement of justice.[21]

This article, however, explores the possibility of securing an overlapping consensus not only on requirements of justice, but on conceptions of *citizenship*. There is clearly an overlap to the extent that one is a citizen of a political system, and each political system is founded on a conception of justice, but as I have shown there is a wide range of questions that relate to membership and belonging that are not covered by justice. The need to examine these questions is particularly strong in the case of communities that, unlike the Amish, Dukhobors, or Haredim, see themselves as adhering to a universal, proselytizing faith.

---

[21] "Justice as fairness honors, as far as it can, the claims of those who wish to withdraw from the modern world in accordance with the injunctions of their religion, provided only that they acknowledge the principles of the political conception of justice and appreciate its political ideals of person and society" (Rawls, *Political Liberalism*, p. 200).

Thus, the first area in which the political theorist would seek consensus is on the terms for legitimating residence in a non-Muslim state. She is not looking merely for Muslim scholars who permit such residence, but who do so for reasons compatible with the aims of a liberal political order, reasons that would give the Muslim citizen authentic and principled reasons for regarding his state of residence as a place he can live along the terms liberalism prescribes. Based on my reading of the treatment of this question in Islamic sources, I submit that a stable and compatible doctrine of residence in a non-Muslim state would require affirmation of the following positions:

R1: *The authoritative texts cited in favor of the prohibition on residence do not necessarily dictate the conclusions advanced by those jurists; there are other authoritative texts that lead to contradictory rulings and there are reasons to regard these are more authoritative than the texts cited by pro-*hijra *jurists.*

R2: *It may be possible to fulfill the basic duty to "manifest one's religion" even in the absence of sovereign Muslim political authority and under non-Muslim political and legal authority.*

R3: *Although great benefits to Islam, including its possible spread and the strengthening of Muslim communities, can be gained by living in non-Muslim lands, this is not the only way in which Muslims are permitted to regard their life in those societies.*

Loyalty to a Non-Muslim State

Residing in a non-Muslim state, even on the "right" terms and for the "right" reasons, does not by itself amount to a doctrinal affirmation of citizenship. A second aspect of the affirmation of belonging required of minority ethical or religious communities is the question of competing loyalties between the state of citizenship and other states or communities. The questions that we are interested in here are what it means to be loyal to one's state, what other loyalties may be consistent with that loyalty, and for what reasons it is legitimate to refuse to fight. This also requires some elaboration with special reference to Islamic concerns. These questions have traditionally been addressed in response to the pacifism of certain Christian sects, to refusal in the vein of Hobbesian individualism, and to liberal humanist or cosmopolitan objections to injustice against other humans. The Islamic case is special, however, since objections to fighting come not from pacifism, individual self-preservation or cosmopolitanism, but rather from a doctrine of loyalty to the global political community of fellow Muslims (the *umma*). The concern arises that refusal may point to nothing more than a rejection of civic commitment to a non-Muslim society.

Given that there has been a debate amongst jurists about whether Muslims are even permitted to reside permanently in non-Muslim states, it is understandable that rendering loyalty to them will be particularly controversial from an Islamic standpoint. It is instructive to note the sections in the books of law under which Muslim scholars discuss questions of residence and behavior in non-Muslim lands: those on *jihad*. Although it is indeed too simplistic to assume that all juridical discussions of non-Muslim polities and communities can be reduced to a blanket justification of aggression or antagonism, it is certainly the case that jurists view the Islamic political community as an entity towards which Muslims have ethical obligations (even when it is not constituted as a state). This political community is one with universal aspirations and is assumed to be, at the very least, in a state of competition with other communities. Given this basic assumption, it is not surprising that the idea of service in a non-Muslim army is considered aberrant. The Western analogue is not Christian or secular doctrines of *jus ad bellum* or *jus in bello*, but rather perennial state-centered expectations of civic loyalty. It is akin to asking, Are there doctrines of nationalism, patriotism or republicanism that can themselves provide justificatory reasons for serving a foreign state? The question either meets with baffled silence or complete hostility.

Muslim citizens thus have traditional doctrines prohibiting service in a non-Muslim army and discouraging identification with the interests of a non-Muslim state. In the interests of being systematic, I present the following five specific points of Islamic doctrine as covering the range of potentially incompatible positions on the question of civic loyalty to a non-Muslim state.

The first position is perhaps the most uncontroversial in Islamic legal and ethical traditions:

(1) *A Muslim may never kill another Muslim, especially in the service of unbelievers.*

There is direct scriptural foundation for this prohibition. The Qur'an proclaims: "Never should a believer kill a believer; but (if it so happens) by mistake (compensation is due) .... Whosoever slays a believer intentionally his reward is Hell forever, and the wrath and curse of God are upon him, and a dreadful penalty is prepared for him" [Q. 4:92–93]. Also regarded as "scriptural" in the sense of emanating from the Prophet's judgment is the following rule established by Muhammad as part of the "Constitution of Medina" for governing the various tribal and religious communities in that city during his exile from Mecca: "A believer shall not slay a believer for the sake of an unbeliever, nor shall he aid an unbeliever against a believer. Believers are friends one to the other to the exclusion of outsiders."[22] Muslim jurists have extrapolated from these sources not only a clear prohibition against helping non-Muslims in combat against Muslims (whatever the cause) but often the ruling that doing so constitutes apostasy, which is punishable by death according to those sources.[23]

[22] Alfred Guillaume, *The Life of Muhammad: A Translation of Ishaq's* Sirat Rasul Allah (London: Oxford University Press, 1955), p. 232.

[23] See Muhammad Rashid Rida, *Fatawa al-Imam Muhammad Rashid Rida*, ed. Salah al-Din al-Munajjid and Yusuf Q. Khuri, (Beirut: Dar al-Kitab al-Jadid, 1980), v. 5, p. 1749–50; Qaradawi, *Fi fiqh al-aqalliyat* and Sulayman Muhammad Tubulyak, (transliteration from Bosnian of "Sulejman

(2) *A war for the sole purpose of expanding the space ruled by Islam and Islamic law is a just war, a legitimate form of* jihad.

The classical theological-juridical position was that the basic status of relations between the Islamic and non-Islamic worlds is one of war and permanent nonrecognition.[24] A war waged by a legitimate Islamic ruler (*imam*) for no other purpose than bringing new territories into the abode of Islam was not only regarded as permissible by classical jurists, but in some accounts even one of the just ruler's requirements of office.[25] Modern "fundamentalists" or "revivalists" are explicit in their view that the classical doctrine is still valid. Sayyid Qutb makes clear that the classical doctrine of nonrecognition of non-Muslim polities ought to be revived by Muslims as part of the renewal of their religion: "When there is a divine code requiring complete submission to God alone, and there are alongside it human systems and conditions that are man-made, advocating submission to human beings, it is right that the divine system should move across barriers to liberate people from enslavement by others."[26] "No peace agreement may be made [with non-Muslims] except on the basis of submission evident by the payment of a special tax which gives them the right to live in peace with the Muslims. They are not given a peaceful status unless they are bound by covenant with the Muslim community on the basis of paying the submission tax."[27]

(3) *It may be the duty of every individual Muslim, even those residing outside of the Islamic polity to contribute to a legitimate* jihad, *if so called by the* imam.

A just life for a Muslim does not only consist in performing acts of worship or avoiding sin, but in serving the community of believers in any way required of him, including (perhaps especially) in war for the cause of Islam,[28] The classical doctrine held that waging the above-described "expansionist" *jihad* is a "collective duty" (*fard kifaya*), that is, something that must be discharged by the entire community, not necessarily every individual believer. However, when an Islamic state or community is under attack by infidels, defending them and Islam becomes an "individual duty" (*fard 'ayn*) for all Muslims. Some Islamic scholars have held this individual

---

Topoljak"), *al-Ahkam al-siyasiyya li'l-aqalliyat al-muslima fi al-fiqh al-Islami* (Beirut: Dar al-Nafa'is, 1997), p. 122.

[24] See Majid Khadduri, *War and Peace in the Law of Islam* (Baltimore, Maryland: Johns Hopkins Press, 1955), p. 145; Bassam Tibi, "War and Peace in Islam," in *Islamic Political Ethics*, ed. Sohail Hashmi (Princeton, N.J.: Princeton University Press, 2002), p. 176.

[25] Some medieval works on public law asserted that a just ruler must wage "raids" into unbelieving lands at least once a year.

[26] Qutb, *In the Shade of the Qur'an*, v. VIII, p. 28

[27] Ibid., v. VIII, pp. 101–02.

[28] Q. 4:95: "Not equal are those believers who sit [at home] and receive no hurt, and those who strive and fight in the cause of God with their goods and their persons. God has granted a grade higher to those who strive and fight with their goods and persons than to those who sit [at home]. Unto all has God promised good, but those who strive and fight has He distinguished above those who sit [at home] by a special reward."

duty to override all other obligations to a non-Muslim state of residence[29]; this is also, of course, the intellectual foundation for present-day jihadi movements that have used Muslim citizens of non-Muslim states in attacks against those states.[30]

(4) *A Muslim may not advance the cause of unbelievers or uphold non-Islamic rulings and truth-claims.*

One finds in juridical sources a frequent antipathy to Muslims helping non-Muslims when it is viewed that the cause is the advancement of a non-Islamic faith or conception of truth. The roots of this antipathy are manifold: not only might such help be seen as directly detracting from the Islamic cause, but even if there is no direct harm to Islam or Muslims, advancing the cause, increasing the strength, or upholding the rule of unbelievers is something prohibited to Muslims. Thus, a contemporary Islamic scholar submits that if Muslims find themselves fighting on behalf of non-Muslims against other non-Muslims, "it is necessary that Muslims *intend* by engaging in such fighting only to bring about benefit to Muslims, and to elevate the word of God, without intending to bring about the strengthening of the unbelievers, befriending them or elevating the word of unbelief."[31] This view is echoed in the explanations of two medieval scholars of the ban on such fighting: "[It is not lawful for Muslims to fight on the side of non-Muslims] because the jurisdiction of the unbelievers prevails there and Muslims cannot enforce non-Muslim rulings."[32] And: "Because the laws of idolatry are dominant over them Muslims are not able to rule by the laws of Islam, and thus any fighting on their part would take the form of exaltation of the word of idolatry and this is not permitted unless they fear for their lives from the invaders, in which case there is no sin incurred in fighting to defend themselves rather than fighting to exalt the word of idolatry."[33]

(5) *A Muslim may not sacrifice his life for other than certain causes.*

The previous quotation is preceded by the following statement: "If there is a group of Muslims in the abode of war and that country is attacked by another non-Muslim country, then the Muslims are not allowed to fight, for fighting involves exposing oneself to danger which is only allowed for the purpose of exaltation of the Word of God, may He be glorified, and the glorification of religion, which are not present in this case." This suggests, to me, a very specific theological point: God has made a Muslim's life sacred and a believer is only allowed to risk or sacrifice it

---

[29] Sayyid Abul 'Ala Mawdudi, *Towards Understanding the Qur'an* (Leicester, United Kingdom: The Islamic Foundation, 1990), v. III, pp. 209–10.

[30] See Shaykh Muhammad Afifi al-Akiti, *Defending the Transgressed by Censuring the Reckless against the Killing of Civilians* (Aqsa Press, 2005) for a presentation – and refutation – of these positions.

[31] Tubulyak (Topoljak), *al-Ahkam al-siyasiyya*, p. 117.

[32] Muhammad ibn al-Hasan al-Shaybani, *The Islamic Law of Nations: Shaybani's Siyar*, trans. Majid Khadduri, (Baltimore, Maryland: Johns Hopkins Press, 1966), p. 193.

[33] Muhammad ibn Ahmad al-Sarakhsi, *Kitab al-Mabsut* (Beirut: Dar al-Kutub al-'Ilmiyya, 2001), v. 10, p. 106.

for very specific ends; protecting a non-Muslim state, whatever else we believe about that believer's obligations to that state, is simply not one of those expressly sanctioned ends.

Without making any assumptions about the popularity of these positions among any present-day Muslim community, it is plain that there is a very explicit doctrinal background that could cause a Muslim to doubt the legitimacy of her loyalty to a non-Muslim state. From the perspective of political liberalism, the most problematic views are the following: that a Muslim may not recognize his non-Muslim state's unqualified right to existence, that he may not regard himself as under any personal duty of restraint towards his state of citizenship, and that he may not feel he can defend his state of residence, even against a non-Muslim aggressor, solely because of the non-Islamic character of that society's political system. What then would a Muslim citizen have to proclaim in order for it to be said that that he is balancing both his loyalties to his community of fellow believers and his duty to his state of citizenship?

Two obvious, or near-obvious, positions can be immediately established:

L1: *Hostilities on the part of Muslim forces against a non-Muslim state are justified only in self-defense or to counter aggression and not to facilitate the spread of Islam or to change the government of a state in which Muslims are not oppressed.*

I will argue below that there is considerable scope for reasonable disagreement on just war theory; however, there can be no question that a citizen who holds that it may be just for another state to invade his state for the sole purpose of changing its political system, when that political system does not oppress him, is not being reasonable, in the most basic sense of proposing and being willing to abide by fair terms of social cooperation. Of course, the fundamentalist may feel that merely in being forced to live under non-Islamic law she is being "oppressed." But this is not inconsistent with her acknowledging that she enjoys equal civil rights and liberties to those of all other citizens. She may feel, following Qutb, that her *non-Muslim* fellow citizens are oppressed *as well* in being "forced to live under man-made law." It is also not inconsistent with her recognizing that being denied equal liberal rights (to property, fair trial, freedom of religion, freedom of expression, and so forth.) would be an additional and different form of oppression. Thus, it is understood that L1 refers to a situation in which Muslims are treated as free and equal citizens within a secular political regime. Controlling for what the Qutbian and the liberal would both regard as "oppression" (unequal civil rights), the reasonable Muslim citizen regards the fact of secular legislation as insufficient grounds for forcible regime change.

Note that L1 excludes from an overlapping consensus the following variation on the above position (2):

> (2a) *A war for the sole purpose of expanding the space ruled by Islam and Islamic law is a just war, a legitimate form of* jihad. *However, not every single Muslim is required to join in such efforts or regard his participation as an individual duty. Muslims residing in*

non-Muslim states are required to uphold their tacit or express promise to those states not to harm them.[34]

While asserting (2) or (2a) need not qualify as a crime, there is no question that the views in those statements characterize doctrines well outside the most flexible and inclusive possible overlapping consensus. In terms of a *doctrine* of citizenship, our understanding of the requirement that religious or cultural minorities see their membership in a liberal society as legitimate would obviously imply the principled condemnation of violence used against it, not just personal abstention from such violence.

A second principle of loyalty thus follows:

L2: *In conflicts between a non-Muslim state in which Muslims live and a Muslim force, a Muslim may forswear on grounds of principle any active aid to the Muslim force and promise to engage in no violent activities against their non-Muslim state.*

My phrasing of this principle is neutral as to the cause and moral status of the war. That is, should the Muslim or non-Muslim state be regarded as the aggressor, a Muslim citizen should regard a liberal state of citizenship as inviolable in this way. From the Islamic perspective, this in fact involves two separate positions: that a Muslim need not contribute to the fulfillment of the collective duty (*fard kifaya*) to expand the realm of Islam, and that a Muslim need not discharge his individual duty (*fard 'ayn*) to contribute to the self-defense of Muslim lands by attacking his state of residence or citizenship. It is clearly the latter that is more problematic from an Islamic standpoint (although, as cited above, even many of the more radical Islamist groups operating in Western countries affirm it). However, even from a liberal perspective, it requires justification and clarification.

Consider a citizen who feels that his state is waging an unjust war or maintaining an unjust law. Liberalism holds that political obligation does not always require obedience in these cases.[35] Refusal to fight in an unjust war or to obey an unjust law is thus not generally considered a rejection of one's citizenship in what is otherwise a liberal democracy. Two questions then confront us: on what grounds may a citizen regard a war (or law) as unjust, and what forms of opposition to these injustices in addition to refusal are consistent with affirmation of one's citizenship in such a state?

[34] This is the position, for example, of the British group "al-Muhajiroun" ("The Migrants"), which supports terrorist attacks against the United Kingdom and the United States, but only by Muslims not legally residing in those countries. See al-Akiti, *Defending the Transgressed*, p. 17.

[35] "A person may conscientiously refuse to comply with his duty to enter the armed forces during a particular war on the ground that the aims of the conflict are unjust. It may be that the objective sought by war is economic advantage or national power. The basic liberty of citizens cannot be interfered with to achieve these ends. And, of course, it is unjust and contrary to the law of nations to attack the liberty of other societies for these reasons. Therefore a just cause for war does not exist, and this may be sufficiently evident that a citizen is justified in refusing to discharge his legal duty" (Rawls, *A Theory of Justice* [Cambridge, Mass.: Harvard University Press, 1971], p. 381).

On the first question, the first observation from the liberal perspective is that although the burdens of judgment will result in reasonable pluralism about the moral status of certain wars, some objections to war will be clearly unreasonable, or incompatible with the basic moral reasoning of other citizens. For example, a common Islamic response to the wars in Afghanistan and Iraq is that they are unjust simply because of the religious identities of the parties: a Muslim must oppose these wars simply because they are *non-Muslims* attacking *Muslims*. This view makes no distinctions based on cause, war aims or conduct within war. The view is that a Muslim may not regard his non-Muslim state's use of force against any Muslim as legitimate for any reason, even self-defense. This form of reasoning is thus outright unreasonable in failing to recognize fellow citizens as enjoying a basic moral status. Thus, any further reasoning about the permissibility of various forms of resistance to "unjust wars" already rests on premises that reveal a basic unreasonableness and, thus, a lack of affirmation of liberal citizenship.

However, this form of unreasonableness need not be the case. First, it may be the case that there is reasonable disagreement on the actual motives and necessity of a given war.[36] Thus, an unreasonable citizen says the United States acted unjustly in responding to the September 11 attacks by invading Afghanistan because a non-Muslim state may never attack Muslims. There is no disputation here that the September 11 attacks were the work of an entity in Afghanistan, or that military response would be an effective prevention of future attacks, or even that a military response would involve unjust collateral damage. A reasonable citizen, on the other hand, might say that the United States acted wrongly in invading because it was not necessary or effective for preventing future attacks, or that it could not be done without intolerable collateral damage. We may regard this citizen as wrong or as not demonstrating to a sufficient degree that his position proves the invasion unjust, but concede that he advances reasons that are consistent with recognizing his fellow citizens' legitimate rights.

Also, it may perfectly well *be* the case that a domestically liberal state acts illiberally, even unjustly, abroad. There might be a consensus between various just war doctrines that *in this case* the war was unprovoked, or disproportionate, or motivated by some other purpose such as power, glory, domination, economic gain or territorial expansion. Even if a Muslim citizen who advances this objection is largely motivated by the fact that of *Muslim suffering* (she does not raise similar objections or skepticisms about her state's wars against non-Muslim states, or not so vociferously), she may still be supported by a range of comprehensive doctrines in her view

---

[36]This is of course a nuance not raised by Rawls, who assumes that is it "may be sufficiently evident" whether the war is just. But this is a genuine problem and one not caused only by the plurality of comprehensive doctrines in a society. When does a country proclaim a war to be about economic advantage or national power and fail to provide a justification that is persuasive to many of its citizens? But in present circumstances this assumption is unwarranted. Consider the rise in wars of intervention that claim a humanitarian justification, a justification based on the need to fight nonstate terrorism, or a justification based on the need to prevent future threats from states. These wars are deeply disputed as to their nature, purpose and necessity in ways that both wars of self-defense after a direct invasion and open military adventures are not.

that the war is unjust, just as some Black Nationalists in the 1960s may have been largely motivated by particularist sentiments but still correct in their condemnation of racist policies.

So let us grant that a Muslim citizen may regard one of her state's wars as unjust, and may be strongly supported in this view by other just war doctrines. The question then arises, What forms of disobedience or opposition are compatible with support for liberal citizenship? (Again: the question is not simply what ought to be *permitted* in a liberal society, but whether we think a citizen who *believes* that x is justified is capable of giving support to liberal terms of social cooperation.) The most plausible argument that one could take up violent action against their liberal state of citizenship yet still not be advancing a general doctrine incompatible with citizenship in that state would be something like the following:

I. To view something as unjust may be also to will it to cease. To will something to cease must also imply that some actions taken toward that end are willed. Unjust actions may thus be countered with actions designed to stop them.

II. Such actions, to be morally permissible, must be necessary, proportionate and directed at the morally responsible agents.

III. Many unjust actions involve violence. Peaceful acts of resistance may be either ineffectual or impose further unbearable costs on those already transgressed against. Violent acts may thus be more effective than nonviolent ones and, if proportionate to the original injustice and directed only at morally responsible agents, not instances of a further injustice.

Let us pause here. What I think is fairly uncontroversial is that a loyal citizen may wish for his state's unjust actions to cease and recognize that certain countervailing actions may be necessary. In the case of an unjust war of aggression, he may also recognize the right of other peoples to resist, just as he claims this right for himself. Thus, I see no incoherence or disloyalty in his recognizing that the violence directed against his state's military forces by other forces legitimately resisting is legitimate. In this recognition, he is merely expressing his wish for his liberal state to act more justly.

However, our question deals with such a citizen taking a further step and actively helping the resistance to injustice, specifically through direct violent action. The argument would thus have to involve something like:

IV. All moral agents have a duty to advance justice. If violent action in resistance to initial aggression is deemed to be justified in principle, no autonomous moral agent's action in support of this justified resistance can be deemed unjustified, as long as it remains within the bounds of proportionality and is directed at morally responsible agents.

The argument here is essentially that if the liberal state of citizenship acts so unjustly in the first place, it surrenders any legitimate expectation of loyalty. An apposite example is that of John Brown (or, rather, "John Brown," since I do not wish to be responsible for complete accuracy or nuance in historical interpretation). Can it be said that "John Brown" in violently attacking agents of slavery when the responsible political authorities had failed to do so is thereby demonstrating adherence to a comprehensive doctrine incompatible with liberal citizenship? That is, why is an ideal-typical position "I pledge loyalty to my political community and promise to defend it against aggressors but make no commitment to supporting or even tolerating its own injustices" so different from the position "I consent to obey the laws of my society legitimately enacted so long as they do not violate fundamental principles of justice"? And if the former is not *obviously* of a different nature morally from the latter, could we not imagine that an ideal-typical Islamic position something like the following would meet similar standards of reasonableness: "I pledge loyalty to my non-Muslim state of residence so long as it respects my rights, provides me with security and does not transgress egregiously against my brother Muslims"?

In order to understand why something like L2 is still required, we must accept certain beliefs about the relationship that is formed by citizenship and the nature of democratic commitment. To be committed to citizenship in a liberal democracy is, perhaps, to be committed primarily to realizing certain values and principles. That is why loyalty to a state or nation can never be absolute, because such a state or nation is only worthy of loyalty as much as it itself is loyal to those principles over a long period of time. However, an affirmation of citizenship, rather than a commitment to justice, is not just an affirmation of those principles in the abstract, but an affirmation of a particular long-term project of realizing those principles. Moreover, political community, however intimately defined in terms of principles of justice, is also an exercise and a practice of pursuing many other things besides justice, such as welfare, solidarity and prosperity, and all of this in the real cauldron of history and through the actions of real people with the normal range of human motivations.

Thus, the traditional liberal justification of civil disobedience and the refusal to fight presumes a certain stance of "loyal opposition" where the citizen disobeys or refuses not out of either selfishness or rejection of her membership in the political community, but precisely in affirmation of that membership. The citizen who disobeys out of principle does not do so lightly or in response to every policy with which she disagrees. Furthermore, she often expects and accepts punishment for this disobedience, not just resignedly or even for propagandistic effect, but to express her overall commitment to the rule of law and the democratic community that sustains it. This stance also draws on (but in turn is limited by) the belief in the capacity of democratic institutions to (eventually) rectify injustices and in the citizen's long-term commitment to the community's development in the direction of justice.

By contrast, violence represents an exit from the community and disavowal of the democratic process that disobedience and refusal (including, say, a refusal to pay the proportion of one's taxes that support an unjust war) do not. This is not to say that such exit may never be a morally reasonable response. It may. But it is not "citizenship." It is not a commitment to sustaining, supporting and reforming the institutions of a political system that one endorses. It is not a commitment to a long-term relationship that may at times disappoint, but in balance satisfy more than any other. Of course a political system may prove itself over a sufficiently long period of time to be too corrupt or too indifferent to its historical ideals. But with exit via the resort to violence in such a case it is no longer clear that we are dealing with our central concern: endorsement of reasonable terms of social cooperation in a liberal democracy. This may be the case with my above reference to "John Brown."

To return to our specific inquiry, I will use a current example. A Muslim citizen who regards the present U. S. occupation of Iraq as unjust would not be advancing an unreasonable view. Furthermore, Islamic doctrine gives this citizen far more resources for defending this view than the simplistic "non-Muslims may never attack Muslims" attitude I presented earlier. She may give reasons similar enough to those non-Muslim citizens may offer: the war was unprovoked, it has resulted in intolerable civilian casualties, and the United States is not obviously materially disinterested. These views could result in the reasonable position that violent resistance against this occupation is morally justified (which is not to say that it is the only or the most reasonable position). As I argued above, this conclusion is susceptible to the further argument that, therefore, any moral agent is justified in aiding this just resistance, even violently. On this view, it is the unjust war, not the citizen's unreasonable comprehensive doctrine, that has produced this situation.

According to my reasoning above, the response of the political liberal can only be that this person has given up on the capacity of democratic communities to correct their mistakes, and has demonstrated a certain disinterest in her own long-term investment in the community's moral progress. And this, to be clear, all presumes the *charitable* interpretation of the citizen's reasoning: that it is based on considerations of justice that are potentially part of an overlapping consensus, and not a cruder form of Muslim communalism or in-group solidarity. We thus defend L2 on these grounds: if a Muslim citizen regards a war waged by his state of citizenship as unjust for reasons that are potentially reasonable or principled, then his decision to oppose this war through violent action reflects, if not itself injustice, then a repudiation of the long-term relationship that characterizes citizenship; if this citizen regards a war waged by his state of citizenship as unjust for reasons that reflect rather a basic lack of recognition of that state's legitimate rights, then his comprehensive doctrine is not reasonable to begin with in the way required by political liberalism.

We come now to a much more complicated set of questions about when it becomes unreasonable for Muslim citizens to fight in or otherwise support the self-defense efforts of the society that has guaranteed them security and equal rights and liberties, and in general provided for the conditions of their daily life. Let us begin by assuming that affirming the right of one's political community to defend itself against aggression (L1) is both a necessary and *sufficient* just war doctrine for a citizen to hold. That it is sufficient suggests that this is all a citizen must proclaim; a citizen who refuses to fight in an unjust war abroad cannot be accused of holding a doctrine incompatible with liberal citizenship. I accept as established the traditional liberal right to conscientious refusal to fight in wars that can be regarded as unjust from a moral perspective.[37] Even a citizen who refuses to fight in a war that may be just but not one of self-defense – think of humanitarian invasions or preventative wars – can hardly be accused of denying that his society enjoys the basic right to self-defense.

Thus, whether requests for conscientious objection may be part of a comprehensive moral doctrine compatible with liberal citizenship can only be problematic if the war is one of self-defense and if the reasons that motivate certain citizens to so refuse reflect an underlying unwillingness to propose and abide by fair terms of cooperation and lack of recognition of their political community's basic legitimate rights.[38] The concern in the case of Islam as a comprehensive doctrine is that since it commands believers to defend their Muslim-majority political community, their unwillingness to fight for their non-Muslim political community may reflect an indifference to, lack of commitment to, or, in the worst case, contempt for that community's legitimate interests.

Let us begin with the most difficult situation from an Islamic perspective, when a Muslim may be required to defend a state of citizenship against a Muslim force. Based on the original Islamic positions (1) and (2) we might encounter the following position:

> (1') *No Muslim is permitted to fight in a non-Muslim army, even to defend a territory in which he or she lives and is not oppressed, when the opposing force is a Muslim one.*

Here we pick up where our discussion in defense of L2 left off. This position seems to strain the boundaries of tolerance, and appear analogous to an ethnic or national minority during a war between his state of citizenship and the country of his co-ethnics. What distinguishes the two cases, however, is that in the national minority case we have a *simple* clash of loyalties between national communities: the minority would prefer to live with its co-ethnics and makes no pretence of membership in another *nation*. In the Muslim case, however, we might be dealing with a religious obligation never to kill another Muslim. He might not reject the host community as such, and might be willing to defend it against non-Muslim aggressors, but faces a conflict of obligations and prefers not to shed certain kinds of blood. He seems not to have clearly chosen his fellow citizens over his fellow Muslims, but it is also not yet clear that he has done the reverse.

If he proclaims himself unwilling to kill fellow Muslims, but also unwilling to aid them or damage his fellow citizens by any acts of commission (i.e., he affirms L2), we may just be willing to recognize this neutrality as a sufficient declaration of

[37] An individual "can maintain that, all things considered, his natural duty not to be made the agent of grave injustice and evil to another outweighs his duty to obey" (Rawls, *A Theory of Justice*, p. 380).

[38] "There are likely to be moments when all residents, aliens and citizens alike, are morally obligated to defend the state that defends their everyday social life. ... The existence of borderline cases does not call the original distinction into question" (Walzer, "Political Alienation and Military Service," in *Obligations*, p. 105–6).

civic loyalty. To even consider a position like (1′) for inclusion in an overlapping consensus, we would first require that it be combined with L2 in something like the following way:

> (1a) *No Muslim is permitted to fight in a non-Muslim army, even to defend a territory in which he/she lives and is not oppressed, when the opposing force is a Muslim one. However, if the Muslim has been given security, treated fairly and allowed to manifest his/her religion in that territory, he/she may not join the forces of the invading Muslim army and may not engage in any acts of sabotage or obstruction of the non-Muslim state's efforts to defend itself.*

What we are specifically looking to establish is that the citizen does no harm to the society's vital interests by any of his actions or refusals to act, and that he is committed to no declaration of the illegitimacy of the acts performed by his fellow citizens (i.e., he also affirms L1). The latter requirement refers again to the *reasons* used by a citizen to justify positions such as (1′) or (1a). We want to know both that the citizen seeks exemption because of a specific divine imperative not to kill fellow Muslims (rather than out of a desire to see his state of citizenship conquered) and that his promise to engage in no acts of sabotage or betrayal are advanced for *principled* reasons (rather than a desire to avoid punishment).

Thus, the following statements might support the claim that a citizen can assert (1′) and (1a) and still be holding a doctrine eligible for the overlapping consensus:

> (1b) *No Muslim is permitted to fight in a non-Muslim army, even to defend a territory in which he/she lives and is not oppressed, when the opposing force is a Muslim one because the* Qur'an *and* hadith *have proclaimed it a sin for a Muslim to kill a fellow Muslim.*

This position makes it clear that he fears angering God by doing something rather than supports the efforts of an invading Muslim force to conquer a non-Muslim state. Similarly, we prefer an elaboration of (1a) along the following grounds:

> (1c) *If the Muslim has been given security, treated fairly and allowed to manifest his/her religion in that territory, he/she may not join the forces of the invading Muslim army and may not engage in any acts of sabotage or obstruction of the non-Muslim state's efforts to defend itself because he/she has to that point accepted the protection and benefits of living in that state and thus contracted himself not to harm it.*

This addendum to (1a) makes it clear that the Muslim citizen feels a certain moral obligation to the non-Muslim society and his non-Muslim fellow citizens, insofar as he considers the duty not to violate contracts or promises a moral obligation derived from religion. He not only fears worldly punishment for acting against the interests of his state, but also divine punishment for committing a sin. For our purposes, this demonstrates that he is capable of proposing and abiding by fair terms of social cooperation.

However, let us consider that the liberal state has enacted a policy of *conscription* for the war of self-defense. The argument might be made then that what the dissenting citizen is requesting is an unfair exemption from the duty to perform an act that all citizens have the obligation to perform, like paying taxes. Why should a citizen's personal conscience not be grounds for an exemption from all demands of commission? What is additionally problematic is that the citizen has not declared certain acts as unjust per se but only when done to certain people. It might thus be claimed that the individual does not in fact have a conscientious objection at all because he does not assert universal principles applying to the conduct of war but rather arbitrary principles depending on the identity of the agent and the object. Our question is, thus, whether this privileging of a claim of another community over the claim of one's fellow citizens is a violation of the duties of citizenship.

I want to consider the idea that it depends on the precise weight of each claim. If one's moral claim to an individual whom he regards as a fellow member of a special community of humans is not to kill him or do him grave damage, and the claim to another political community (in which he enjoys protection and freedom) is that of discharging his individual share of a collective duty that does not rely for success on his individual performance, then our specifically *liberal* conception of citizenship ought to tolerate exemption on these grounds. By contrast, declaring that one's lack of recognition of the political community (even one in which one is not oppressed) forbids one from contributing to its welfare through the paying of fair taxes demonstrates an indifference to the community and its legitimate interests in a way that refusing to kill for it does not. The point here is that the (Islamic) duty not to kill fellow Muslims is not symmetrical to the (civic) duty to discharge one's share of a collective obligation. The former is far weightier than the latter. What I believe this suggests is that holding specifically the above position (1b) does not commit the Muslim in question to the position that he has no obligations to his state of citizenship or that *any* duty to fellow Muslims (no matter how trivial) outweighs *any* duty to fellow citizens (no matter how weighty). Thus, what is determinant in this case are three factors: (a) that the duty to fellow Muslims is particularly weighty in a moral sense (the duty not to kill); (b) that his exemption from a collective duty will itself not result in the society's inability to achieve a legitimate and necessary goal; and (c) that he has not proclaimed the *illegitimacy* of a non-Muslim society's efforts to defend itself, even against Muslim forces. Thus, we may say that a Muslim citizen who affirms L1 and L2, who explains his support for L2 though a statement like (1c) (i.e., that his promise not to harm his political community is *principled*) and who explains his request for exemption through a statement like (1b) (i.e., that it is based on a desire to avoid sin and next-worldly punishment, not a desire for the defeat of his political community) is affirming reasonable views about the rights of his political community and his duties towards it.

This discussion has, however, revealed the precise limits of the balancing act between the two competing loyalties. The preceding discussion assumes that the reasonable Muslim citizen is making an earnest effort to discharge both his civic and religious obligations, and that there may be an equilibrium where he does no vital harm to either community. This equilibrium is disturbed, however, when it is imagined that the self-defense efforts of a society require for success the contribution of all adult citizens. Let us also suppose that he regards noncombatant service as impermissible, say, according to the *hadith*: "he who kills a believer by even half a word will meet God with no hope of His mercy written on his face." However improbable this may be given modern warfare, let us suppose that a Muslim community does vital damage to its political society even by remaining passive, and does so for no other reason than the narrow one of wishing not to kill fellow Muslims. Only here does it become clear that the failure to choose between communities becomes, in fact, a choice. The Muslim may assert no wish for her society to be conquered (L1) but is in fact wishing for this *less* than she wishes to obey God, as she imagines God requires. Here she joins the class of semi-citizens/semi-aliens along with all committed pacifists.

From the perspective of political liberalism, the most blatantly problematic request for exemption is when a non-Muslim state is seeking to defend itself against the aggression of another *non-Muslim* force. We can synthesize the sentiments expressed in the Islamic positions (4) and (5) from above into the following plausible statement:

> (4') *No Muslim is permitted to fight in any non-Muslim army, even to defend a territory in which he/she lives and is not oppressed, even when the aggressing force is not a Muslim one.*

This case appears to represent the repudiation of citizenship in this state, and perhaps even the form of loyal resident alienage that Walzer discusses. It is enough to say that a doctrine that declares it impermissible for Muslims to help defend a society in which they live, are not oppressed, and are not facing a conflict of loyalties, to be a failure to recognize the legitimacy of the political community and its reasonable interests. What is decisive in this case is that the Muslim citizen seems to have no absolute doctrine of pacifism and no conflicting moral or religious obligation to another community or agent that is being violated in the act of aiding the legitimate self-defense of the community. The weakness of the reasons for refusal seems to suggest a simple failure to regard the community in which he lives as one in which he has a stake and the welfare and security of which is of crucial importance to him, both attitudes that are foundational to the spirit of citizenship.

However, even this case may be more complicated than it appears. The crucial factor in determining whether a Muslim can assert (4′) and still be said to hold a doctrine of citizenship compatible with that of political liberalism are the types of reasons cited in defense of it. Consider the following synthesis of the earlier quotations supporting position (4):

> (4a) *No Muslim is permitted to fight in any non-Muslim army, even to defend a territory in which he/she lives and is not oppressed, even when the aggressing force is not a Muslim one because it is impermissible for him/her to advance the cause of unbelievers or to uphold the laws of unbelief.*

In this case the reasons advanced in support of a refusal to contribute do, in fact, reveal an utter lack of solidarity with fellow citizens, and something approaching an attitude of contempt. Non-Muslims cannot be supported no matter what their treatment of Muslims, simply because of their comprehensive doctrine. However, consider:

> (4b) *No Muslim is permitted to fight in any non-Muslim army, even to defend a territory in which he/she lives and is not oppressed, even when the aggressing force is not a Muslim one because his/her life has been made sacred and it is impermissible to expose oneself to danger except for the purpose of exaltation of the Word of God, and the glorification of religion, which are not present in this case.*

This justification seems at first glance similar if one understands "the exaltation of religion" as a euphemism for fighting for Muslim communal interests. However, what if one understands it to be a divine imperative not to expose something sacred and inviolable (a Muslim's own life) to mortal danger except in a few expressly delineated cases? We might interpret the Muslim invoking (4b) as saying: "Strictly speaking, we cannot die for this cause because God has not permitted it and it would thus be a sin to do so; however, under the terms of citizenship we are not allowed to violate your legitimate interests through any form of betrayal and we are allowed to contribute in noncombatant capacities." Here it becomes clear that the reasons invoked for exemption: (a) are sincerely held and of a principled nature; (b) are not grounded in indifference or contempt for one's non-Muslim fellow-citizens: and (c) are not incompatible with contributing to the state of citizenship in nonviolent ways also on principled grounds. In fact, as with the above case of refusing to fight against an aggressing Muslim force when the survival of the society depends on such contribution, the Muslim citizen whose *only reason* for refusing to fight is his belief that God has not allowed him to die for this reason is approaching the traditional grounds for refusal advanced by Quakers or other Christian pacifists. In such a case, we might judge that (4b) represents a doctrine compatible with political liberalism but creating a hybrid citizen/alien doctrine, whereas (4′) alone and (4a) are blatantly incompatible.

If this is correct, and if it is also correct that a Muslim's abstention from a war of self-defense against an aggressing Muslim force is reasonable when he has affirmed L1 and L2, and explained his abstention according to (1b) and (1c), then the only additional principle of civic loyalty required from Islamic sources would be the following:

L3: *In conflicts when the non-Muslim state in which Muslims live is under attack by another non-Muslim force, and thus no conflict of loyalty or theological imperative is at stake, it is permissible to contribute in some substantive way to the self-defense efforts of the non-Muslim state.*

Leaving the meaning of "substantive contribution" vague enough to include both combatant and noncombatant service, I submit that this position represents an equilibrium between the concerns of political liberalism and those of Islamic doctrine. Note that it is always possible that a Muslim could affirm on principled, Islamic grounds such noncombatant service even against an aggressing Muslim force (especially if he asserts L1), which would represent a more robust version of this position.

Recognition of and Solidarity with Non-Muslims

Much of what was discussed in the previous two sections suggests an attitude of recognition on the part of Muslims towards non-Muslims, insofar as we require Muslims to view non-Muslims not *merely* as potential converts and non-Muslim societies as potential objects of loyalty. Affirmation of the inviolability of non-Muslim property, honor and life as a basic religious duty arising from contract between two parties would go a long way towards grounding the recognition of equality in the public sphere, which is a basic requirement of citizenship in a pluralist society. The topics covered in the previous section do not, however, necessarily lead to a doctrine of recognition or civic solidarity, understood as a willingness to contribute to common social and political goals in a condition of equality. Such willingness, I submit, would suggest a more robust recognition of the other as a civic equal than does the mere recognition of the state as having valid claims on subjects enjoying its protection. The latter could conceivably be achieved under a rubric of relations between distinct communities or units, as it has indeed traditionally been conceived in Islamic juridical and political theories.

It will be recalled from the section on residence in a non-Muslim state that there is a tradition in Islamic jurisprudence that prohibits living in a non-Muslim state because Muslims are forbidden from forming bonds of friendship or solidarity with non-Muslims. This view is often thought to be an injunction based on a number of Qur'anic verses, including:

> Let not the believers take the infidels for their allies in preference to the believers – for who does this has nothing to do with God – unless it be to protect yourselves from them in this way. God warns you about Himself and the final goal is to God [3:28].

> Oh you who have believed! Do not take for your intimates other than your own kind. They will continually cause you turmoil and love anything that will distress you. Loathing has already come forth from their mouths and what is concealed in their breasts is even greater. We have made the signs clear to you if you will use your reason [3:118].

These verses (see also: Q. 5:51, 60:1, 4:139, 4:144) use term the *awliya'*, which has been rendered here as "friends" or "allies," or *muwalah* as an abstract noun. Qur'anic commentators spend very little time in specifying the range of legal relationships covered by the verses prohibiting *muwalah* with non-Muslims. If they do it is usually by way of enumerating synonyms or other general concepts like "keeping company," "befriending," "mutual consultation," or "revealing the intimate concerns of believers to them."[39] Modern commentators (as well as Muslim Qur'an translators) also treat the term generally and as a synonym for loyalty and friendship. The present-day Lebanese legal scholar, Khalid 'Abd al-Qadir, who attempts to appropriate the classical jurists as faithfully as possible in his seven-hundred-page treatment of Muslim minority issues, defines the concept in terms of "affection," "help" "alliance," "friendship," "following," "being neighbors," "proximity," and so forth.[40]

Treating these verses and this concept as bearing on liberal citizenship would thus indeed appear to have some justification since our understanding of citizenship and solidarity covers the range of meanings of *muwalah*: we are concerned with

[39] See Isma'il ibn 'Umar Ibn Kathir, *Tafsir al-Qur'an al-Azim* (Beirut: Dar al-Kutub al-'Ilmiyya, 1998), v. 2, p. 390.

[40] Khalid 'Abd al-Qadir, *Fiqh al-aqalliyat al-Muslima* (Tripoli: Dar al-Iman, 1998), p. 626.

both the legal and political agreement to accept a non-Muslim state's protection, and the bond of mutual concern between fellow citizens, which we might indeed consider to be a form of alliance or civic friendship.

For those who read the *muwalah* verses as having both a literal and a general application, and thus discouraging all forms of solidarity with non-Muslims, these verses are underpinned, clarified or explained primarily by three ethico-political principles: that putting one's trust in unbelievers is a form of rejection of God and His promises[41]; that alliance and friendship with unbelievers is a betrayal of Muslims and the Islamic community on earth[42]; and that unbelievers are inherently untrustworthy and will ultimately seek to subvert Muslim faith. For many Muslim scholars, from conservative-traditionalists to more radical revivalists, secular self-restraint on the part of non-Muslim states does not mitigate the basic mistrust, given the view that both the general society and the state ought to be the locus for the implementation of the Islamic good life in a way that requires a particular form of cooperation and trust with others. The trust sought is not a form of mere promise-keeping, but a shared commitment to upholding substantive moral values and combating behaviors that contradict them. Thus, we have a family of positions that caution against solidarity with non-Muslims on the basis of a liberal social contract. Scholars inclined towards this position who still see residence in non-Muslim lands as permissible tend to recommend some form of self-segregation for Muslim communities, or endorse political obligation on the grounds that these lands will someday have Muslim majorities. A very small number take the medieval designation of non-Muslim lands as the "abode of war" literally, and claim that the ethics of war permit Muslims to regard non-Muslim life, property and honor as licit.[43]

This is the Islamic background to our emphasis on the need to ground Islamically a doctrine of recognition and social solidarity. The very idea of forming meaningful bonds of affection and cooperation with non-Muslims is rejected by some classical and contemporary fundamentalist thinkers. Bearing this in mind, what would political liberalism require by way of an alternative Islamic doctrine of recognition and solidarity?

A general doctrine of recognition, I argue, would consist of two main pillars: first, recognition of a right not to be Muslim and some acceptance of pluralism and difference as a potentially permanent feature of social life; and, second, an affirmation of relationships based on justice between communities. Together, these two

---

[41] Qutb on Q. 3:28: "We have this very stern warning in verse 3:28, making it absolutely clear that a Muslim disowns Islam if he forgoes a relationship of alliance or patronage with someone who refuses to acknowledge God's revelation as the arbiter in life. He has cut himself off from God." (Qutb, *In the Shade of the Qur'an*, Salahi and Shamis, trans., v. II, pp. 62–3).

[42] This theme is particularly salient given the generally accepted context for the revelation of the verses in question, which is the betrayal of the Islamic community by the "hypocrites," those who pretended to be Muslim before the fall of Mecca but in fact maintained loyalties and allegiances with their Christian, Jewish and erstwhile pagan brethren. See Muhammad Rashid Rida, *Tafsir al-Manar al-hakim al-shahir bi-tafsir al-manar* (Beirut: Dar al-Ma'rifa, 1973), v. 3, pp. 276–7, for a summary of the various theories of the context of revelation for 3:28 and 60:1.

[43] See Fadlallah, *al-Hijra wa al-ightirab*, pp. 80–81, for a presentation and refutation of this view.

pillars would contribute towards a positive conception of recognition and respect for non-Muslims, beyond mere tolerance in the "negative" sense. Building on this, a doctrine of solidarity with a non-Muslim polity further requires an affirmation of the legitimacy of Muslims actively contributing to the welfare of such societies and participating in their political life. To avoid confusion, it is not my argument that the belief must be held that such contribution and participation are intrinsic to an Islamic conception of the good life, or that they are aspects of virtue. Such assertions would be a very thick affirmation of citizenship; but what the comparative theorist in this case is interested in establishing is merely an Islamic foundation for the belief that contributing to the welfare of non-Muslim societies and participating in their political life are permissible and not in conflict with any core Islamic conception of the good or of justice.

I have discussed briefly the problems the liberal theorist has with Islamic justifications of sharing political space with non-Muslims solely on the grounds that they may some day become Muslims. One the one hand, the fact of reasonable pluralism is a central organizing principle for liberal justification. Political liberalism goes to great lengths to convince nonliberals, particularly religious believers, that it advances no truth claims contrary to their metaphysical beliefs and, thus, that believers need not repudiate their own claims to truth. However, a core feature of reasonableness is being able to see fellow citizens as free and equal, self-authenticating sources of claims and interests. One of the implications of this view is that, given the burdens of judgment, diversity in beliefs and life choices is an inevitable feature of free and open societies. Thus, although liberalism upholds the freedom to proselytize on the basis of the right to revise one's conception of the good, it is doubtful that a citizen can support liberal citizenship to even a minimal degree without *accepting* that his fellow citizens may never convert to Islam. Mutual recognition between citizens thus requires that this diversity be accepted, even as we try to win adherents to our way of life. I thus submit that the first pillar of a doctrine of recognition would include as an extension of the earlier principle R3 an acceptance of religious pluralism something like the following.

RP: *Religious disagreement is an inevitable feature of human life, perhaps divinely ordained. Although a Muslim has a duty to make the Islamic message known and to call to it, it is understood that not all unbelievers will hear or heed this call. It is permissible to live in societies even where there is little or no prospect of Islam becoming a majority religion, and it is permissible to maintain civic relationships with unbelievers even after they have heard and failed to accept the invitation to Islam.*

I have phrased this rather deliberately to express the idea of diversity and minority status as a potentially permanent condition. Although this principle could have many varieties, the idea is to exclude from an overlapping consensus those (rather common) justifications of political obligation that rest on the premise that some day (even centuries hence) present-day non-Muslim societies will have Muslim majorities that can thus create Islamic states. A further important note is that Abrahamic fraternity or shared monotheism are not sufficient grounds for civic solidarity in a politically liberal society that does not distinguish between citizens on the basis of metaphysical beliefs. Recognition must also be extended to atheists, agnostics and non-Abrahamic believers.

That Muslims have reason to believe that sharing social space with non-Muslims is a permanent condition to be tolerated, or a necessity out of which virtue can be made, implies very little about the nature of relations between communities in that social space. It certainly does not imply that members of different communities have the same moral standing or that they are entitled to the same standards of treatment. Medieval Islamic public law granted non-Muslims in Muslim states significant rights to noninterference, but nothing approaching equality of rights or status. Thus, as a second building block of our doctrine of recognition of the other, we require Islamic reasons for regarding relations with non-Muslims in a single society as relations of justice between equals. This requirement opens up extremely complex questions of the substantive content of justice (see my discussion below on this in relation to political participation), but a doctrine of mutual recognition would not be complete with something like the following:

J: *Relations between Muslims and non-Muslims are governed by standards of justice, rather than the ethics of war. Minimal standards of justice require civic equality and procedural impartiality toward all persons regardless of their religious identity.*

I submit here, however, that these more passive aspects of recognition must also be supplemented with a more positive doctrine of solidarity. Rawls has referred to liberal society as a "fair system of cooperation," that is, as one based on *reciprocity* as opposed to mutual advantage, impartiality, mere socially coordinated activity, a fixed natural order or a system of traditional hierarchy justified by religious authority or aristocratic values. For Rawls, *reciprocity* is the idea that "all who are engaged in cooperation and who do their part as the rules and procedure require, are to benefit in an appropriate way as assessed by a suitable benchmark of comparison,"[44] a conception that lies between both impartiality (being moved by the general good) and mutual advantage (everyone benefiting with respect to their present or expected future situation). I am not concerned here to vindicate a particular conception of distributive justice but merely the basic idea of citizenship as social cooperation: of contributing to the welfare (directly and indirectly) of fellow citizens (including those who do not share your conception of the good), and of sharing political sovereignty. One cannot speak of a comprehensive doctrine as affirming citizenship in a society when at the same time it seeks to avoid contributing to the welfare of fellow citizens merely because they do not share a conception of truth or of the good. This willingness to so contribute is what I have in mind by "solidarity."

We have seen throughout this article that contributing to the welfare and strength of non-Muslims is something to which some Muslim jurists and exegetes have objected. They have objected to contributing to the material well-being of non-Muslims both because this increases the relative strength of non-Muslim states and

[44] Rawls, *Political Liberalism*, p. 16.

societies over Muslim ones and also because they see such mutual aid as belonging to a relationship of love and solidarity that can only be established with fellow Muslims. A Muslim has no libertarian objection to the redistribution of his wealth in principle, but may have such an objection when it occurs across confessional boundaries and through the coercive powers of a non-Muslim state. However, it is unavoidable even in a Nozickian minimal state that sharing political space involves in countless ways sharing the burdens of social life. We contribute to one another's welfare not only through forced redistribution but even as a double-effect of pursuing our own goals. Given the sources we have encountered that discourage contributing to the welfare of non-Muslims, an overlapping consensus would require some contrary declaration such as:

CW: *It is permissible for a Muslim to form common social, economic and civic goals with non-Muslims. It is understood that in sharing social and political space Muslims benefit from this and in turn contribute to the material welfare of non-Muslims, to which there is no Islamic objection.*

In addition to the willingness to contribute to the material welfare of non-Muslims, a crucial aspect of solidarity relates to sharing political sovereignty. With the question of political participation we reach a hinge between the two broad problems with citizenship in non-Muslim liberal democracies: one, in those states being *non-Muslim* in character, both socially and politically; two, in those states being *liberal* in character. It is readily conceivable that a Muslim could affirm residence on liberal terms, forswear any assistance to aggressive foreign powers (including Muslim ones), recognize the acceptability of religious pluralism and even gladly contribute to the secular welfare of non-Muslims, yet find it impermissible to contribute to the formulation of non-Islamic legislation or the administration of non-Muslim political authority. Even if this person disavowed any interest in using political institutions to impose an Islamic conception of government, his comprehensive doctrine would still not be fully supportive of an overlapping consensus because of it is prescribing alienation from domestic political institutions, for "to be a citizen is to be committed to a political system, not merely to the survival of the society that system organizes, but to the survival of the particular organization and also to all those purposes beyond survival that the organization sets for itself. Residence alone cannot and does not generate such a commitment."[45]

Yet, when speaking of the legitimacy of political institutions, we immediately enter into very deep and complex questions of justice. The question from the Islamic perspective immediately becomes whether any non-Islamic forms of rule can be just. That none can is not an obvious or universally accepted Islamic position. To be sure, any reconstruction of a comprehensive Islamic doctrine of citizenship in a liberal democracy (Muslim-minority or not) would require addressing this; however, doing so satisfactorily would require exceeding the constraints of the present inquiry. Nonetheless, there is an important way in which we can address this ques-

---

[45] Walzer, "Political Alienation and Military Service," in *Obligations*, p. 105.

tion here, and that is in the context of solidarity with non-Muslims. (Thus, my reference to political participation as a "hinge" issue.)

Although a citizen need not consider political participation as part of her conception of the good in order to be regarded as holding a doctrine of citizenship, she should at least regard it as *permissible* in relation her conception of the good, and if she in fact does not participate, then her reasons should be such that they do not constitute rejection of or ingratitude toward what other citizens do when they perform the necessary task of political participation. Most crucially, her reasons for participating must be such that they do not undermine or reject the liberal terms of social cooperation. In addition to long-term strategies to Islamize political institutions that include political participation in the present institutions as an acceptable tactic, more ambiguous attitudes would be those that reveal unease with liberal institutions but justify political participation only as a means of securing certain benefits *for Muslims*. Let us suppose that the benefits in question are themselves compatible with liberal conceptions of justice and a well-ordered society; might such a justification be compatible with liberal citizenship?

Consider the following three positions:

1. "My conception of the good is based on the pursuit of purely private happiness. I have no objection to the political order around me – it provides me with all the security and freedom I need to be happy – but nor do I feel the need to be a part of it. Should this political order be threatened by forces that would replace it with one more hostile to my interest in security and freedom, I would have no objection to defending it, but otherwise I am happy to let others handle the administration of things."
2. "My conception of the good is based on the pursuit of happiness. I have certain interests that I share with some citizens but not with all. Influencing politicians through various forms of political participation is an important way in which I advance those interests. Otherwise, where our group interest is not affected I have very little interest in political participation."
3. "My conception of the good is based on the pursuit of salvation, which I think can be best achieved through government on the basis of a divine law. I understand that in this society the majority of the population does not share my understanding of what divine law requires. This society gives me the security, freedom and dignity to follow my most important religious practices and, thus, I would defend it against harm and destruction. I do not begrudge my unbelieving fellow citizens their worldly happiness and I do not resent my contribution to their welfare. However, while I will obey all laws of this society that do not oppress me, I do not feel any need to contribute to the making of those laws. For me, political participation is only justified to pursue social benefits for co-religionists, which may or may not overlap with the interests of others."

The first and third statements are expressions of nonparticipation based on one's conception of the good that, I believe, are nonetheless affirmations of citizenship (as opposed to mere resident alienage) because of the way they affirm the legitimacy of what other citizens do when they participate in political life (and even a certain gratitude for it). If we can assume that many non-Muslim citizens of contemporary liberal democracies hold conceptions of the good conforming to the first or second templates, then an Islamic argument that views nonparticipation as the norm and participation justified only to pursue Muslim self-interest is equally compatible with liberal citizenship *if it presumes an argument something like the third template as the underlying Islamic position*, rather than a position of gradual Islamization or complete indifference to non-Muslims. (This argument presumes that the individual in question is also affirming all the previously mentioned beliefs about the permissibility of loyalty, recognition, tolerance and contributing to non-Muslim welfare.) What is decisive is that although the motivation is largely to advance Muslim communal interests, this citizen does not view benefits that accrue to non-Muslims as a double-effect as something otherwise impermissible or unfortunate. Thus, the final aspect of a doctrine of recognition and solidarity would be an affirmation of the permissibility of participating in a non-Muslim political system along the following lines:

PP: *It is permissible for a Muslim to participate in a political system not based on Islamic justice or public justification. Such participation is an appropriate way to advance certain interests of Muslim communities, particularly in worldly matters, interests that may overlap with non-Muslim fellow citizens.*

Conclusion

A morally diverse society is composed of citizens with a variety of life goals and authoritative standards for resolving moral disputes. A regime committed to a public conception of justice similar to Rawls's political liberalism passes judgment on those goals and authoritative standards only insofar as they impinge on the equal rights of other citizens, or obstruct society's efforts to secure socially necessary goods, such as security, order, public health, or general welfare. Just as political liberalism requires a certain self-restraint on the part of citizens in their use of power to advantage a particular conception of the good, so does it impose on itself self-restraint in how it interferes in citizens' ordering of their own souls. For this reason, political liberals understand that not all citizens, perhaps not even most, will order their souls in such a way that their duties as a citizen, and as a *liberal citizen* at that, receive lexical priority over their other goals and duties.

This article is an attempt, from a liberal perspective, to respond to the concerns about citizenship in a liberal state emerging from Islamic doctrine. There are a few areas where I believe that our understanding of liberal citizenship may emerge altered. Our discussion of loyalty and military service is one such area. Although remaining committed to a few firm basic principles, such as that of a society's right to defend itself and its right to expect the contribution of citizens who benefit from the security and welfare it provides, we accept that there are a variety of ways in which those principles can be upheld. In the case of Muslims who believe it is a sin to kill fellow Muslims and do not wish to carry arms against them, we return to our basic principles and ask what is truly fundamental: that a citizen must always obey his state, or that the citizen must be willing in principle to discharge his civic duties and recognize his society's legitimate rights? With the slightest degree of sympathy for the conflicted, divided citizen, the one who actually wishes to be both a good citizen and a faithful believer, a liberal state finds itself willing to find alternative ways of discharging civic duties, and also of regarding those duties.

Let us look at it in a more abstract way: what if a minority community's recognition of a political form of liberalism depended on the extent to which that liberal regime allowed for the free practice of its religion? Community *c*, not normally known for its respect for individual autonomy or some other liberal value, is induced to find the resources from within its authoritative texts to see individual freedom as justifiable because of the myriad other benefits offered within a free society. The free practice of religion requires, in the case of community *c*, however, the freedom to engage in, or refrain from, which in turn requires a certain form of exemption from public duties. Our consideration of whether the exemption is justifiable will certainly not hinge merely on community *c* wanting it, but in the event that we find such an exemption compatible with fundamental liberal principles, our appreciation of the importance of that exemption will undoubtedly alter our conception of the proper balance between church and state, religious liberty and civic equality, communal solidarity and individual freedom. We might, in essence, end up understanding the minimum or proper demands of citizenship in a new way because of the specific exemption required by a specific community.

However, it is not to be assumed that everything we "learn" about liberalism consists of an accommodation to comprehensive doctrines. In some cases, we are made aware of attitudes or ends particular to a given comprehensive doctrine that might call for a stiffening of our liberal spines. A prime example from the present article of such an attitude is the role prescribed by Muslim theorists for proselytizing (*da'wa*). On the face of it, political liberalism would be expected to regard favorably a community's acknowledgment of liberalism's guarantee of religious liberty and free speech. A justification of life lived within a particular political space on the grounds of its more expansive religious freedom would appear to be just the foundation for an overlapping consensus sought by political liberalism. However, when the discourse on *da'wa* is examined more closely, one often finds an express desire to Islamize non-Muslim societies and states and a recognition of non-Muslims only as potential converts. The latter results in our concerns (expressed earlier in this article) that a justification of citizenship based on the space to "call" non-Muslims to Islam may reveal a shallow commitment to democratic rights and a lack of recognition of non-Muslim fellow citizens.

Clearly, a wide range of topics related to justice and citizenship in liberal democracies remain undiscussed here, particularly the question of individual autonomy and a community's self-restraint toward its own members. What I wish to draw attention to in this article, in addition to my substantive arguments on the three main topics addressed, is the role of this form of comparative political theory in helping to elucidate not only the contours of various comprehensive doctrines but also the precise nature of our liberal beliefs.

Bibliography

Abu Zakariyya' al-Nawawi. (2000). *al-Majmu' Sharh al-Muhadhdhab*. Beirut: Dar al-Fikr.

Ahmad ibn Yahya al-Wansharisi. (1981). In M. Hajji (Ed.), *al-Mi'yar al-Mu'rib wa al jami' al-mughrib 'an fatawa ahl Ifiiqiya wa'l-Andalus wa'l-Maghrib* (Vol. 2, pp. 121–138). Rabat: Ministry of Religious Endowments and Islamic Affairs.

Bilgrami, A. (2004). Secularism and relativism. *Boundary, 2*, 31.

Cohen, J. (1993). Moral Pluralism and Political Consensus. In D. Copp, J. Hampton, & J. E. Roemer (Eds.), *The idea of democracy* (pp. 274–275). Cambridge: Cambridge University Press.

Crone, P. (2004). *God's rule: Government and Islam*. New York: Columbia University Press.

Gaus, G. F. (1996). *Justificatory liberalism: An essay on epistemology and political theory*. Oxford: Oxford University Press.

Gaus, G. F. (n.d.). The rational, the reasonable and justification. *Journal of Political Philosophy, 3*(3), 234–258, at p. 255.

Guillaume, A. (1955). *The Life of Muhammad: A Translation of Ishaq's*. In: Sirat Rasul Allah (Ed.), London: Oxford University Press.

Isma'il ibn 'Umar Ibn Kathir. (1998). *Tafsir al-Qur'an al-Azim*. Beirut: Dar al-Kutub al-'Ilmiyya.

Kekes, J. (1993). *The morality of pluralism*. Princeton: Princeton University Press.

Khadduri, M. (1955). *War and peace in the law of Islam*. Baltimore: Johns Hopkins Press.

Khaled Abou El Fadl. (1994). Islamic law and Muslim Minorities: The juristic discourse on Muslim Minorities from the second/eighth to the eleventh/seventeenth centuries. *Islamic Law and Society, 1*(2), 141–187.

Khalid 'Abd al-Qadir. (1998). *Fiqh al-aqalliyat al-Muslima*. Tripoli: Dar al-Iman.

March, A. F. (2007). Islamic foundations for a social contract in non-Muslim liberal democracies. *American Political Science Review, 101*(2), 235–252.

Muhammad Husayn Fadlallah. (1999). *al-Hijra wa al-ightirab: ta'sis fiqhi li mushkilat al-luju' wa al-hijra*. Beirut: Mu'assasat al-'Arif lil-Matbu'at.

Muhammad ibn Ahmad al-Sarakhsi. (2001). *Kitab al-Mabsut*. Beirut: Dar al-Kutub al-'Ilmiyya.

Muhammad ibn al-Hasan al-Shaybani. (1966). *The Islamic law of nations: Shaybani's Siyar* (M. Khadduri, Trans.). Baltimore: Johns Hopkins Press.

Muhammad Rashid Rida. (1973). *Tafsir al-Manar al-hakim al-shahir bi-tafsir al-manar*. Beirut: Dar al-Ma'rifa.

Muhammad Rashid Rida. (1980). *Fatawa al-Imam Muhammad Rashid Rida*. In: Salah al-Din al-Munajjid, & Yusuf Q. Khuri (Eds.). Beirut: Dar al-Kitab al-Jadid.

Rawls, J. (1971). *A theory of justice*. Cambridge, MA: Harvard University Press.

Rorty, R. (1989). *Contingency, irony, and solidarity*. Cambridge: Cambridge University Press.

Salih ibn Muhammad al-Shithri. (n.d.). *Hukm al-luju' wa'l-iqama fi bilad al-kuffar*. Riyad: Dar al-Habib.

Sayyid Abul 'Ala Mawdudi. (1990). *Towards understanding the Qur'an*. Leicester: The Islamic Foundation.

Sayyid Qutb. (2001). *In the shade of the Qur'an* (Adil Salahi, & Ashur Shamis, Trans. and Eds.). Leicester: The Islamic Foundation.

Shaykh Muhammad Afifi al-Akiti. (2005). *Defending the transgressed by censuring the reckless against the killing of civilians*. Aqsa Press.

Sulayman Muhammad Tubulyak. (1997). *al-Ahkam al-siyasiyya li'l-aqalliyat al-muslima fi al-fiqh al-Islami*. Beirut: Dar al-Nafa'is.

Tibi, B. (2002). War and peace in Islam. In S. Hashmi (Ed.), *Islamic political ethics*. Princeton: Princeton University Press.

Walzer, M. (1970). *Obligations: Essays on disobedience, war, and citizenship*. Cambridge, MA: Harvard University Press.

Yusuf al-Qaradawi. (2001). *Fi fiqh al-aqalliyyat al-muslima*. Cairo: Dar al-Shuruq.

Correction to: The Ethics of Citizenship in the 21st Century

David Thunder

Correction to:
D. Thunder (ed.), *The Ethics of Citizenship in the 21st Century*, https://doi.org/10.1007/978-3-319-50415-5

The chapters "What Is the Use of an Ethical Theory of Citizenship?" and "An Ethical Defense of Citizenship" were previously published non-open access. They have now been changed to open access under a CC BY 4.0 license and the copyright holder updated to 'The Author(s)'. The book has also been updated with these changes.

The updated online versions of these chapters can be found at:
https://doi.org/10.1007/978-3-319-50415-5_1
https://doi.org/10.1007/978-3-319-50415-5_6

D. Thunder (ed.), *The Ethics of Citizenship in the 21st Century*,
https://doi.org/10.1007/978-3-319-50415-5_10

The manufacturer's authorised representative in the EU is Springer
Nature Customer Service Centre GmbH, Europaplatz 3, 69115 Heidelberg,
Germany. If you have any concerns regarding our products, please
contact ProductSafety@springernature.com

Printed and bound by CPI Group (UK) Ltd, Croydon, CR0 4YY
30/09/2026
02225650-0002